FLOYD CLYMER'S MOTORCYCLIST'S LIBRARY

The Book of the
PUCH MAXI
Models 'N' and 'S'

R. H. Warring

ANNOUNCEMENT

By special arrangement with the original publishers of this book, Sir Isaac Pitman & Son, Ltd., of London, England, we have secured the exclusive publishing rights for this book, as well as all others in THE MOTORCYCLIST'S LIBRARY.

Included in THE MOTORCYCLIST'S LIBRARY are complete instruction manuals covering the care and operation of respective motorcycles and engines; valuable data on speed tuning, and thrilling accounts of motorcycle race events. See listing of available titles elsewhere in this edition.

We consider it a privilege to be able to offer so many fine titles to our customers.

FLOYD CLYMER
Publisher of Books Pertaining to Automobiles and Motorcycles

2125 W. PICO ST.   LOS ANGELES 6, CALIF.

PUCH MAXI 'N' & 'S'

A Compilation of 3 major publications that cover the overhaul, repair and maintenance of the Puch Maxi 'N' & 'S'

Maxi N

1 - A reprint of the 1974 Motorcyclist's Library 'The Book of the Puch Maxi'

2 - A reprint of the 1977 Factory 'Instructions' manual

3 - A reprint of the 1976 Factory 'Spare Parts' manual

Maxi S

A Floyd Clymer Publication 2021 by VelocePress.com

INTRODUCTION

Welcome to the world of digital publishing ~ the book you now hold in your hand, while unchanged from the original edition, was printed using the latest state of the art digital technology. The advent of print-on-demand has forever changed the publishing process, never has information been so accessible and it is our hope that this book serves your informational needs for years to come. If this is your first exposure to digital publishing, we hope that you are pleased with the results. Many more titles of interest to the classic automobile and motorcycle enthusiast, collector and restorer are available via our website at www.VelocePress.com. We hope that you find this title as interesting as we do.

NOTE FROM THE PUBLISHER

The information presented is true and complete to the best of our knowledge. All recommendations are made without any guarantees on the part of the author or the publisher, who also disclaim all liability incurred with the use of this information.

TRADEMARKS

We recognize that some words, model names and designations, for example, mentioned herein are the property of the trademark holder. We use them for identification purposes only. This is not an official publication.

INFORMATION ON THE USE OF THIS PUBLICATION

This manual is an invaluable resource and a 'must have' for owners interested in performing their own maintenance. However, in today's information age we are constantly subject to changes in common practice, new technology, availability of improved materials and increased awareness of chemical toxicity. As such, it is advised that the user consult with an experienced professional prior to undertaking any procedure described herein. While every care has been taken to ensure correctness of information, it is obviously not possible to guarantee complete freedom from errors or omissions or to accept liability arising from such errors or omissions. Therefore, any individual that uses the information contained within, or elects to perform or participate in do-it-yourself repairs or modifications acknowledges that there is a risk factor involved and that the publisher or its associates cannot be held responsible for personal injury or property damage resulting from the use of the information or the outcome of such procedures.

WARNING!

One final word of advice, this publication is intended to be used as a reference guide, and when in doubt the reader should consult with a qualified technician.

Preface

THE STEYR Puch Maxi is one of the most successful mopeds produced to date, offering economy "motoring" with safe, reliable performance. The two models, the Maxi N and Maxi S, are both powered by a 49 c.c. engine with single speed drive through an automatic clutch, and are essentially similar technically. The principal difference with the Maxi S is that the frame design has been changed to accommodate rear springing.

The Puch Maxi was first imported into Britain in 1969, and both the "N" and "S" models are available. These differ in slight details from their Continental counterparts, such as in the light bulbs fitted, but engineering-wise can be considered identical.

The servicing, maintenance and strip-down and adjustment details given in this book follow recommended Steyr-Puch workshop practice and the illustrations are largely based on the company's own works drawings. The descriptions should cover virtually all the requirements of a Puch Maxi owner wishing to undertake his (or her) own servicing work. Where major servicing is undertaken, a copy of the Maxi Spare Parts Catalogue will be invaluable in identifying parts required as replacements by works part numbers. Failing this, a Puch Maxi Service Agent should be able to identify the parts required from the exploded diagrams in this book.

Extensive stocks of Puch Maxi spares are held in this country by the importers—Steyr-Daimler-Puch (Great Britain) Ltd.—and are readily available through authorized service agents (*see* Appendix for addresses).

The author is particularly grateful for the generous help given by Steyr-Daimler-Puch (Great Britain) Ltd., in the preparation of this book, which it is hoped is as complete as the Puch Maxi owner is likely to require.

OLD BOSHAM
SUSSEX, 1974

R. H. WARRING

Contents

CHAPTER		PAGE
1	The Puch Maxi moped—General	1
2	Routine and simple maintenance	9
3	Fault finding	13
4	Decarbonizing	17
5	Cables and handlebar controls	19
6	Wheels, hubs and brakes	23
7	Pedals and chains	28
8	Forks and frame	32
9	Carburettor	38
10	The engine group	43
11	Flywheel magneto-generator	55
12	The electrics	60
	Appendix: Importers and Distributors and Service Agents	65
	Index	67

1. The Puch Maxi moped—General

THE PUCH Maxi is an extremely well-designed and constructed moped, powered by a 49 c.c. two-stroke engine driving through a centrifugal clutch to provide single gear "automatic" transmission. The pedals are used for starting, with start or clutch engaged; or as an alternative method of propulsion with the engine not running (when the centrifugal clutch is automatically disengaged).

Two models have been introduced in Britain—the Maxi "N" and Maxi "S". These are virtually identical in technical specification except that the Maxi "S" has hydraulic rear suspension, to accommodate this the rear frame design has been modified, together with the rear mudguard and associated parts. The engine and other parts are identical for both models, except for detail changes as noted in later chapters.

The Maxi frame is of all-welded pressed steel construction, with integral fuel tank incorporated in the front section. The engine is mounted horizontally, with the head facing forward, and bolts to a U-shaped bracket welded to the bottom of the frame tank section. Cooling is by direct airflow produced by forward motion of the moped. Thus there is minimum cooling when the engine is running with the moped stationary. Engine construction is of light alloy with a hard chromed bore.

The engine group comprises engine, flywheel magneto-generator, clutch, and final drive sprocket on a countershaft driven from the crankshaft through spiral gears. Drive is taken to the rear wheels by a chain. The two-shoe centrifugal clutch automatically starts to engage at an engine speed of about 1,200–1,500 r.p.m. and becomes fully engaged at 2,600–3,000 r.p.m. Maximum engine speed is 4,500 r.p.m. When reducing engine speed, the centrifugal clutch disengages at 1,500–1,400 r.p.m.

The clutch can also be operated directly by pulling the starter lever on the handlebars, connecting pedal drive to engine. At the same time this movement also operates a decompressor, admitting air into the cylinder and thus making it easy for the engine to spin over. Starting procedure is to pedal off (when the engine will automatically be disengaged), and once in steady motion pull the starting lever in. At the same time the throttle twist grip should be turned to about one third open. This will spin the engine over, when the starting lever is released and the engine should fire and start. The engine cannot start and run, even though being turned over, all the time the starting lever is held in because the decompressor is also in

Fig. 1.1 Puch Maxi Model S with sprung rear suspension. Tax and fully comprehensive insurance should be obtainable for well under £10 annually

Fig. 1.2 Puch Maxi Model N differs mainly in having a fixed rear frame. Another distinguishing feature is the slightly different shape of the fairing panels

THE PUCH MAXI MOPED—GENERAL

operation. Accidental operation of the starting lever when the engine is running is to be avoided as this will decompress the cylinder, causing the engine to slow or stop. With normal running the pedal drive "freewheels" at the rear hub, bicycle style, so that the pedals remain substantially stationary to act as footrests.

Hub brakes are fitted to both the front and rear wheels, these being of internal expanding type operated by cables from the handlebar levers. The front brake lever is on the right handlebar and the rear brake lever on the left handlebar. The twist-grip throttle is on the right handlebar and the starting lever on the left handlebar (*see* Fig. 1.3).

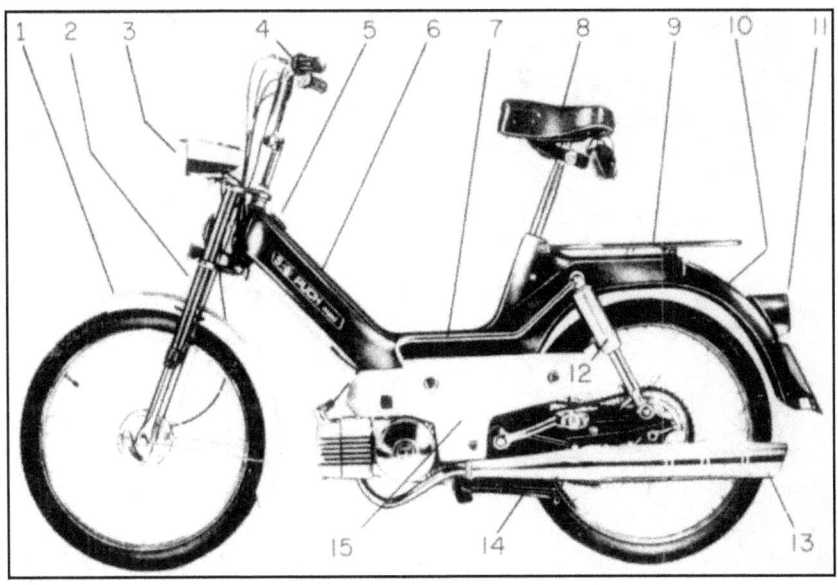

Fig. 1.3a   Puch Maxi features

1 front mudguard
2 number plate
3 headlamp
4 starter lever and rear brake lever
5 fuel tank filler
6 fuel tank (integral with frame)
7 lifting handle (each side)
8 saddle
9 luggage grid
10 rear mudguard
11 tail lamp
12 sprung rear suspension
13 silencer/exhaust
14 centre stand
15 detachable fairing

The choke is located on the top of the carburettor. For starting from cold the choke is pressed in and the "tickler" also operated a few times to provide the engine with a richer mixture (Fig. 1.4). Depending on the temperature the choke can be left operated for as long as necessary for the engine to warm up sufficiently to give smooth running. The choke is disengaged *automatically* by fully opening the throttle momentarily.

4   THE BOOK OF THE PUCH MAXI

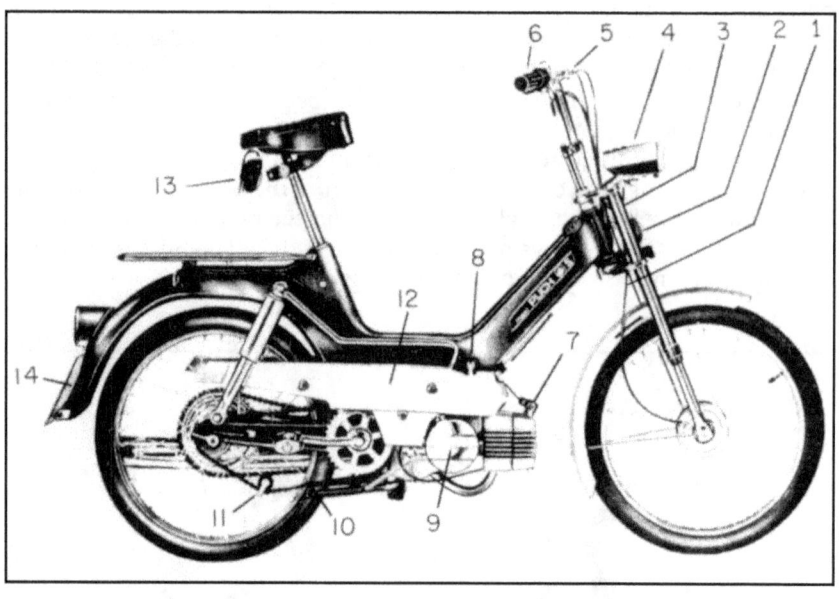

Fig. 1.3b Puch Maxi features

1 speedometer drive
2 horn
3 front forks
4 speedometer
5 front brake lever
6 twistgrip throttle
7 spark plug
8 fuel tap
9 automatic clutch
10 pedal chain
11 pedal chain tensioner
12 detachable fairing
13 tool bag
14 rear number plate

General Driving Instructions

Speed is controlled by the twist-grip throttle. The Maxi can be driven continuously at maximum throttle, but it is generally recommended that after using maximum throttle opening for acceleration up to top speed (approximately 28 m.p.h.), the throttle should be backed off to about three-quarters opening. This will result in very little loss of speed but will appreciably reduce the fuel consumption.

The engine is stopped by closing the throttle and then pulling and holding the starting lever in to operate the decompressor.

Procedure for stopping and parking is to close the throttle then apply brakes to come to a standstill. Pull the starter lever in and hold in until the engine stops, then release. Dismount and pull the machine onto its stand. Close the fuel tap and use the key to operate the steering lock, if the moped is to be left unattended. For the lock to operate the handlebars must be turned to the right, the key inserted in the lock and turned to the left. Key and lock can then be pushed downwards. In this position turn the key to the right and pull out. Unlocking follows the reverse procedure.

THE PUCH MAXI MOPED—GENERAL

Note: the moped should not be laid on its side, or in a position where it may fall over, with the fuel tap left on. This can induce flooding of the engine, making for difficult starting.

Reducing the throttle from maximum or cruising setting will provide engine braking, but this will only be effective down to an engine speed of 1,500 r.p.m., when the engine will automatically disengage from the drive. Brakes must thus be applied to slow the moped at reduced throttle settings. Normal braking technique is to reduce or close the throttle, at the same time applying both brakes. Avoid fierce application of the brakes, particularly on poor or wet road surfaces. If driving conditions are bad, it is safer to use the rear brake only for slowing.

Fig 1.4 Carburettor tickler (arrowed)

More careful attention to braking is required on downhill runs. If the throttle is closed too much, the braking effect of the engine will be lost by the automatic clutch disengaging. Also prolonged low throttle running of the engine may starve it of petrol-oil mixture, resulting in loss of lubrication. Thus it is generally desirable, as far as possible, to tackle descents—especially long hills—at a speed where engine braking is still effective. If speed has to be reduced by further braking on a long descent, the throttle should be opened occasionally to suck petrol-oil into the cylinder to maintain satisfactory lubrication.

Apart from familiarity with the controls, and the mastering of "optimum" braking technique, no special skills are required to master driving the Maxi moped. Anyone who can ride a bicycle should have no trouble converting to its "powered" equivalent. The large 21 in. diameter wheels with 2 in. tyres, light weight and low centre of gravity, combine with good technical design to give the Puch Maxi very safe handling characteristics.

Running-in

It is not good practice to race a new engine or to let it run for long periods at the same speed—fast or slow. Two-stroke engines, however, are not particularly critical about running-in requirements.

The main points to observe are:

1 Make absolutely sure that the correct petrol:oil mixture is used.
2 Avoid using more than three-quarter throttle opening when driving for the first 200–250 miles.
3 Drive at varying speeds as far as possible.
4 During the next 250 miles, full throttle running for short periods at a time will be helpful.

Service checks required after the first 500 miles are detailed in the table in Chapter 2 (p. 12). The engine can be regarded as "run-in" after the first 500 miles, but performance may continue to improve slightly on the next 1,000–2,000 miles. Change of main jet size (*see* Chapter 9) should be delayed until the engine has obviously settled down to consistent running.

GENERAL SPECIFICATIONS

Engine: single-cylinder, air-cooled, two-stroke.
Die-cast light alloy cylinder and head, chrome cylinder bore, light alloy piston, with two rings.
Displacement: 48·8 c.c.
Bore: 1·49 in. (38 mm).
Stroke: 1·69 in. (43 mm).
Maximum output: 2·2 b.h.p. at 4,500 r.p.m.
Maximum torque: 2·75 ft/lb (0·38 mkg).
Compression ratio: 11:1.
Transmission: Primary transmission through centrifugal clutch to helical toothed gears (5·05:1 reduction).
Clutch and gears running in oilbath. Secondary transmission by $\frac{1}{2}$ in. $\times$ $\frac{3}{16}$ in. chain, reduction 2·81:1. Pedal chain $\frac{1}{2}$ in. $\times$ $\frac{1}{8}$ in. tensioned by spring-loaded jockey sprocket, reduction ratio 1·8:1.
Frame: All-welded pressed steel incorporating integral tank.
Suspension: Front—telescopic forks incorporating coil springs. Rear—pivoted fork, hydraulically damped (Maxi "S" only).
Fuel: 25:1 petrol:oil mixture (one third pint oil per gallon of petrol). Oil specified SAE 40 or SAE 50 (or equivalent two-stroke mixture).
Fuel tank capacity: 0·7 gallon (3·2 litres).
Gearbox lubrication: automatic transmission fluid—recommended types BP Automatic Transmission Fluid, Castrol TQ, Esso ATF55, Mobil Fluid 200, Shell Donax T6.
Gearbox capacity: new filling 150 c.c.
by oil change approx. 120 c.c
Tyres: Front and rear 2·00 × 21 in.
Tyre Pressures: Front 25 lb/in.^{2}
Rear 32 lb/in.^{2}

Weights and Dimensions:

Overall length 66·9 in. (1700 mm).
Overall width 27·1 in. (690 mm).
Overall height 39·3 in. (1000 mm).

THE PUCH MAXI MOPED—GENERAL

Weights and Dimensions contd.

Wheelbase	44·1 in. (1120 mm).
Ground clearance (unloaded)	3·9 in. (100 mm).
Dry weight	86 lb (39 kg).

Performance and consumption:

Top speed	28 m.p.h. (45 km/h).
Hill climbing ability	15 per cent.
Fuel consumption	177 m/Imp. gal. (1·6 litres/100 km).

Identification numbers:

Specification plate—on right hand side of frame, immediately above cover.
Engine number —engraved on top of crankcase on right hand side.
Frame number —engraved on top of frame strut, right hand side.

STANDARD EQUIPMENT

Tyre pump and tool bag—located behind offside (right hand) engine/chain cover. Tools comprise:

> wrench 8/10 mm
> 2 single ended spanners
> screwdriver
> socket wrench for spark plug
> set of gaskets
> touch-up paint.

SPECIAL TOOLS

Part No.	Tool and purpose
905.6.31.106.2*	Jig to support engine unit in vice.
905.6.34.102.0*	Extractor for crankshaft main bearings, countershaft bearings and clutch housing.
905.6.33.105.0*	Tool for extracting and re-fitting small end bush.
320.1.20.012.2	Supporting plate for pressing on new main bearings.
050.7012	Flywheel puller.
905.0.36.101.2	Peg spanner to hold flywheel.
350.1.70.012.0	Sleeve for pressing on new bearings on crankshaft and countershaft.
905.6.35.401.1	Spanner for spoke nipples.
905.6.35.402.1	Spanner for hub cones.
905.0.12.101.0	Ignition timing instrument.
905.6.35.404.0	Rear wheel sprocket tool.

* These tools are specially made for the Puch Maxi.
The other tools listed are standard Puch workshop tools.

TECHNICAL DATA

Carburettor

Carburettor adjustment		
	main jet	70, 68 or 64 may be fitted as standard (next size down jet is also included in the tool kit).
	needle jet	220.
	needle position	2nd notch from top.

Electrical

Breaker point gap	0·014–0·017 in. (0·35–0·45 mm).
Pole shoe interruption	0·275–0·433 in. (7–11 mm).
Ignition timing	0·630–0·709 in. (16–18 mm).
Spark plug	Bosch W 145 T 1.
Spark gap	0·015–0·019 in. (0·4–0·5 mm).

Tightening Torques

Engine:	Cylinder head	6–7 ft/lb (0·9 mkp).
	Flywheel magneto nut	25 ft/lb (3·5 mkp).
	Clutch hub	20·53 ft/lb (2·7 mkp).
	Crankcase screws	6 ft/lb (0·8 mkp).
	Engine suspension	24 ft/lb (3·2 mkp).
Bodywork:	Suspension unit bearing	16–17 ft/lb (2·3 mkp).
	Rear wheel mounting	20 ft/lb (2·7 mkp).
	Brake cam mounting	50 ft/lb (0·7 mkp).
	Handlebar mounting	20 ft/lb (2·6 mkp).
	Twist grip mounting	5–6 ft/lb (0·8 mkp).

2 Routine and Simple Maintenance

For convenience of reference, routine maintenance requirements are listed in two tables—one covering maintenance involving inspection and/or adjustment if necessary; and one covering routine lubrication requirements. The number of adjustments, etc. which can be carried out by the owner depends to some extent on his or her mechanical ability. Most of the basic checks and adjustments necessary as a matter of routine are simple and straightforward, and can be undertaken by anyone. Specific information on adjustments, stripping down where necessary, and detailed servicing information will be found in subsequent chapters under specific headings.

Regular attention to routine maintenance and routine lubrication should provide long, trouble-free operation. The materials recommended differ somewhat from those given in the owner's manual, but represent a practical coverage of most requirements. Attention to servicing may, however, be needed at any time when a fault is suspected, or apparent. The troubleshooting charts of Chapter 3 can be a useful guide here.

Lubricants and Lubrication

All *oiling* points can be lubricated with SAE 20 or SAE 30 oil (the latter being the recommended grade). Grease nipple points can be lubricated with a grease gun filled either with SAE 90 oil or grease, as preferred. Chain lubrication is described separately (*see* Chapter 7).

The crankcase "gearbox" unit is lubricated with transmission fluid, and only a recommended fluid should be used.

The positions of some lubricating points are shown in Fig. 2.1. Other diagrammatic or text references are given in the lubrication table.

To check the oil level in the gearbox, the moped should be stood upright on its stand, the offside (right hand) cover removed and the oil level plug on the right hand side of the crankcase unscrewed (Fig. 2.2). The oil in the crankcase should come up to the lower level of this hole. If lower, remove the filling plug on the top of the crankcase and add new oil until it just starts to flow out of the oil level hole. Replace both plugs tightly.

To change the gearbox oil the engine should be run for a time to warm up (or oil changed immediately after a normal run). Unscrew the filling plug, level plug and drain plug (at the bottom of the crankcase). Tilt the moped slightly to the right to ensure complete draining.

Replace the drain plug and fill through the filler with 150 c.c. (approx.

¼ pint) of new transmission fluid, or until fluid just starts to flow from the level plug hole with the moped upright. Replace level and filler plugs *only* after oil has stopped flowing out of the level plug hole.

Fig. 2.1 Main lubricating points. For unnumbered reference points, consult the appropriate reference(s) given in the Lubrication Table.

Fig. 2.2 Crankcase plugs. f—fill; l—level; d—drain

ROUTINE AND SIMPLE MAINTENANCE

RECOMMENDED ROUTINE LUBRICATION

Part	Ref.	Lubricant	When
Gearbox	Fig. 2.2	Transmission fluid BP Automatic Transmission fluid Castrol T9 Esso ATF 55 Mobil Fluid 200 or Shell Donax T6	(i) check level weekly or monthly (ii) change every six months
Chains	Chap. 7	SAE 90 oil or Chain Grease	Need for *cleaning* and *lubricating* chains depends on amount of use and conditions For *average* conditions—every 3 months For *dirty* or wet conditions—every 1–2 months or as thought necessary
Steering bearing	Fig. 8.1	Grease	Every 6,000 miles or every 6 months
Wheel bearings	Fig. 6.2, 6.3	Lithium base grease	Every 6,000 miles or every 6 months
Front forks: Plastic guide bushes	Fig. 8.1	SAE 30 oil	Every 6,000 miles or every year

Chassis points
Brake adjuster, front
              rear
Choke cable adjuster
Pedals
Decompressor cable adjuster
Chain tension adjuster
Brake lever points,
              front
              rear
Centre stand
	Fig. 5.1
	Fig. 5.1
	Fig. 2.1 (4)
	Fig. 5.1
	Fig. 2.1 (1)
	Fig. 2.1 (3)
	Fig. 2.1 (2)
		SAE 30 oil	Every 6,000 miles or every 3 months

Cables:
Front brake: nipple
              wheel end
Rear brake: nipple
              wheel end
Throttle: top end
              oiler
              bottom end
Starter: bottom end
Decompressor: ends
	Fig. 5.1	SAE 90 oil or grease
		SAE 30 oil
		SAE 90 oil or grease
		SAE 30 oil
		
		SAE 30 oil
		SAE 30 oil
		SAE 30 oil
			Every 3,000 miles or every 3 months

Contact breaker felt pad	Fig. 11.5	SAE 90 oil or grease	Every 6,000 miles

RECOMMENDED ROUTINE MAINTENANCE

Component	Action	Daily	Weekly	Period		
				Every 1,000 miles or monthly	Every 3,000 miles or 3 monthly	Every 6,000 miles or 6 monthly
Tyres	check pressure	○	●			
	check for cuts, etc.			○	●	
Wheels	check spokes				○	●
	wheel bearings					●
Air filter			○	●		
Brakes	check and adjust			○	●	
Carburettor	adjust idle				●	
	clean				○	●
Fuel tank, tap filler cap	clean				○	●
Starter control	adjust				●	
Spark plug	check			○	●	
Ignition	check				●	●
Lighting	check				○	●
Steering bearing	adjust (and lubricate)				○	●
Engine and silencer	decarbonize				○	●
	check nuts for tightness				●	
Chain tension	check			○	●	

○ for unfavourable operating conditions (e.g. winter, bad roads, etc.).
● for average operating conditions.
Note: if the moped is to be serviced regularly by a garage or Puch Maxi agent, recommended period for servicing is every 3,000 miles.

500 MILE MAINTENANCE FOR NEW MACHINES
(Normally carried out by supplier or service agent)

Chain	— clean, lubricate and check tension
Engine	— change gear oil
	check and tighten nuts
	clean fuel taps and line
	clean and adjust carburettor (replacing main jet with next number down)
	check spark plug
	clean air filter
Cables	check and adjust starter control
	check other cable movements
Lighting	— check system
General	— lubricate chassis
	check hub bearings and adjust as necessary
	lubricate steering bearing and adjust as necessary
	check brakes and adjust as necessary

3 Fault Finding

THIS chapter is planned as a general guide to tracing and curing faults which may develop in the engine and/or ignition system of the Puch Maxi. Remedial action applicable to other faults, such as poor braking, lack of proper response to lever control movements, etc., will be more obvious and dealt with in separate chapters dealing with these particular components. Engine and/or ignition faults can be more obscure, and so possible faults and their causes, and the action necessary, are given in tabular form for quick and easy reference. It should then only need a little elementary "detective" work to eliminate possible causes one by one, until the actual cause is found and the necessary remedial action taken. To make this as easy as possible, the "possible causes" are listed in the order in which they are most likely to occur, e.g. 1, 2, 3, etc.

It cannot be emphasized too strongly that the most common cause of *any* fault developing is lack of attention to regular maintenance, regular lubrication, regular attention to cable adjustment—and regular cleaning as recommended under Routine Maintenance in Chapter 2. Also should any fault develop it should be located and remedied immediately, even if apparently of only minor nature. Any definite fault which is neglected can only lead to increasing trouble, and possibly the development of serious and costly damage.

Simple checks

The basic causes of most engine faults are "fuel" and "electrics". Starting point for "fuel" faults are simply:

1 Lack of fuel—ranging from the obvious (empty tank, or fuel tap not turned on), to partial obstruction of the fuel supply through dirt or a fault developing in the carburettor.

2 Too much fuel—which is far less likely (unless the choke is left in operation continuously).

3 Use of the wrong fuel mixture. It is *imperative* that only 24:1 petrol: oil mixture should be used in the tank—never just petrol alone.

The "electrics" can be checked quite simply by removing the spark plug and setting the moped up on its stand. The body of the plug is then held against the cylinder and the starting lever pulled in and the pedals turned by hand to rotate the engine. This should produce a strong white spark across the gap in the plug with each revolution of the engine.

If no spark appears, detach the lead from the plug and hold the end of the lead about ¼ in. (not more) away from the cylinder. Crank the engine over, when a spark should jump from the end of the lead to the cylinder for every revolution of the engine. This will prove that the high tension supply is O.K. to the end of the spark plug lead. Hence the lack of spark is due to a faulty plug (or dirty plug). Replace with a new (or cleaned) plug.

If no spark can be obtained from the end of the plug lead, then the fault lies in the magneto-generator unit—e.g. probably dirty or badly adjusted contact breaker points. Check the action required in Chapter 11.

TROUBLE SHOOTING TABLE

Fault	Possible cause(s)	Action
Engine does not start:	(i) lack of choke (starting from cold)	(a) check that choke is operated: also operate tickler
	(ii) lack of fuel	(a) check that fuel tap is open (b) check that there is fuel in tank (c) check that fuel line to carburettor is O.K. and not pulled off (d) operate tickler to check that fuel is flowing from tank (e) if (a), (b), (c) and (d) O.K., possible fault in carburettor
	(iii) weak or no spark	(a) check plug for spark (b) if no spark at plug, check plug lead for spark (c) if (b) O.K., clean plug and check gap, or fit new plug (d) if no spark at lead, check contact breaker points (e) if (d) appears satisfactory, check flux gap and cable connections
	(iv) engine flooded (chief causes—use of choke and/or tickler starting warm engine; or moped laid on its side with fuel tap open)	remove spark plug. If very wet suspect flooding (and/or weak spark) (a) to clear, start with throttle full open (b) if badly flooded, remove drain plug in bottom of crankcase to clear engine first
	(v) starting lever not adjusted properly	(a) check and readjust as necessary for proper decompression and starting clutch action
Engine fires, but stops	(i) choke not operated	(a) always use choke when starting cold engine
	(ii) lack of fuel	(a) check fuel supply for blockage, or lack of fuel
Engine difficult to start	(i) poor spark	(a) spark plug damp: wipe dry (b) spark plug dirty—clean (c) spark plug gap too big—adjust (d) wrong type of spark plug—change to correct type (e) flux gap requires adjustment
	(ii) lack of fuel	(a) partially blocked carburettor—clean jets
Engine backfires when starting	(i) ignition timing incorrect	(a) check ignition timing to see if too far advanced. Readjust timing if necessary
Engine backfires when running	(i) incorrect plug	(a) plug too hot, change to next heat grade down (b) plug dirty
	(ii) carbon deposits on head or plug	(a) decarbonize top end

FAULT FINDING

TROUBLE SHOOTING TABLE

Fault	Possible cause(s)	Action
Engine misfires when running and stops	(i) lack of fuel	(a) check that fuel tap is open (b) check that there is fuel in tank (c) if (a) and (b) O.K., check for other possible causes of fuel starvation
	(ii) weak spark	(a) check plug for condition and correct gap (b) check contact breaker gap, also condition of points (c) check flux gap
	(iii) water, dirt or air in fuel supply	(a) clean carburettor; check for air leaks on carburettor assembly and fuel line
Engine stops when throttle is opened	(i) lack of fuel (main jet clogged)	(a) clean main jet (b) check for dirt or water in carburettor; clean and wash out with petrol
Engine runs erratically	(i) ignition fault	(a) check spark plug (gap and condition) (b) check contact breaker (gap and condition) (c) check ignition leads for possible faults
Engine runs too rich	(i) black and oily looking spark plug (see also "Carburettor faults" in Chapter 9)	(a) change main jet to next number down (b) check that correct type of spark plug is fitted (change to next highest heat range)
Engine runs too lean	(i) white deposit on spark plug—electrodes may be pitted and burnt (see also "Carburettor faults" in Chapter 9)	(a) check that correct type of spark plug is fitted (change to next lowest heat range) (b) change main jet to next number up
Engine lacks power	(i) carburettor fault (ii) engine/exhaust coked up (iii) wrong fuel mixture (iv) ignition timing incorrect (ignition retarded) (v) excessive wear	(a) see "Carburettor faults" in Chapter 9 (b) decarbonize head, exhaust port and exhaust system (a) if in doubt, drain tank via fuel pipe removed from carburettor and refill with correct mixture (a) check ignition timing and readjust if necessary (a) major service may be required
Engine pinks	(i) ignition timing incorrect (too far advanced) (ii) unsuitable fuel	(a) check timing and readjust if necessary (a) use higher octane petrol in petrol:oil mixture
Engine develops mechanical "knock"	(i) excessive wear	disassemble and check wear on: (a) piston rings and bore (b) big end bearings (c) gudgeon pin (d) crankshaft bearings
Engine runs with a "hissing" noise	(i) air leak	(a) check that spark plug is tight (b) check that cylinder head gasket is not leaking; check head nuts for tightness (c) check that crankcase drain plug is tight (d) check that breather screw is tight (e) check other engine bolts for tightness
Engine runs with excessive noise	(i) silencer fault	(a) disassemble silencer and replace faulty part(s)
Engine overheats	(i) insufficient lubrication (ii) insufficient air cooling (iii) carbon deposits in engine	(a) check that correct mixture is being used (e.g. tank not topped up or accidentally filled with petrol only) (a) keep cylinder fins clean to maintain sufficient cooling area for heat dissipation (a) decarbonize engine

TROUBLE SHOOTING TABLE

Fault	Possible cause(s)	Action
Engine stops suddenly when running normally Excessive fuel consumption	(iv) mixture incorrect (see "Carburettor faults" in Chapter 9) (v) ignition timing incorrect (too far advanced) (i) lack of fuel (most common cause) (ii) electrical failure (iii) plug fouled (i) choke not functioning correctly (ii) carburettor fault (iii) fuel supply leakage	(a) check that correct or optimum main jet is fitted to carburettor (a) check ignition timing and correct if necessary (a) check that fuel tap is open (b) check that there is fuel in tank (a) check for disconnected plug lead or wiring lead (a) remove and clean plug (a) use momentary full throttle to release choke after engine has warmed up (b) check that choke release movement is operating correctly (a) check for leaking float valve (a) check for fuel leakage at tap, fuel line end and carburettor

4 Decarbonizing

The makers specify that decarbonizing should be carried out every 5,000 km (3,000 miles), but this need imply only a top overhaul—decarbonizing of cylinder head, top of piston and silencer. This can be done without removing the engine from the frame.

Remove the plug lead and plug after first giving the cylinder unit a thorough clean with petrol or paraffin. Release the nipple of the decompressor cable from its slot in the decompressor spring after turning the cable adjuster to obtain enough slack. The four bolts holding the head are then unscrewed, then the head can be lifted after gently tapping to free, if necessary. Remove the head gasket (metal foil) and discard, unless completely new looking and undamaged.

Carbon deposits inside the head can then be removed with a *wooden* scraper with a blunt edge. Do not use any hard or sharp edged tool for this purpose, as otherwise the head surface is likely to be scored. Wash clean in petrol and dry with a soft lint-free cloth.

Turn the engine over via the flywheel until the piston is at its uppermost point relative to the cylinder (TDC). The crown of the piston is now accessible for scraping off carbon deposits with the same sort of wooden tool. "Thorough" scraping down to bright metal is not necessary. Only rough scaly deposits need be removed.

Detach the exhaust pipe (secured to the cylinder by two nuts and washers under the flange), and free the silencer from its fixing point (held by one hexagonal headed bolt), allowing exhaust pipe and silencer to be removed from the machine. The exhaust flange gasket should be discarded.

If the engine is now turned to bring the piston to its bottom position in the cylinder, the exhaust port can be cleaned of any carbon deposits. Wipe out any loose deposits falling inside the cylinder with a lint-free cloth. Smear the cylinder walls with oil and spin the engine over several times. Then check that no deposits remain inside the cylinder. The cylinder head can then be replaced, not forgetting the gasket, and the four head nuts tightened down progressively in diagonal order. (*See Technical Data* for tightening torque, p. 8.)

The silencer unit can be released from the silencer body by unscrewing the two nuts on the central rod (Fig. 4.1). The pipe can be cleaned with a small bristle brush on a string "pull through". Carbon deposits on the other parts can be removed by scraping and the holes in the damping insert cleaned with wire. The silencer units on the Maxi "N" and Maxi "S" differ slightly in detail construction, notably in the length of the central rod and the silencer fixing point.

When reassembling, replace the Belleville washers with new ones if the originals show any signs of damage or deterioration, otherwise they may not provide suitable locking action. The exhaust flange gasket should also be replaced with a new one.

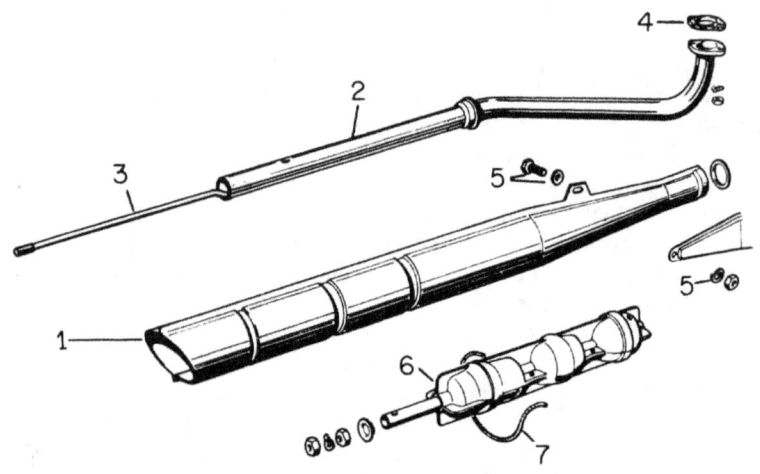

Fig. 4.1 Silencer shown disassembled

1 silencer outer
2 exhaust
3 central rod
4 exhaust gasket

5 silencer fastening belt, washer, spring washer and nut
6 silencer unit (note the holes to be cleaned)
7 asbestos cord

If bottom end decarbonizing is also thought necessary—e.g. after some 20,000 miles, or when performance has gradually deteriorated after long service and heavy carbonization is evident when the head is removed—the cylinder can also be withdrawn for cleaning of piston and rings.

To remove the cylinder the intake silencer and carburettor must first be detached from the frame and engine unit, respectively. The cylinder barrel can then be withdrawn up the four studs, but may first need a gentle tap to "unstick" from the gasket at the base. Once the cylinder barrel has been withdrawn the unsupported piston should be handled with care. It can be disassembled from the connecting rod by removing the circlips on the gudgeon pin and then carefully pushing the gudgeon pin out. See also Chapter 10 (p. 44) for detailed information on disassembling the engine unit.

5 Cables and Handlebar Controls

THE five cables on the "Maxi" are as follows:
From the right hand handlebar:
1 Front brake from lever to front hub.
2 Throttle cable from twist grip to carburettor.
From the left hand handlebar:
3 Rear brake from lever to rear hub.
4 Starter clutch control from starter lever to clutch operating lever.
From clutch to cylinder:
5 Decompressor control (connecting starter lever movement via clutch operating lever to decompressor).

Cables 1, 2, 3, and 5 have soldered nipples at each end of the cable. The clutch cable 4 has a soldered nipple at the lower end only. The upper end of the cable inner is plain and is anchored in the starter lever with a grub screw.

The decompressor cable 5 is virtually an extension of the clutch cable 4, so that movement of the starter lever operates both clutch and decompressor. This requires fairly precise adjustment of the two cables to ensure that the movement is correct. The *first* 0·8 in. (2 cm) movement of the

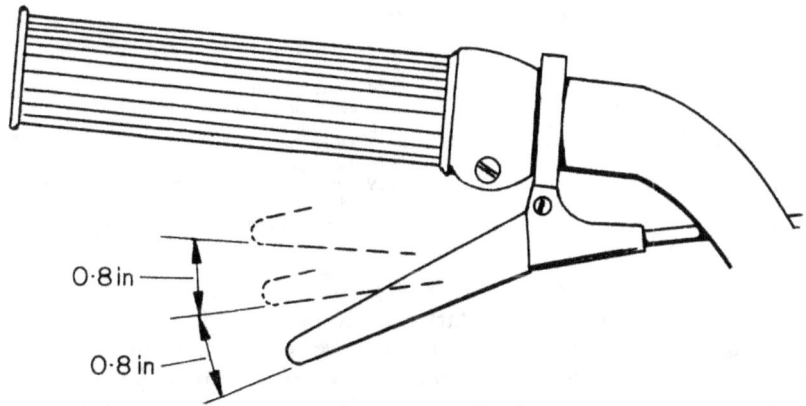

Fig. 5.1 Correct starter lever movement. First 2 cm (0·80 in.) of movement opens decompressor; second 2 cm (0·80 in.) movement engages starter clutch

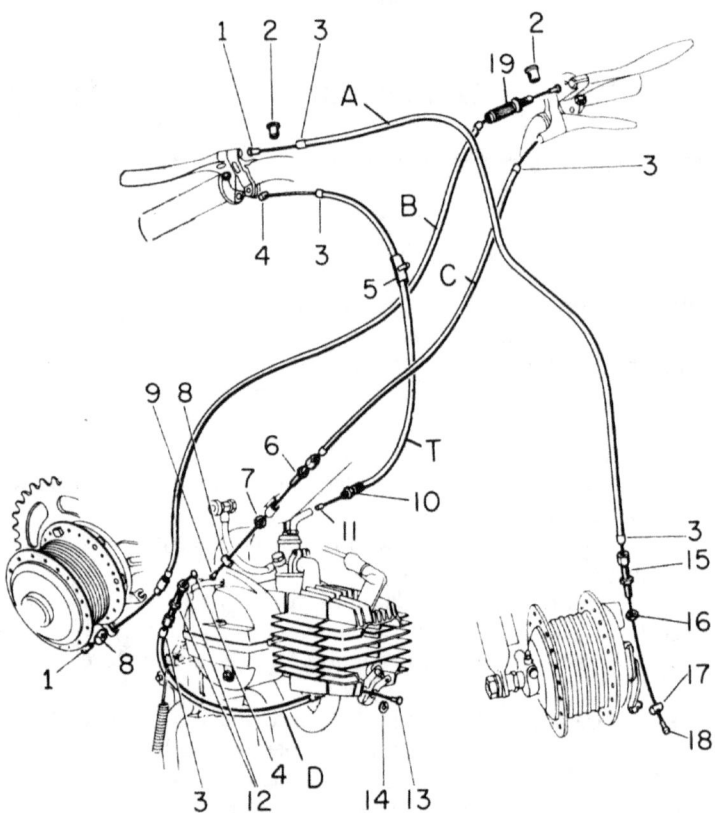

Fig. 5.2 Cables. A, front brake; B, rear brake; C, clutch;
D, decompressor; T, throttle

1 soldered nipple
2 nipple holder
3 shell
4 soldered nipple
5 oiler (throttle control cable only)
6 cable adjuster (starter clutch cable)
7 locking nut
8 nipple holder
9 soldered nipple
10 throttle cable adjuster
11 soldered nipple
12 cable adjuster (decompressor cable)
13 soldered nipple
14 slotted washer
15 cable adjuster (front brake)
16 locking nut
17 nipple holder
18 soldered nipple
19 cable adjuster, rear brake cable. Note: on Maxi N adjuster is at wheel end of cable; also a return spring is fitted over the cable at this end and end fittings differ

starter lever should open the decompressor, and the next 0·8 in. (2 cm) movement should engage the starter clutch (*see* Fig. 5.1).

The appropriate adjusters are on the lower end of the clutch cable and the upper end of the decompressor cable (i.e. adjacent to the clutch operating lever in both cases). Accurate adjustment is necessary if either cable is replaced. Also adjustment should be checked against lever movement periodically—e.g. three monthly intervals, or earlier if starting troubles are experienced.

CABLES AND HANDLEBAR CONTROLS

Adjusters for the other cables are:

    Front brake—at wheel hub end of cable.
    Rear brake—at wheel hub end of cable on Maxi "N"
                adjacent to handlebar lever on Maxi "S"
    Throttle control—at carburettor end of cable.

See Fig. 5.2 for detailed information on the cable runs and components.

If an inner cable breaks or frays, the cable run should be replaced as a complete unit. In the case of the Maxi "N" it is necessary to specify the model number as the cable support was modified from machine No. 9914184 on. Models with an earlier serial number have a screwed on cable support; and models with a serial number from 9914184 on an integral cable support.

Front brake and throttle cables are identical on the Maxi "N" and Maxi "S". The rear brake cables are different on the two models.

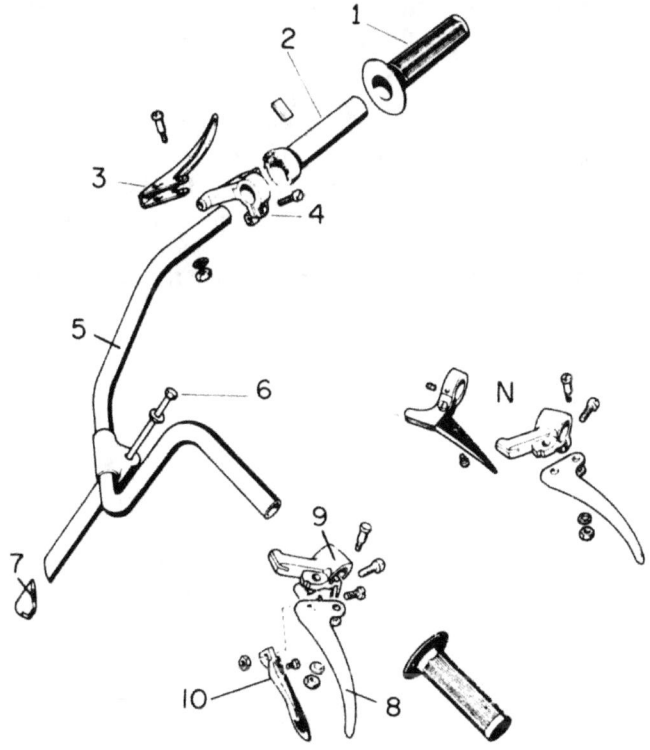

Fig. 5.3   Handlebar group

1 throttle grip
2 throttle twistgrip tube
3 brake lever
4 housing
5 handlebars
6 clamping bolt
7 clamp wedge
8 brake lever
9 housing
10 starter lever
    detail N—housing and starter and brake lever on Maxi N

For lubrication purposes, the brake cables are provided with a nipple at the handlebar end for grease lubrication (or SAE 90 oil used in a grease gun). The lower ends of the cables, and pivot points, can be lubricated with SAE 20 or SAE 30 oil. The throttle cable also has an oiler incorporated in the run, which can readily be found by tracing the cable run down from the handlebar end.

Handlebar Controls

The handlebars and handlebar controls are shown in exploded detail in Fig. 5.3. The throttle twistgrip assembly may be of two different manufacturers (Magura or ZKW), but all parts are interchangeable. Components are also identical on Maxi "N" and Maxi "S" models.

The diagram should provide all the information necessary for stripping down individual units and reassembly in correct order, should this be necessary. The handlebars themselves are secured by a clamping bolt with a hexagonal head at the top of the stem. This engages with a clamp wedge locking the handlebars to the front fork. Unscrewing the clamp bolt enables the handlebars to be removed from the forks.

To free the handlebars it is necessary to disconnect all control cables from the control levers and throttle twist grip, and remove the horn button. All wires must be disconnected from the terminals on the switch. The reflector can then be removed, after first removing the front of the headlamp, and remaining wires pulled down out of the lamp casing. The lamp casing can then be removed complete with speedometer head and cable drive. Finally remove the horn and/or disconnect the horn wires from their terminals.

6 Wheels, Hubs and Brakes

BOTH front and rear wheels have a rim diameter of 17 inches, to fit 21 × 2·00 in. tyres. Two different rim profiles are used—the Kromag or Schürmann (*see* Fig. 6.1). These also differ in the length of the spokes on the front wheel—188 mm to fit the Kromag rim, and 190 mm to fit the Schürmann rim. Both types have 36 spokes, on both front and rear wheels, and all other parts are common to both rim profiles.

Fig. 6.1 Alternative rim profiles used
A—Kromag   B—Schürmann

The rear wheel differs from the front wheel in the hub design, also incorporating a 20-tooth idle gear sprocket (freewheel) and a 45-tooth chain sprocket. The rear wheel of the Maxi "S" also differs slightly in detail design from that of the Maxi "N", notably in the shape of the brake cover plate and the fitting of a return spring on the brake lever assembly.

Both front and rear wheel hubs are alloy castings, that of the rear wheel being appreciably wider, with a flange on the nearside to which the sprocket is bolted and an extension on the offside to which the idler sprocket is fitted. Brake drums are cast into the hubs.

THE FRONT WHEEL

Removing the Front Wheel. Detach the speedometer drive by unscrewing the nut holding it to the small gearbox on the offside fork housing. Disconnect the brake cable on the opposite side and then unscrew the spindle nuts on each side. Remove the mudguard stays from the spindle, when the wheel can be dropped out of the forks.

Refit the front wheel in reverse sequence.

Front Hub. The bearings are of cup and cone type with loose balls (22 in each side, 7/32 in. diameter balls). Bearing "play" is adjusted via the cone, which is then locked by a hexagonal nut (*see* Fig. 6.2).

24 THE BOOK OF THE PUCH MAXI

To disassemble the front hub the wheel should be gripped in a vice with soft jaws by the offside axle nut (the wheel then being horizontal). Unscrew the nearside axle nut, now uppermost, and remove the brake cover plate and washer. The cone locking nut can now be removed, followed by the cone, when the hub can be lifted from the axle.

To clean the bearings, lift off the cover washers and remove the balls. Wash balls and bearing shells with petrol and regrease before reassembly. If the bearing shell is damaged, this can be prised out and replaced, pressing back carefully with a suitable arbor.

The cover washers which protect the bearing can prove tricky to reassemble. It is recommended that a length of metal tube which is a loose fit on the spindle be used as a driver to slide them in place.

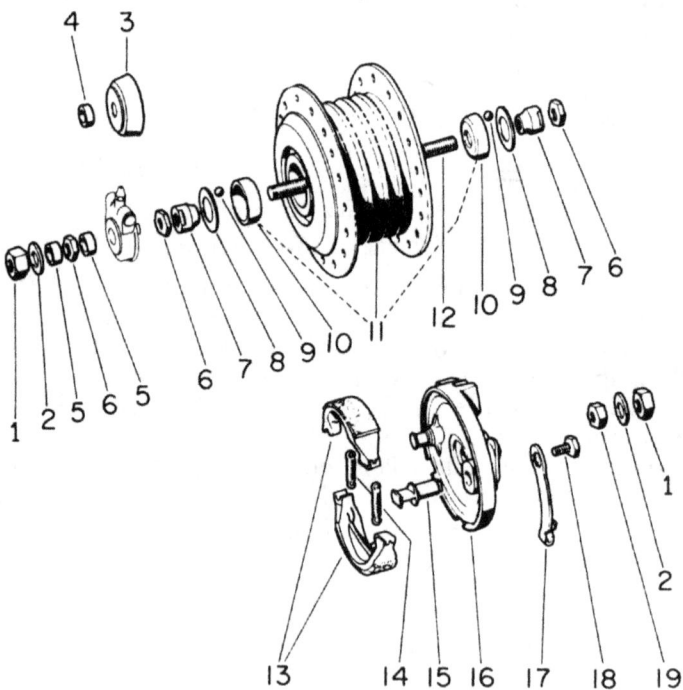

Fig. 6.2 Front hub and front brake exploded detail

1 hexagon nut
2 washer
3 cover cap
4 spacer ring
5 spacer ring
6 hexagon nut
7 cone
8 cover
9 ball
10 bearing shell
11 front wheel brake hub (with pressed-in bearing cups)
12 front wheel spindle
13 pair of brake shoes with bonded lining
14 brake shoe spring
15 brake cam
16 brake cover plate
17 brake lever
18 hexagon bolt
19 hexagon nut

Assembly follows in the reverse order. Adjust bearing play from the brake side first, then take up play on the other side. Tighten until the spindle is stiff to turn. Then loosen by ¼ to ½ turn. This should provide free movement with no appreciable play, when adjustment can be secured with the lock nut.

THE REAR WHEEL

Removing the Rear Wheel. Both covers have to be removed to gain access to the rear wheel. Loosen both spindle nuts and the chain adjuster. Loosen the brake cable adjuster and detach the brake cable, pulling the cable adjuster out of its guide. The wheel can now be slid forward out of the frame and tilted to one side as necessary to remove the two chains from their sprockets. Push the spring loaded chain tensioning sprocket forwards, if necessary, to obtain the necessary slack on the pedal chain.

Reassembly follows in the reverse order, taking particular care to ensure that the peg on the brake cover plate engages in the recess in the frame. Also, of course, chain tension must be checked and adjusted as necessary.

Rear Hub. Disassembly follows essentially the same procedure as described for the front hub. Bearing adjustment is also identical. Component parts and their respective positioning can be identified from Fig. 6.3.

If the sprocket wheel or idler sprocket has to be replaced, this can be done without disassembling the rear hub. The main sprocket wheel is simply secured to the hub with six screws. To remove the idling sprocket the appropriate special tool should be used to hold the sprocket against rotation as the two securing nuts holding the sprocket on the spindle are removed. This sprocket is intended to be replaced as a complete unit.

BRAKES

The brake shoes have bonded on linings and so in the case of worn linings the shoes are replaced. The shoes can easily be removed once both brake springs have been detached with a screwdriver.

Scoring or damage to the brake drums call for a replacement hub, the drum being cast in with the hub.

In the event that both linings and drum surface have become highly polished, brake efficiency can be improved by roughening these surfaces by rubbing with emery paper. Accumulation of dust inside the drum can also affect brake efficiency. Thus whenever the brake is disassembled for examination (or replacement of shoes), the drum should be cleaned by blowing out.

Within normal wear limits, brake efficiency is basically dependent on proper positioning of the brake lever, which should not be more than 90 degrees to the run of the brake cable when the brakes are fully operated (*see* Fig. 6.4). This angle will gradually increase as the brakes are adjusted to compensate for wear, but the lever position can be adjusted so as not to exceed a 90-degree angle within wear limits, this adjustment being made on the indents locating the brake lever on the brake cam.

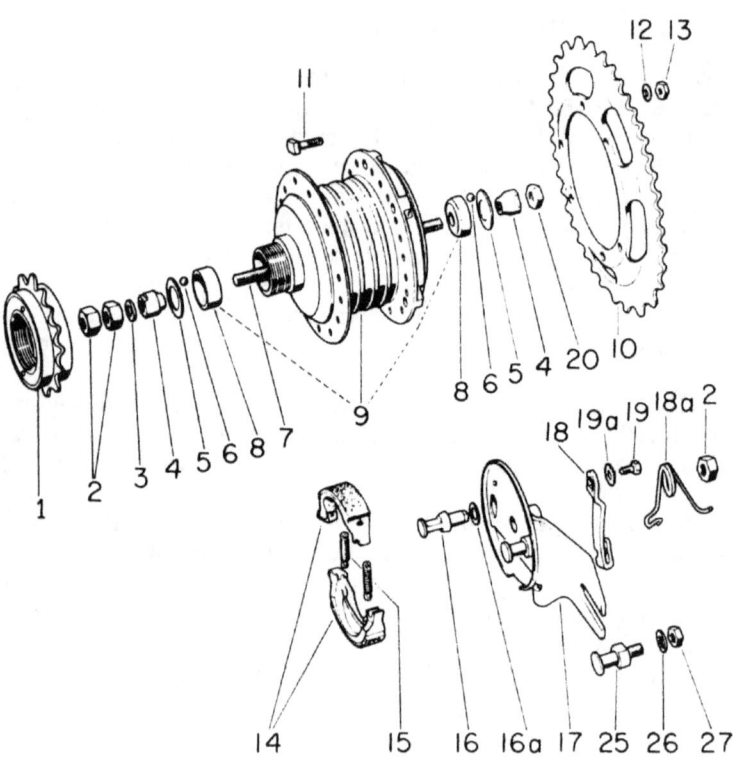

Fig. 6.3   Rear wheel hub and brake detail—Maxi S
(Maxi N differs slightly in the shape of the brake cover plate and brake lever: return spring is on brake cable)

1 idle gear sprocket (20 teeth)
2 hexagon nut
3 washer
4 cone
5 cover disc
6 ball
7 rear wheel axle
8 bearing cup
9 rear wheel brake hub (with pressed-in bearing cups)
10 chain sprocket (45 teeth)
11 retaining bolt
12 serrated lock washer
13 hexagon nut
14 pair of brake shoes with bonded lining
15 brake shoe spring
16 brake cam
16a washer
17 brake cover plate
18 brake lever
18a return spring
19 hexagon bolt
19a lock washer
20 hexagon nut
25 brake supporting bolt
26 toothed washer
27 hexagon nut

WHEELS, HUBS AND BRAKES

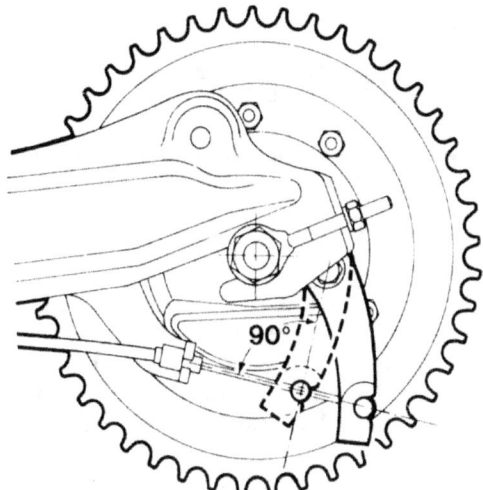

Fig. 6.4 Correct attitude of brake lever for optimum movement

Wear limits specified by the manufacturers are:

Drum diameter: nominal size 3·1500 in. (80 mm)

wear limit 3·1893 in. (81 mm)

Brake shoes assembled: nominal dia. 3·1103–3·1300 in. (79·0–79·5 mm)
wear limit 3·0394 in. (77·2 mm)

THE TYRES

Tyre Changing. The wheel is first removed to change a tyre. The tyre is then deflated as completely as possible by pressing down the valve, when the rim nut is unscrewed and the valve pushed through the hole in the rim.

One bead of the tyre should then be separated from the rim, pressing the side opposite to the valve into the rim grooves. This should give enough slack at the valve position to lift the bead over the edge of the rim with a tyre lever. Using one lever to hold the bead at this position, a second tyre lever can then be slid around the edge of the rim to lift out the complete circumference of the bead. The inner tube can then be withdrawn. If necessary, the complete tyre can then be removed by lifting the second bead over the rim.

When replacing the inner tube, first check that the rim tape is lying in its proper position, covering the ends of the spoke nipples. It is generally helpful to inflate the inner tube slightly before fitting, and also dust lightly with French chalk.

7 Pedals and Chains

THE pedal and chain components are shown in Fig. 7.1. There is also a second chain connecting the engine drive sprocket to the rear wheel (*see* Fig. 6.3, Chapter 6, p. 26). The pedal chain is on the right hand side (offside) of the moped; and the engine chain on the left hand side (nearside).

Two types of pedal wheels have been fitted—one with 36 teeth used on Maxi "N" models up to machine No. 9610282, and one with 37 teeth used on subsequent Maxi "N" models, and Maxi "S" models. In the case of Maxi "N" models, the chain has 87 links to match the 36-tooth wheel; and 88 links to match the 37-tooth wheel. The Maxi "S" chain has 80 links.

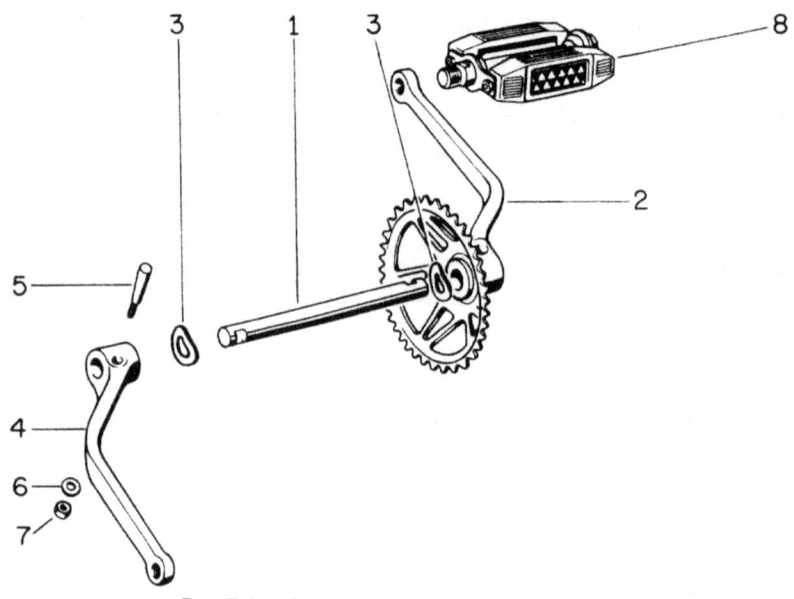

Fig. 7.1 Pedal spindle, cranks and pedals

1 pedal spindle
2 crank with 36 or 37 teeth sprocket, depending on model (see text)
3 Belleville washer
4 pedal crank (left-hand side)
5 cotter pin
6 washer
7 nut
8 pedal

PEDALS AND CHAINS

The pedal spindle runs in two nylon bushes pressed into a steel tube welded to the main frame. Wear is unlikely on these bearings (any wear will usually be on the spindle rather than the nylon bushes), but if replacement is thought desirable the bushes can readily be prised out and new ones fitted.

Tension is maintained in the pedal chain by a spring loaded jockey sprocket (chain tensioner) and is thus self-adjusting (Fig. 7.2). The only requirement in this respect is that the chain tensioner arm should be inclined *slightly* forward to work effectively—a point to be watched when adjusting the engine drive chain.

Fig. 7.2 The pedal chain is automatically tensioned by a jockey wheel (j)

Tension of the engine drive chain is adjusted by adjusters on the rear forks (one each side just above the spindle nuts) (Fig. 7.3). Tension is correct when the engine drive chain has between $\frac{3}{8}$ in. and $\frac{5}{8}$ in. slack at the mid-point.

To adjust the engine chain tension, the rear wheel spindle nuts must be loosened to permit the chain adjusters to be screwed in to move the wheel back slightly (or screwed out to allow the wheel to move forwards slightly, if the chain is too tight). An exactly equal amount of adjustment should be made on each chain adjuster, so that the correct alignment of the rear wheel is maintained. When the chain tension has been adjusted satisfactorily, the spindle nuts are tightened.

Fig. 7.3a   Drive chain adjuster (arrowed) right-hand side

Fig. 7.3b   Drive chain adjuster (arrowed) left-hand side

Fig. 7.3   Drive chain tension is adjusted by moving the rear wheel inwards or outwards, using the chain adjusters (arrowed)

PEDALS AND CHAINS

A limit to engine chain adjustment is reached when the rear wheel has moved so far back that the pedal chain tensioner arm is inclined too far forward, and no longer effective in providing automatic tensioning of the pedal chain. In this case there are two possible solutions:

1 Lengthen the pedal chain by the insertion of an additional link, which should restore the chain tensioner arm to its optimum position.

2 Replace the engine drive chain.

Method 1 is recommended practice, unless there is obviously considerable wear on the engine drive chain, when it would be best to replace this chain.

Cleaning Chains. Regular cleaning and relubrication of the chains is essential, to secure maximum chain life. Chains should be removed for cleaning, i.e. by detaching the spring plate on the master link and removing this link, not cleaned in position as this can only be partially effective.

Chains should be cleaned by washing in a dish of paraffin, assisted by brushing with a stiff brush. Wipe dry and lubricate before replacing. Lubricate by dipping in SAE 90 oil, or in a container holding chain grease which has been heated until the grease is molten. Surplus lubricant can be wiped off before refitting the chain.

It is equally important that the sprocket wheels be cleaned, to remove dirt, etc. between the teeth and on the sides of the teeth, before the chains are refitted.

After refitting, engine chain tension should be adjusted correctly. Check also the position of the spring plate on the master links. The *closed* end of this plate must always point in the direction of travel of the chain.

Intervals for chain cleaning and relubrication depend largely on the amount of vehicle use, and operating conditions, but cleaning at least every three months should be regarded as a strict necessity, and at shorter intervals if using the moped under wet or dirty conditions.

8 Forks and Frame

THE frame on the Maxi "N" and Maxi "S", and also the rear fork in the case of the Maxi "S" are of all-welded assembly from pressed steel components and if damaged in any way (other than very minor damage) are not repairable. The front fork should also be replaced as a unit if damaged —e.g. it is not possible to straighten twisted forks without the possibility of seriously reducing their strength. Maintenance work is therefore limited to checking for trueness and alignment if thought necessary (e.g. after a minor accident), and replacement of any wear parts. Major damage is treated by replacing the units affected.

Front Fork

The front fork is of telescopic type and essentially maintenance free. Only the plastic guide bushes require periodic lubrication, and the steering bearing.

To disassemble the front forks, remove the front wheel. The fork tubes can then be released from the top bridge by unscrewing the two bolts (washers underneath). The sliding tube can then be pulled out complete from each tube, exposing the spring and guide bushes (*see* Fig. 8.1). If either of the latter are to be removed the lower end of the sliding tube should be clamped in a vice with soft jaws when the spring can be removed by unscrewing in a clockwise direction. The guide bushes can be sprung open by inserting a screwdriver in the slots and slid off.

Plastic bushes and springs are regarded as "wear" parts and should be replaced if outside the following wear limits:

Spring: new length 7·244 in. (184 mm)
        wear limit 6·889 in. (175 mm)
Spring tension [when compressed to 2·284 in. (58 mm) length] should be at least 110 lb.
Plastic guide bush: new diameter 1·0609 in. (26·95 mm)
        wear limit 1·0433 in. (26·5 mm)

Replacement of parts and reassembly is straightforward provided care is taken to ensure that the spring is screwed right home (anti-clockwise) in each bottom tube. Each tube should then be inserted with a straight push upwards, without twisting, into the fork tube.

The alignment of the upper unit (tubes and bridge) can be checked by

FORKS AND FRAME 33

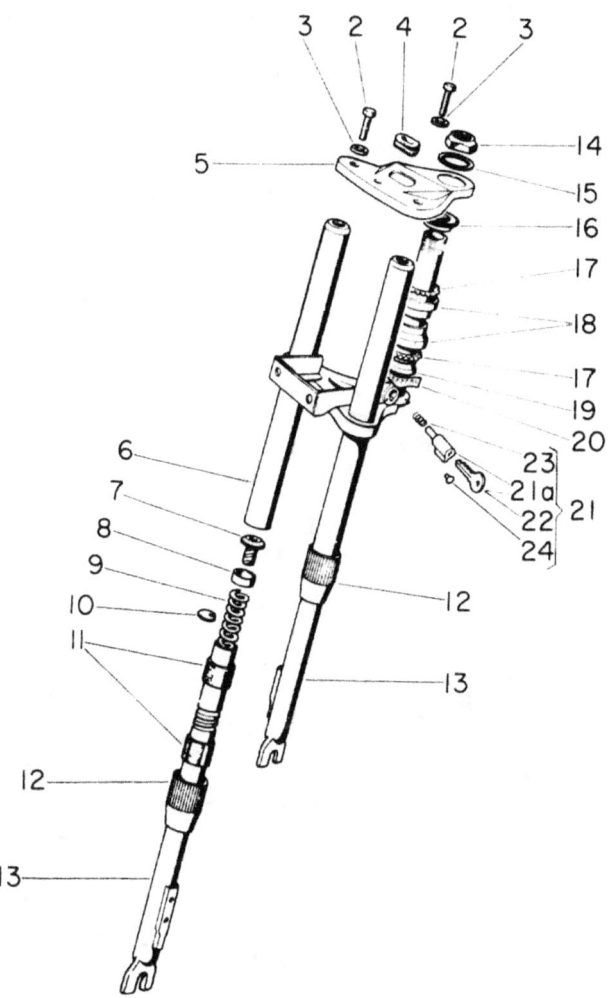

Fig. 8.1 Front fork in exploded detail

2 hexagon head screw
3 washer
4 grommet
5 top bridge
6 bottom bridge
7 threaded coupling
8 damping stop
9 thrust spring
10 washer
11 guide bushing
12 grooved shell
13 sliding tube

14 fork shaft nut
15 washer (only on models to No: 9681671)
16 top guide bushing
17 ball retainer
18 bearing cup
19 bottom guide bushing
20 spring strap
21 lock
22 key
23 thrust spring
24 notched rivet

laying on a level bench surface with the bridge overhanging the edge. Parallelism of the tubes can be checked by observation, and also measurement. If any misalignment is present this will be caused by a twist in the bridge and the unit must be replaced. It cannot be straightened and maintain full strength.

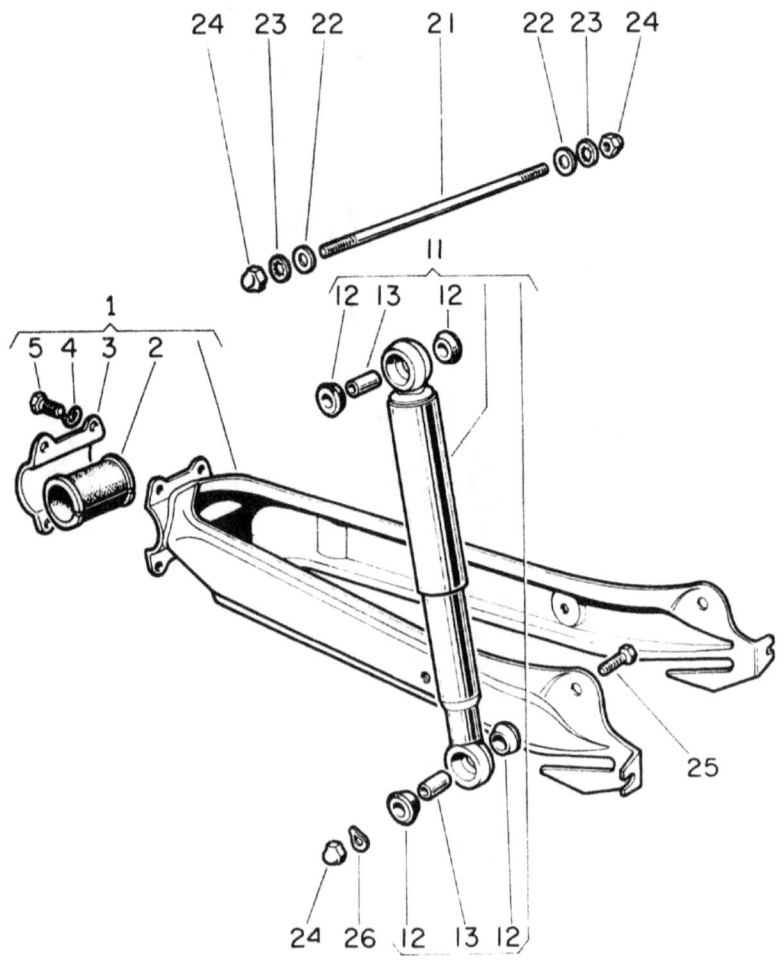

Fig. 8.2 Rear suspension of Maxi S

1 pivoted fork (complete)
2 rubber bearing
3 bearing bush
4 spring ring
5 hexagon screw
11 suspension unit (complete)
12 rubber bearing (two)
13 sleeve
21 bolt
22 washer
23 toothed lock washer
24 domed nut
25 hexagon screw
26 Belleville washer

FORKS AND FRAME

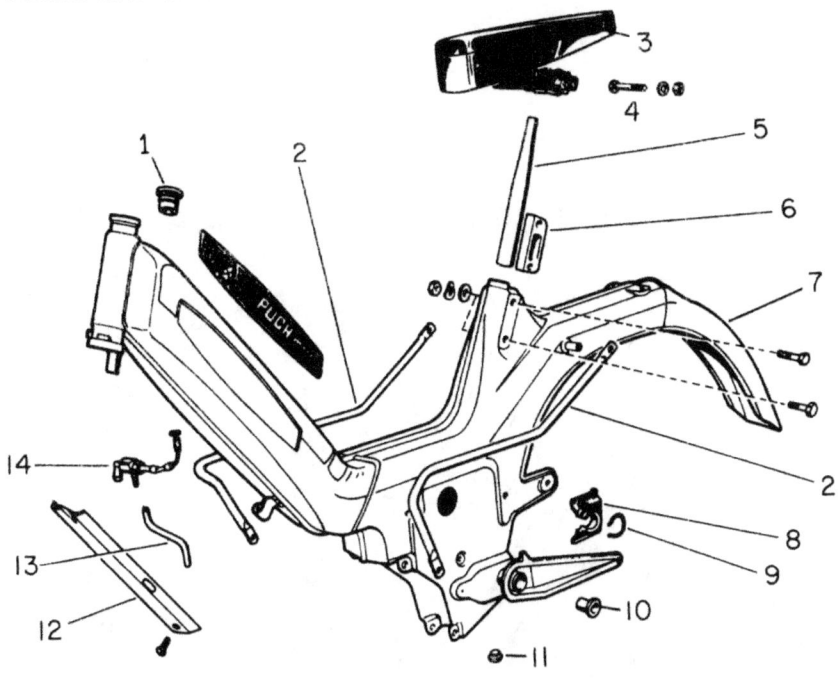

Fig. 8.3a Frame components—Puch Maxi S

1 fuel tank filler cap
2 lifting handles
3 saddle
4 saddle fixing bolt
5 saddle stem
6 saddle stem clamp
7 rear mudguard
8 chain guide
9 circlip for chain guide
10 pedal spindle bush
11 stand stop (rubber)
12 fairing for cables
13 fuel line
14 fuel tap

Steering Head

To gain access to the steering head bearings, remove the front forks, as described above; and the handlebars (*see* Chapter 5). Undo the large nut at the back of the bridge (washer underneath) when the steering column can be withdrawn from the frame tube, downwards.

Steering head bearings are of cone and cup type with loose balls (0·4 mm diameter).

Rear Fork

The Maxi "S" is fitted with a pivoted rear fork (*see* Fig. 8.2) with a telescopic suspension unit pivoted to each side at the rear. The front end of the fork pivots on a rubber bearing. The latter is a "wear" part which may need replacement after a considerable period of operation.

The suspension units are virtually maintenance free, although the top and bottom rubber bearings (one each side at each pivot point) are also "wear" parts and may eventually need replacement.

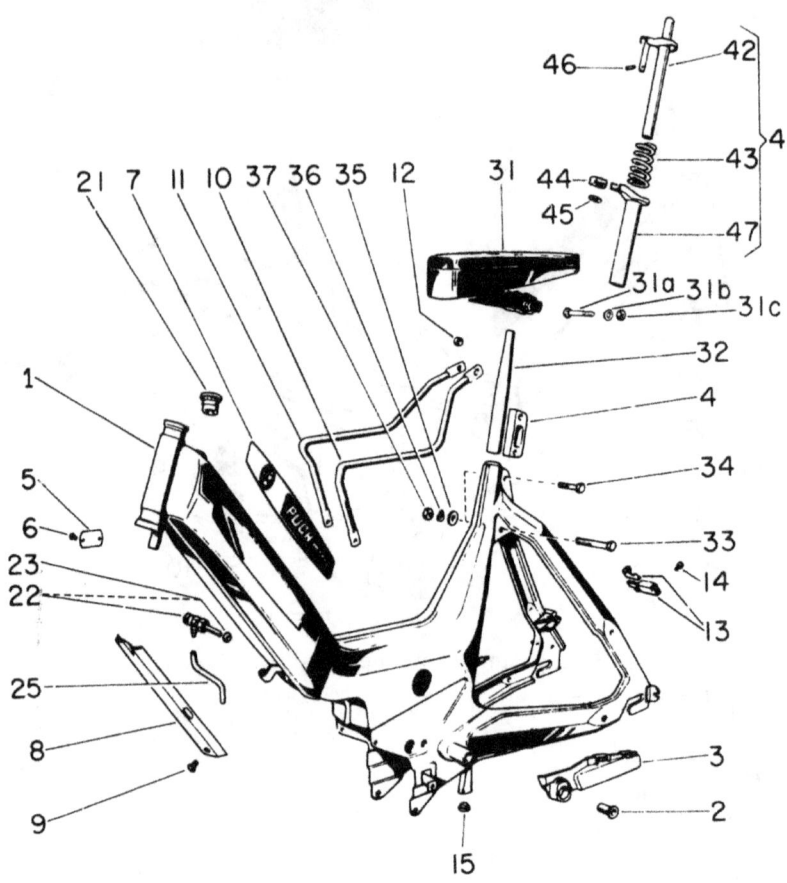

Fig. 8.3b Frame components—Puch Maxi N

1 frame (complete)
2 pedal spindle bushes
3 chain guide
4 clamp for chain guide
5 nameplate
6 bolt
7 decal panel
8 cable fairing
9 countersunk screw
10⎫
11⎭ lifting handles
12 spacer
13 lock
14 cheesehead screw
15 stand stop (rubber)
21 fuel tank filler cap
22 fuel tap (Karco or Orlandi)
23 seal ring
25 fuel line
31 saddle (Giuliari or Denfeld)
31a,b,c saddle fixing bolt washer, nut
32 saddle stem
33⎫
34⎭ hexagon head bolts
35 washer
36 spring washer
37 nut
41 saddle
42 saddle support
43 spring
44 slide bush
45 washer
46 hollow pin
47 saddle tube

FORKS AND FRAME

The suspension units themselves can, however, be disassembled for cleaning and lubrication of the guide bush and plastic ring. Grip the lower end of the unit in a vice with soft jaws and unscrew the lower end cap. Reverse the unit in the vice and unscrew the nut from the guide rod. Once free the spring will tend to shoot out. The sliding leg unit can now be withdrawn.

Reassemble in reverse order.

No replacement parts are available for the suspension units and so if any part is damaged the unit should be replaced as a whole.

Removal of mudguards and luggage carrier should be straightforward, if necessary, and no special instructions are necessary.

The main frame and associated components are shown in Figs. 8.3a and b as a reference, should removal or renewal of individual components be necessary.

9 Carburettor

THE carburettor is a Bing type 1/14/118. It is mounted on top of the engine unit and is readily accessible for maintenance. Attention likely to be required is adjustment of engine idling speed via the mixture screw (Fig. 9.1), and periodic removal of the carburettor for cleaning. It may also be found necessary to change the main jet in order to obtain optimum engine performance.

Fig. 9.1 Carburettor control and adjustment points
  c   choke (press down to operate)
  m   mixture adjustment screw

CARBURETTOR 39

The optimum size of main jet is dependent on the climatic conditions. Models may be found fitted with a no. 70, no. 68, no. 66 or no. 64 main jet (no. 70 being the usual standard). The jet as fitted to new machines is primarily suited to running-in and may ultimately be found to give too rich a mixture for best running. In this case it can be changed for the next jet size down after the running-in period. This next smaller jet size is included in the tool kit. Alternatively an "optimum" main jet size can be established by test (*see Carburettor Tuning*, p. 41).

Adjustment of Idling Speed. Before attempting adjustment of idling speed the engine must be warmed up thoroughly, preferably tackling this job after a run of several miles. The throttle is then closed to "tickover". Unscrew the mixture adjusting screw until the engine is on the point of stalling, then screw in to establish the position for smoothest running. Optimum idling speed range is 800–1,200 r.p.m. (which can be checked with a reed-type tachometer applied to the cylinder barrel, if available).

Once the idling adjustment has been established the play of the throttle cable should be adjusted. Loosen the nut on the cable adjuster and screw out the adjuster as necessary to provide slight play (approximately 0·2 mm or 8 thou.) on the throttle cable. In other words, there is this movement on the throttle cable before the throttle slide is lifted and engine speed increases. If there is insufficient play on the throttle cable, adjustment of the mixture screw will be ineffective. Thus if initial adjustment via the mixture screw appears to have little or no effect, check that play is present on the throttle cable.

Poor tickover, or inability to establish smooth idling via the mixture screw, can also be caused by an excessively large gap on the spark plug or contact breaker.

Carburettor Cleaning. To remove the carburettor for cleaning, turn the fuel tap off, remove the left hand panel (held by three screws), then undo the single screw holding the intake silencer so that it can be pulled out from the frame together with its flexible connecting tube. Pull the plastic fuel pipe off the carburettor, loosen the carburettor clamping screw and twist the carburettor so that the bottom of float chamber points towards the clutch. The carburettor can then be pulled off the intake pipe.

Remove the two screws holding the carburettor cover and remove the top complete with throttle slide, needle and choke. Unscrew the float chamber from the bottom.

The main jet is now visible—and accessible—and can be unscrewed. Clean by blowing through—*never* use a wire to "poke" clean. Other carburettor parts can be cleaned by washing with petrol and the body blown through. If any parts are wiped dry, do not use anything but a soft, clean lint-free cloth.

Before reassembling in reverse order, check that the needle is located

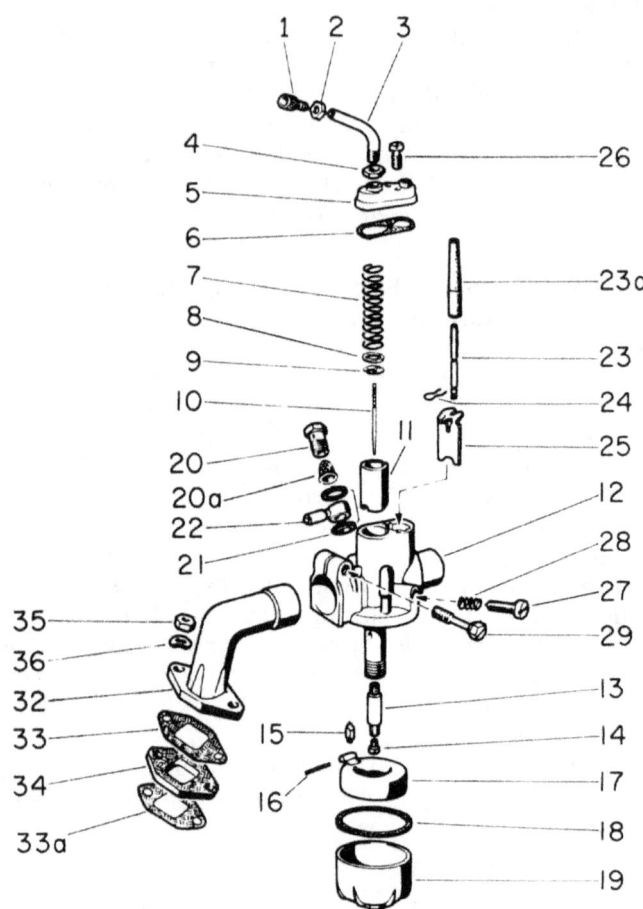

Fig. 9.2 Carburettor components, exploded view

1 throttle cable adjuster
2 locking nut
3 elbow
4 nut
5 carburettor top cover
6 gasket
7 throttle slide spring
8 washer
9 spring clamp
10 needle
11 throttle slide
12 carburettor body
13 needle jet
14 main jet
15 float needle
16 hinge pin
17 float
18 gasket
19 float chamber
20 banjo screw
20a filter
21 fibre washer
22 hose connector banjo
23 thrust pin
23a extension piece
24 clamp spring
25 choke slide
26 carburettor cover screw
27 mixture adjusting screw
28 spring
29 clamp screw
32 connecting sleeve
33 paper gasket
33a paper gasket
34 thick gasket
35 nut
36 Belleville washer

CARBURETTOR

in its second notch from the top. See also Fig. 9.2 for details of carburettor components.

Carburettor Tuning. Carburettor tuning will only be effective if the engine is in good condition (i.e. wear parts within permitted tolerances, engine decarbonized if necessary, and contact breaker and spark plug gaps correct). A change of *main jet* size will affect the *maximum* speed. Altering the *needle jet* position will affect the *medium* speed range.

To establish the optimum main jet size, separate test runs must be made with the next jet sizes up and down and the maximum throttle performances compared. The *optimum* jet size is the one which gives the *next* best performance—i.e. slightly less top speed than the best jet tested.

The optimum mixture for medium speed running can be established by raising or lowering the position of the needle one notch at a time and comparing results. Table I can also be consulted as a guide to carburetion faults and their causes.

The intake silencer/air filter is shown separately in Fig. 9.3. This will require periodic removal for cleaning, the two casing halves being sprung

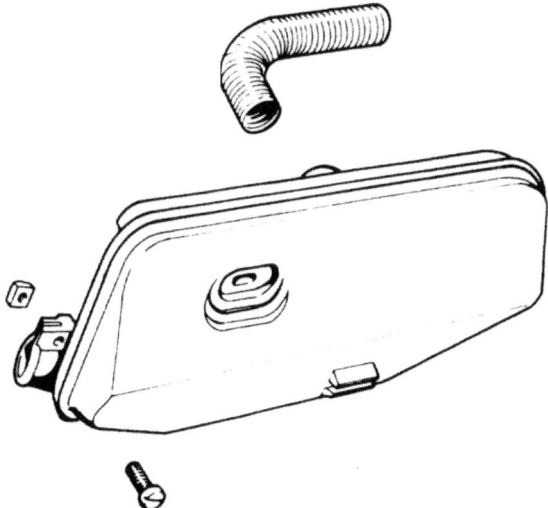

Fig. 9.3 The intake silencer (air filter) can be removed complete. Separate cover parts to remove circular filter for cleaning. (*Note:* filter is retained in position by a coil spring)

apart once the retaining screws have been removed, the filter disc being retained in position by a coil spring. The inside of the casing and the filter can be given an initial wash in petrol and then a dip in petrol:oil mixture, shaking or blowing reasonably dry before reassembly. Check that when the flexible hose is refitted the open end is in a position where it can readily draw in air.

CARBURETION CHECK TABLE

Fault: rough irregular running, poor acceleration, poor pulling power		Fault: engine "pinks", engine overheats, poor top speed performance		Check for possible cause
Spark plug check: plug dark colour or wet		Spark plug check: bright or white colour, burnt electrodes		
Confirms: Mixture too rich at		Confirms: Mixture too lean at		
Medium range	Full throttle	Medium range	Full throttle	
	O			Main jet too big
			O	too small
			O	blocked
	O			loose
O	O			Needle too high
		O		too low
O	O			worn
O	O			loose
O	O			Needle seat leaking
O	O			Float leaking
O				Choke faulty
		O		Air intake blocked
			O	Carb. not fitted properly
			O	Blocked fuel line

10 The Engine Group

THE various components comprising the engine group are shown in Fig. 10.1. Work which can be done with the engine *in situ* is limited to contact breaker adjustment (and removal of the flywheel magneto-generator if necessary), decarbonizing, and piston, piston ring or gudgeon pin replacement (partially stripping the engine as described under Decarbonizing—Chapter 4). For work on the big end bearing, crankshaft, clutch, final drive and main bearings the engine unit must be removed from the machine and disassembled.

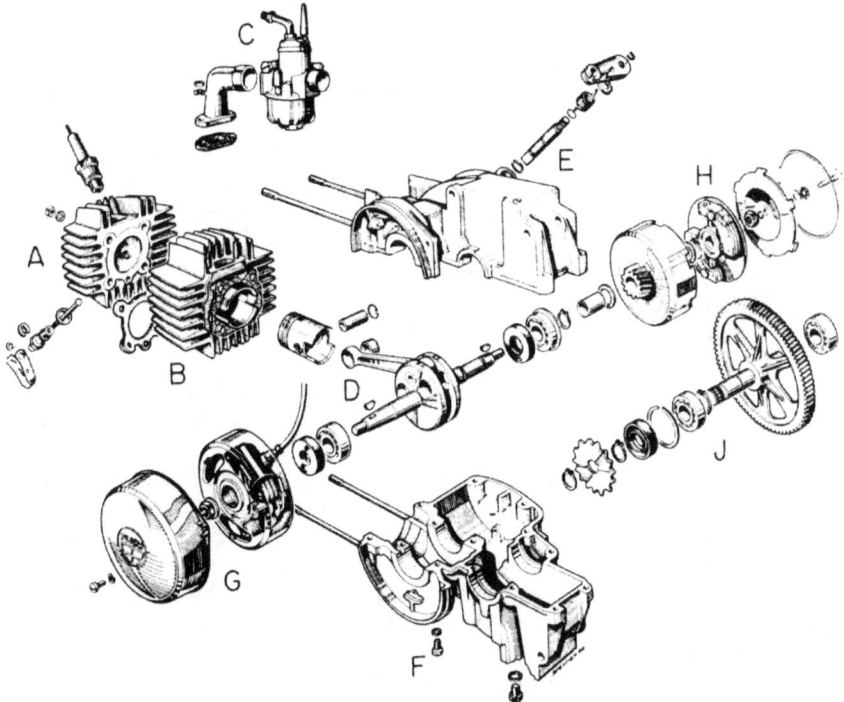

Fig. 10.1 Puch Maxi engine group

A—cylinder head; B—cylinder barrel; C—carburettor; D—crankshaft group; E—crankcase lower half; G—flywheel magneto-generator; H—clutch; J—final drive "gearbox"

Because of its exposed position, *any* dismantling work on the engine group should be preceded by a thorough wash in paraffin or petrol over all external surfaces to remove accumulated dirt.

To free the engine for removal from the frame the following work is necessary:

1 Remove both side covers (chainguards).
2 Close fuel tap and pull hose off carburettor.
3 Loosen air filter retaining screw, pull the rear brake cable out of the way and remove the air filter.
4 Loosen carburettor clamping screw and remove carburettor by twisting; *or* remove the nuts securing the carburettor inlet pipe to the cylinder to detach from the engine unit. The carburettor will now be suspended on the throttle cable, which can be detached.
5 Slacken off the decompressor cable adjuster (or loosen grub screw holding cable at handlebar end to obtain slack on this cable at the lever end).
6 Remove retaining washer on decompressor and detach cable from decompressor.
7 Loosen operating lever clamping screw, pull out cable and disconnect nipple from the lever; *or* remove the engine bolt which is in the way to get enough freedom of movement to remove the cable.
8 Disconnect the yellow wire from the terminal block (or all wires from the terminal block, if appropriate).
9 Remove the complete exhaust system (*see* Decarbonizing for details, although procedure is obvious).
10 Disconnect the clutch cable from the clutch.
11 Remove both chains by springing off the open plate on the master link on each chain, and detaching these links.

Remove the offside (right hand side) pedal complete with sprocket, (held by a nut with a right hand thread. *Note:* the left hand pedal nut has a *left* hand thread).

The engine unit is now "free" and the three fixing screws are readily accessible. It is necessary at this stage to have assistance, or some means of support or slinging, so that the machine can be held clear of the ground. The three engine bolts can then be removed and the engine pulled forwards out of the frame. The centre stand can be removed by unhooking the spring and then undoing the three nuts holding the pivot block to the crankcase. The engine unit can then be stood in a tray and the drain plug removed to drain oil out of the crankcase.

Dismantling work on the engine is much easier if special jig, part no. 905.6.31.106.2, is available. The engine may be bolted to this and held at a convenient height by gripping the jig in a vice. The engine should be mounted in the jig in an upside down position (spark plug facing downwards).

THE ENGINE GROUP

Cylinder and Piston

The cylinder head is removed by unscrewing the four head nuts and withdrawing (after first removing spark plug and lead) (Fig. 10.2). The cylinder barrel can then be drawn off the four studs. The head is sealed with a gasket. The barrel is also sealed by a gasket at the crankhouse end and both may be re-usable.

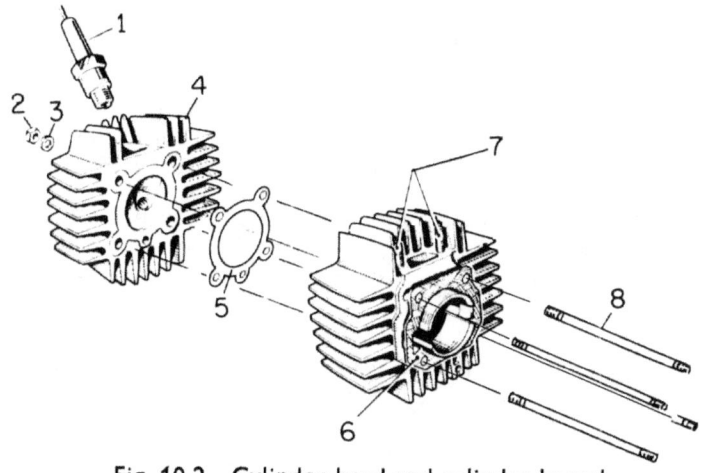

Fig. 10.2 Cylinder head and cylinder barrel

1 spark plug
2 head retaining nut (4)
3 locking washers (4)
4 cylinder head
5 head gasket
6 cylinder barrel
7 studs for exhaust flange
8 studs (to crankcase)

The cylinder bore should be examined for signs of scoring or wear; and the bore can also be measured to check for wear using an internal micrometer. Replacement is required if wear exceeds recommended limits (*see* Table I), or the chrome plated surface shows signs of damage. The cylinder *cannot* be rebored.

TABLE I CYLINDER AND PISTON GROUPS

Group	Cylinder diameter	Piston diameter
1	1·4946–1·4955 in. (37·975–37·985 mm)	1·4939–1·4943 in. (37·945–37·955 mm)
2	1·4955–1·4959 in. (37·985–37·995 mm)	1·4943–1·4947 in. (37·955–37·965 mm)
3	1·4959–1·4963 in. (37·995–38·005 mm)	1·4947–1·4951 in. (37·965–37·975 mm)
4	1·4963–1·4967 in. (38·005–38·015 mm)	1·4951–1·4955 in. (37·975–37·985 mm)
5	1·4967–1·4970 in. (38·015–38·025 mm)	1·4955–1·4959 in. (37·985–37·995 mm)

About 0·000787–0·001576 in. (0·020–0·040 mm) in each case.

The piston should be examined for signs of wear; also worn or broken piston rings. Piston ring wear can be checked by replacing the cylinder and turning the engine to bring the piston to the top of the bore. The gap at this point should be less than 0·020–0·024 in. (0·5–0·6 mm).
Permissible wear limits are:

        Maximum ovality of cylinder 0·000984 in. (0·025 mm)
        Maximum piston ring play 0·00591 in. (0·15 mm)
        Maximum wear limit 0·0197 in. (0·5 mm)

Cylinder and piston must be replaced as a matched pair of the same group, defined by manufacturer's limits. There are five limit groups (*see* Table I). The group number is marked on the top surface of the cylinder flange with a number; and on the crown of the piston with a number.

Note: if piston is removed, or piston rings are removed, it is essential that when reassembled the gaps in both rings should face towards the exhaust port (i.e. downwards if the engine is mounted in the jig).

Gudgeon Pin

The gudgeon pin and piston bearing bore are similarly identified by limits. Gudgeon bore is defined by two groups, identified by a coloured dot on the inside of the piston. Gudgeon pins are marked with one, two or three coloured dots on the end, to identify as group 1, 2 or 3. Matching sizes are shown in Table II.

TABLE II GUDGEON PIN AND GUDGEON BORE GROUPS

Group	Gudgeon pin diameter	Group	Gudgeon bore diameter	Clearance
1	0·4725–0·4724 in. (12·003–12·000 mm)	Yellow	0·4727–0·4726 in. (12·0085–12·006 mm)	0·000118–0·000336 in. (0·003–0·0090 mm)
2	0·4725–0·4724 in. (12·003–12·000 mm)	Blue	0·4726–0·4725 in. (12·006–12·0035 mm)	0·000019–0·000236 in. (0·0005–0·00060 mm)
3	0·4724–0·4723 in. (12·000–11·997 mm)			0·000137–0·000354 in. (0·0035–0·0090 mm)

Little End Bearing

The little end bearing is a bronze bush pressed into the small end of the connecting rod. Limits on diameter are:

        New 0·000315–0·000787 in. (0·008–0·020 mm)
        Wear limit 0·00984 in. (0·025 mm)

The bearing bush must be replaced once this wear limit is reached.
The bush can be removed without disassembling the crankcase by using the special tool no. 905.6.17.101.0. The same tool is used to replace

THE ENGINE GROUP

the new bush. The new bush is then reamed to size, after first drilling the lubricating holes and deburring. Pack the top of the crankcase opening with lint-free rag to prevent swarf dropping inside.

If further work is necessary on the engine, replacement of the little end bush can be undertaken after a complete stripdown.

Particular care is needed to ensure that reaming is "square" so that the connecting rod is accurately centred on the gudgeon pin. A special reaming tool is available, part no. 905.6.17.101.0.

Big End Bearing

Big end bearing wear can be checked by the amount of "float" on the connecting rod, in an up and down direction. There should be a small amount of play only—just detectable. If excessive play is present, then a new crankshaft must be fitted. This is available only as a complete unit. A new crankshaft assembly should also be fitted if there is noticeable binding of the big end bearing, as this would indicate distortion of the crank webs.

This will require further dismantling of the engine.

Decompressor

Decompressor components are shown in Fig. 10.3. The clearance on the movement is quite critical since if this is less than 0·004 in. (0·2 mm) the decompressor may not seal completely, resulting in burning of the valve and valve seat. Slight burning can be treated by replacing the valve and grinding into the seating. If more severe damage is evident, the complete decompressor should be replaced as a unit.

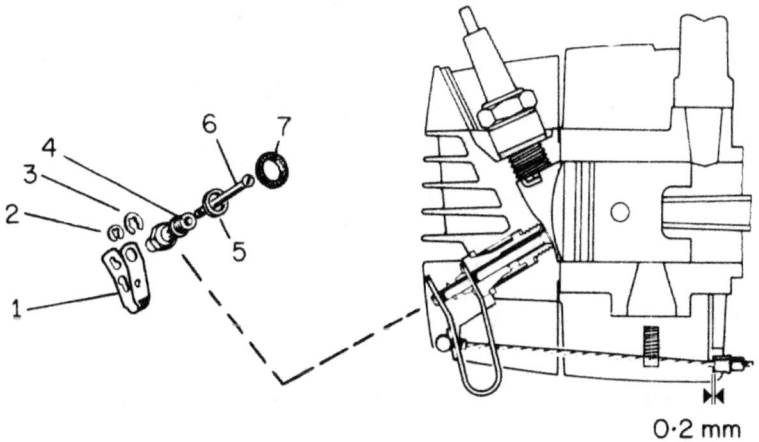

Fig. 10.3   Decompressor—components and adjustment

1 spring bracket
2 small tab washer
3 large tab washer
4 valve guide
5 sealing ring
6 valve
7 seal

If the decompressor is removed (e.g. for inspection), or replaced, always fit new seal rings.

Flywheel Magneto-Generator

The flywheel is keyed to the crankshaft, and also secured in place with a nut. A special tool is needed to hold the flywheel whilst the nut is unscrewed; and an extractor is needed to pull the flywheel off the crankshaft.

Work on the flywheel magneto-generator is detailed in Chapter 11. This unit must also be removed before further disassembly of the engine.

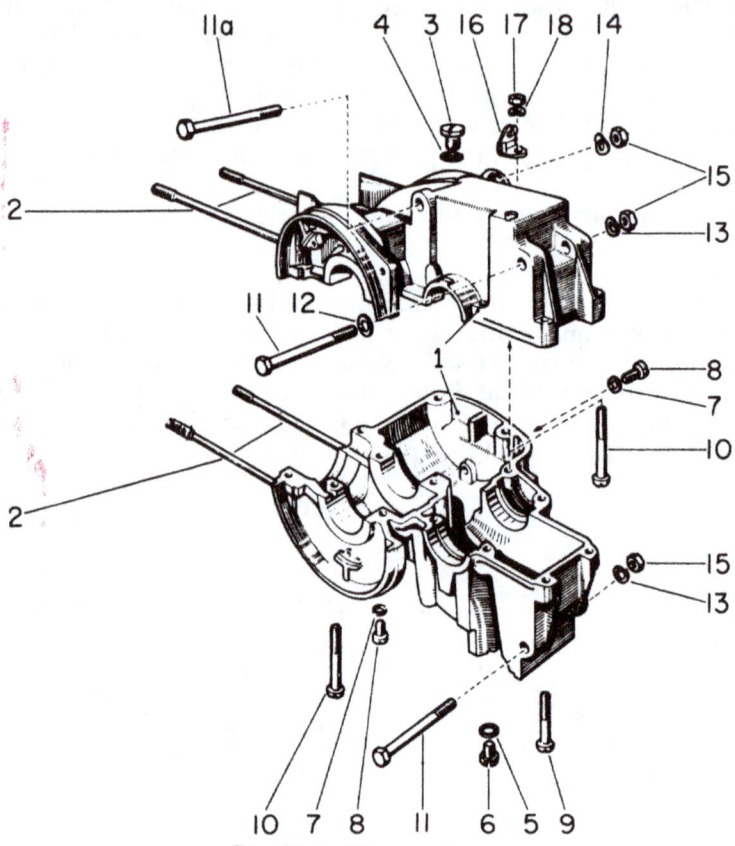

Fig. 10.4   The crankcase

1 crankcase halves
2 cylinder holding studs
3 oil filler plug
4 sealing washer
5 seal washer (oil drain)
6 oil drain screw
7 seal washer
8 oil level screw
9, 10 crankcase assembly screws
11, 11a engine mounting bolts
12 plain washer
13 spring washer
14 Belleville washer
15 nut
16 cable bracket ⎫
17   ⎬ models up to no: 9914183 only
18 washer   ⎭

THE ENGINE GROUP 49

Crankcase (Fig. 10.4)

The crankcase halves are secured with 14 screws (all with slotted heads). All are removed by a screwdriver, except that the screw securing the clutch cable stop bracket must first be freed by undoing the locknut. The screws should be quite tight, and it is very important to use a screwdriver blade of exactly the right width to match the head slots, otherwise the heads can be damaged. It may also be necessary to use an adjustable spanner to grip the flat of the blade to act as a tommy-bar to provide extra torque for loosening the screws.

When all screws are removed the crankcase halves can be separated by lifting off the top half. If stuck, tap lightly around the joint line with a mallet.

Removal of the crankshaft half will expose the crankshaft assembly and bearings, and the countershaft assembly and its bearings. One (or both) may tend to be lifted with the top half of the crankcase, so take appropriate care.

The crankshaft assembly (Fig. 10.5) comprising crankshaft with bearings and oil seals, piston and clutch assembly can now be removed. To remove

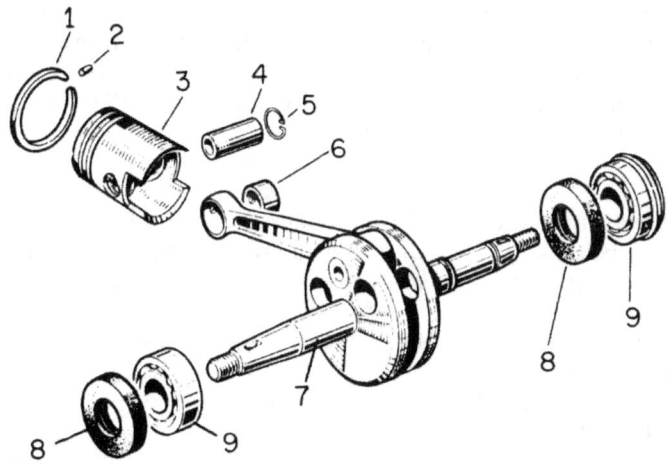

Fig. 10.5 Crankshaft group

1 piston ring
2 locking peg
3 piston
4 gudgeon pin
5 circlip
6 little end bearing bush
7 crankcase (with connecting rod integrally mounted)
8 oil seal
9 ball bearing

the clutch, the assembly must be gripped vertically in a soft jawed vice by the web nearest the clutch, the clutch being uppermost. Remove the thrust bolt and washers from the centre of the outer plate and also the large circlip. The outer plate can then be removed. The nut holding the clutch drum is then accessible and can be removed with a socket spanner (or cranked ring spanner).

A special extractor (tool no. 905.6.34.102.0) is needed to pull the drum off the crankshaft taper. This is secured to the drum with two screws and withdrawing pressure applied by turning the centre bolt on the tool with a spanner. Remove the key from the crankshaft.

Crankshaft Repair Work

The only maintenance work which can be carried out on the crankshaft are replacement of the main bearings and oil seals (if necessary), and replacement of the little end bearings in the connecting rod (as described under Little End Bearing, p. 46).

The flywheel end oil seal is readily removed and replaced. To change the oil seal at the other end, its associated ball bearing must be removed. This is retained by circlips, the larger one serving to locate the crankshaft axially in a groove in the crankcase. Once the circlips have been removed, the bearing can be removed using the special extractor (tool no. 905.6.34. 102.0). The other bearing can be removed with the same tool, after first removing its oil seal.

Two other special tools (nos. 350.1.70.012.0 and 320.1.70.012.2) are needed to fit new bearings to the crankshaft. It is possible to refit bearings using a piece of metal tube as a sleeve and tapping the bearings in position. If this type of tool is used it is imperative that the end of the sleeve bears only on the inner ring of the bearing. If pressure is applied to the outer ring, the bearing will suffer permanent damage.

Clutch

Disassembly of the clutch can be completed by removing the circlip retaining the bell housing, which runs on a floating bush. Note particularly the various washers and their correct positioning for reassembly (*see* Fig. 10.6).

Reassembly of the clutch follows the reverse order, with the crankshaft fitted with bearings and oil seals clamped vertically in a vice by the clutch-end crank web. Fit up the clutch in the following order:

1 Lower circlip.

2 Bush, lower shim washer, clutch drum, upper shim washer and upper circlip.

3 Centrifugal clutch, followed by Belleville washer and nut, tightened to the correct torque (20 lb ft).

4 Small circlip, outer plate, large circlip to lock plate in place.

5 Pressure bolt with washer and needle bearing.

Clutch Clearance

Wear limits on the clutch parts are:

Centrifugal clutch—usable until the metal has worn almost through
Starter clutch—usable until the lining has been worn down to a thickness of 0·040 in. (1 mm).

THE ENGINE GROUP

Centrifugal clutch parts should also be replaced if the drum or linings have become scored or grooved.

Clutch axial movement required for correct clearance is 0·0118–0·0197 in. (0·30–0·50 mm) between the clutch cover and lining; and 0·0078 in. (0·20 mm) between drum and centrifugal clutch—in other words

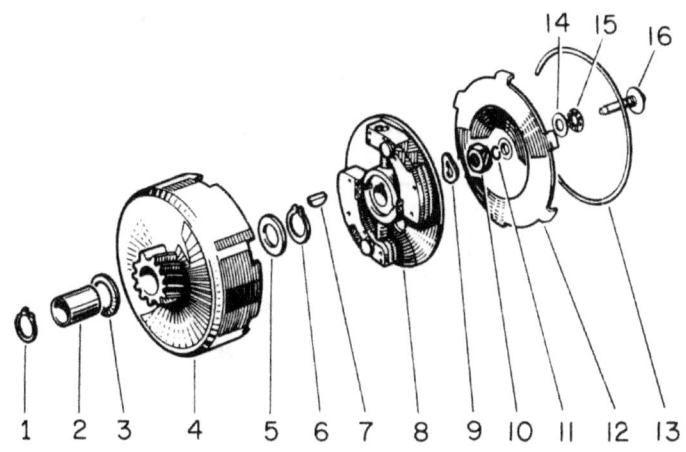

Fig. 10.6 Clutch assembly

1 circlip
2 bush
3 washer
4 clutch drum
5 washer
6 circlip
7 key
8 clutch hub assembly

9 Belleville washer
10 hexagonal nut
11 spring ring
12 clutch cover
13 circlip
14 washer
15 needle bearing
16 thrust bolt

0·30–0·50 mm downwards when centrifugal clutch is pressed downwards as far as it will go; and 0·20 mm upwards when the centrifugal clutch is lifted upwards as far as it will go (*see also* Fig. 10.7). These axial movements are controlled by the thickness of the lower and upper shim washers, respectively. These are available in 0·0078 in. (0·02 mm) thickness graduations. Lower shim washers (readily identified as being of larger diameter and hole size) have an actual thickness range of 0·0433 in. to 0·0669 in. (0·10 mm to 1·70 mm). Upper shim washers have an actual thickness range of 0·0433 in. to 0·827 in. (0·10 mm to 2·10 mm).

The actual thickness of shim washers required can be determined by measurement, if the clutch is first assembled *without* the shim washers. The procedure is then as follows:

1 Press the clutch cover down as far as it will go and measure the distance between the gear on the clutch drum and circlip. Call this distance D.

2 Allow a mean clearance value of 0·016 in. (0·40 mm). Deduct this from D to give the required thickness of the lower shim washer, i.e.

$$T \text{ (lower shim)} = D - 0.016 \text{ in.}$$

3 Lift the clutch cover up as far as it will go, and measure the distance between the gear and circlip, which will now be greater. Call this E.

4 The required axial movement in this direction is 0·0078 in. (0·20 mm). However, since the lower shim washer is not present, this thickness must also be taken into account.

5 Thus the thickness required for the upper shim washer is

$$E - 0.0078 \text{ in.} - T$$

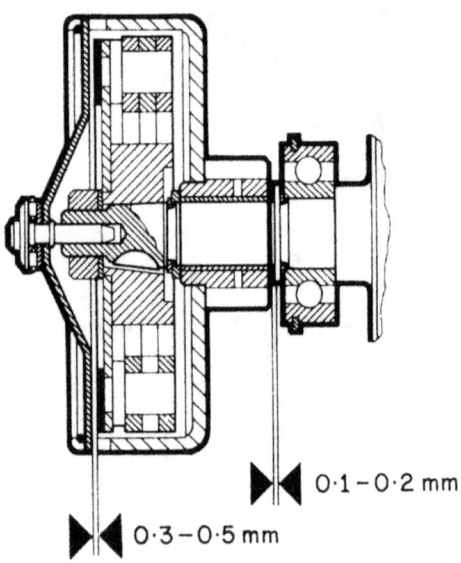

Fig. 10.7 Specified clutch clearances

Countershaft Assembly

The countershaft assembly, which may also be called the "gearbox" can be lifted out of the half crankcase complete and comprises the components shown in Fig. 10.8. There should normally be no need to disassemble this unit, except to replace the oilseal or bearings. Bearings can be removed and refitted using the same special tools required for removal/refitting of the crankshaft bearings.

Countershaft and gear are press fitted together and cannot be separated. If either are damaged or excessively worn they must be replaced as a unit. The chain drive sprocket locks on a splined section of the shaft and is secured with circlips.

THE ENGINE GROUP	53

Reassembly of the Engine Unit

Fully assembled crankshaft and countershaft units are laid in the half crankcase, making sure that bearings and circlips are properly located. All traces of old jointing compound should be removed from both halves of the crankcase by careful scraping, taking care not to scratch into the metal surfaces.

Give a light coating of non-hardening jointing compound to the lower half crankcase rim, then place the other half of the crankcase carefully in place. There are no locating pegs or dowels, so the two crankcase halves have to be positioned initially by sight and feel, until enough bolts can be screwed in finger tight to verify the correct location.

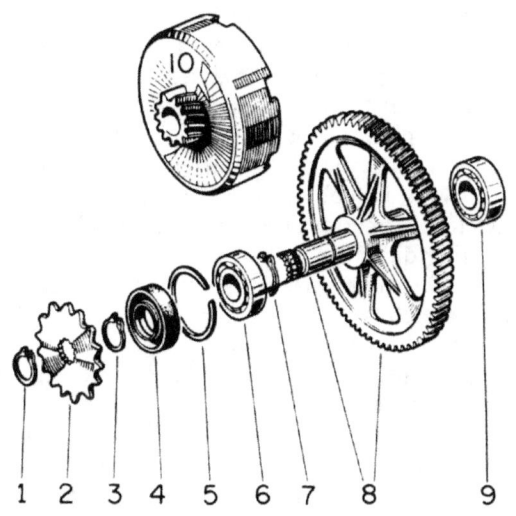

Fig. 10.8 Countershaft Assembly

1 circlip
2 chain sprocket
3 circlip
4 oil seal
5 circlip
6 ball bearing
7 circlip
8 shaft with integral sprocket (mating with pinion on clutch drum 10)
9 ball bearing

Note that the screws are of two different lengths—five long and nine short. Four of the long screws are used to secure the bearing housings, and the fifth positions behind the clutch housing with a locknut and washer holding the clutch cable stop bracket. All screws should be taken down finger tight, and then finally tightened up, working diagonally from side to side.

Cylinder barrel and head should be refitted to the crankcase before replacing the flywheel magneto-generator, to avoid possible damage to the connecting rod. Timing should be checked if the magneto-generator has been disassembled, otherwise the flywheel unit can be aligned against the timing marks (*see* Chapter 11).

The centre stand and its spring should be refitted before the engine unit is removed from its jig, ready for refitting to the frame.

The frame needs to be lifted and supported firmly to allow the engine unit to be inserted in position upwards and backwards, when it can be positioned by the three fixing bolts, as soon as crankcase and frame holes have been aligned. It is generally easiest to insert the upper bolt first, then rock the engine slightly about this as a pivot point to locate and insert the other two bolts. Fit the spring washers and nuts and tighten to recommended torque.

Once the engine unit is secured, the moped can be stood on the centre stand for further assembly work. This should be straightforward, and follows the reverse order of disassembly described earlier.

Particular attention must be paid to adjustment of the starter control movement. The cable must be adjusted to operate the decompressor before the starter clutch (*see* Chapter 5), and the decompressor must have the necessary clearance at the completely engaged starter clutch position. As a guide the starter clutch should operate after approximately 1·18 in. (30 mm) movement of the lever. If the starter clutch is too tightly adjusted, i.e. operates too early, it will act as a brake when the moped is pushed. If too slackly adjusted (i.e. operates too late), the clutch will slip when starting and make starting difficult.

Recommended tightening torques should be observed on flywheel, cylinder head and clutch centre nuts (*see* Technical Data). A tightening torque of 7 lb ft is specified for the crankcase screws, but since these have to be tightened by a screwdriver these are best checked with screwdriver bit in a socket torque spanner.

Specific details required on various assemblies should be easy to follow from the various exploded diagrams. Information on adjustments and other components can be found by referring to other chapters, as necessary.

11 Flywheel Magneto-Generator

A Bosch 0 212 112 061 RBI flywheel magneto-generator is fitted on Maxi "N" models up to machine number 9606164. Subsequent Maxi "N" models, and Maxi "S" models have a Bosch 0 212 112 962 RBI unit. Both have a 6 volt 17 watt rating and are essentially similar in detail construction. Flywheel and crankshaft as matching components are, however, different and thus the two types are not interchangeable.

The flywheel is shrouded by a light cover secured with two small bolts and spring washers. If this cover is removed the contact breaker is visible and accessible, through one of the three cut-outs in the outside face of the flywheel, turning the flywheel as necessary for maximum accessibility.

The correct contact breaker gap is 0·014–0·017 in. (0·35–0·45 mm). To adjust the gap the screw securing the fixed contact mounting plate is slackened. A screwdriver blade can then be inserted in the notch above the screw to adjust the position of the plate (Fig. 11.1).

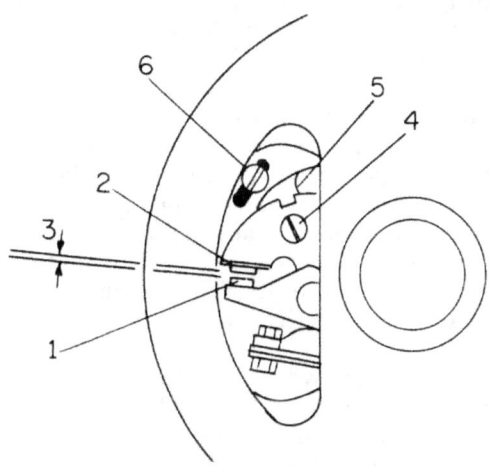

Fig. 11.1 Contact breaker adjustment

1 movable point
2 fixed point
3 gap (0·014–0·017 in.)
4 screw locking fixed point mounting plate
5 setting seat (for screwdriver adjustment)
6 timing adjustment screw (stator fixing screw)

After adjusting the contact breaker gap (gap between points) the *flux gap* should also be checked as this can have a significant effect on the strength of the spark. The *flux gap* is the spacing or gap between the end of the magnetic segment and the coil shoe at the instant when the points open (*see* Fig. 11.2). This gap must always be between 0·275 and 0·433 in. (7

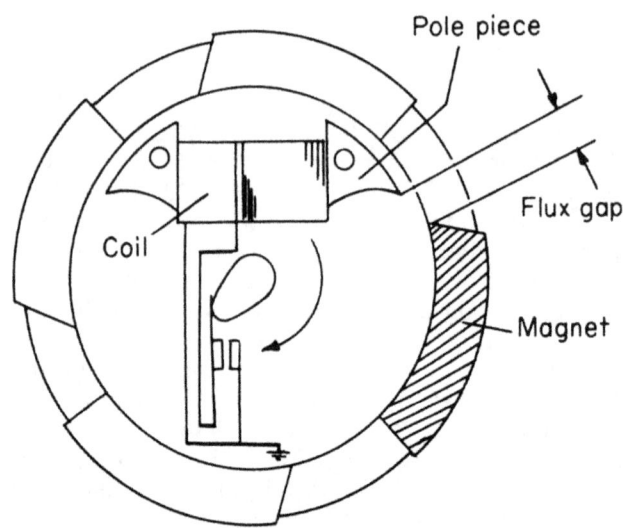

Fig. 11.2 Flux gap is the gap between the magnetic pole shoe and nearest armature edge at the moment contact points open. Permitted range for gap is 7–11 mm (0·275–0·433 in.)

and 11 mm). Adjustment of the points gap alters the flux gap, and thus if the latter is outside the tolerances specified the points gap must be readjusted to bring the flux gap between the specified limits. This should be possible within the tolerance allowed on point gap (0·014–0·017 in.), unless the points or contact breaker heel are badly worn, in which case new breaker parts should be fitted. The general rule is that *reducing* the point gap *increases* the flux gap; and *increasing* the points gap *reduces* the flux gap. The flux gap also has an effect on the voltage output of the lighting coil (*see* Chapter 12).

Adjustment of points gap will also affect timing, which should be rechecked. If necessary, timing can be readjusted by movement of the stator plate, secured by three fixing screws through slotted holes. A simple indicating device for checking the timing comprises a screwdriver connected to a bulb and battery and thence by a wire to "earth" on the engine unit (Fig. 11.3). The screwdriver blade is then rested on the moving point of the contact breaker, through (and clear of) the flywheel cut-out. The bulb will then light up when the points are "made", and go out when the points are open.

FLYWHEEL MAGNETO-GENERATOR

To check and/or adjust the timing, remove the spark plug so that the engine can be turned over freely by the flywheel. The flywheel carries two marks on its rim—OT representing top dead centre, and VZ representing ignition advance. The "indicator point" for these marks is the crankcase joint line.

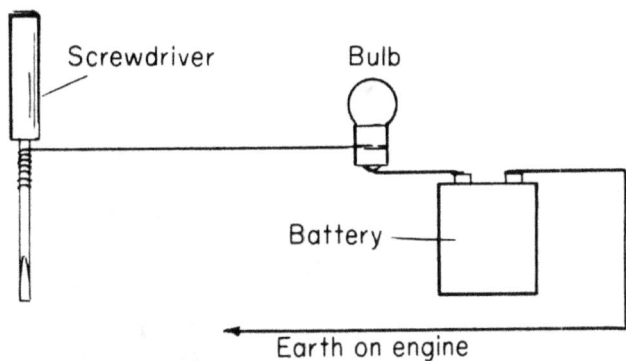

Fig. 11.3 Simple ignition timing indicator

With the indicator circuit connected and the flywheel set to TDC (OT mark against joint line), turn the flywheel anti-clockwise until the points close (as indicated by the bulb lighting). Then turn the flywheel slowly clockwise until the points just open (bulb goes out). If the timing is correct the VZ mark should now be opposite the joint line. If not, the screws holding the stator plate must be loosened and the stator plate rotated to adjust, viz.

1 If the contacts open too early, turn the stator plate clockwise.
2 If the contacts open too late, turn the stator plate anti-clockwise.
Retighten the stator plate screws after adjusting.

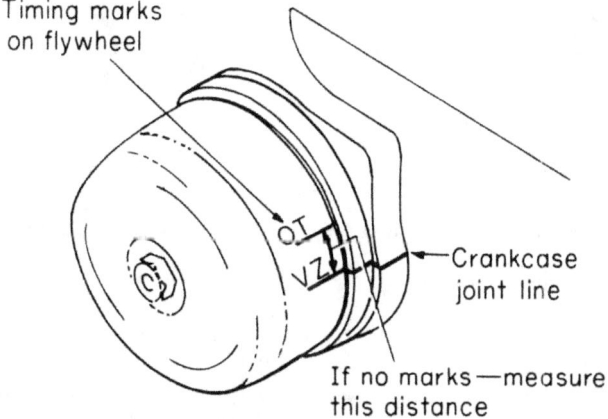

Fig. 11.4 Timing adjustment either by "Marks", or by direct measurement. Joint on crankcase is reference mark.

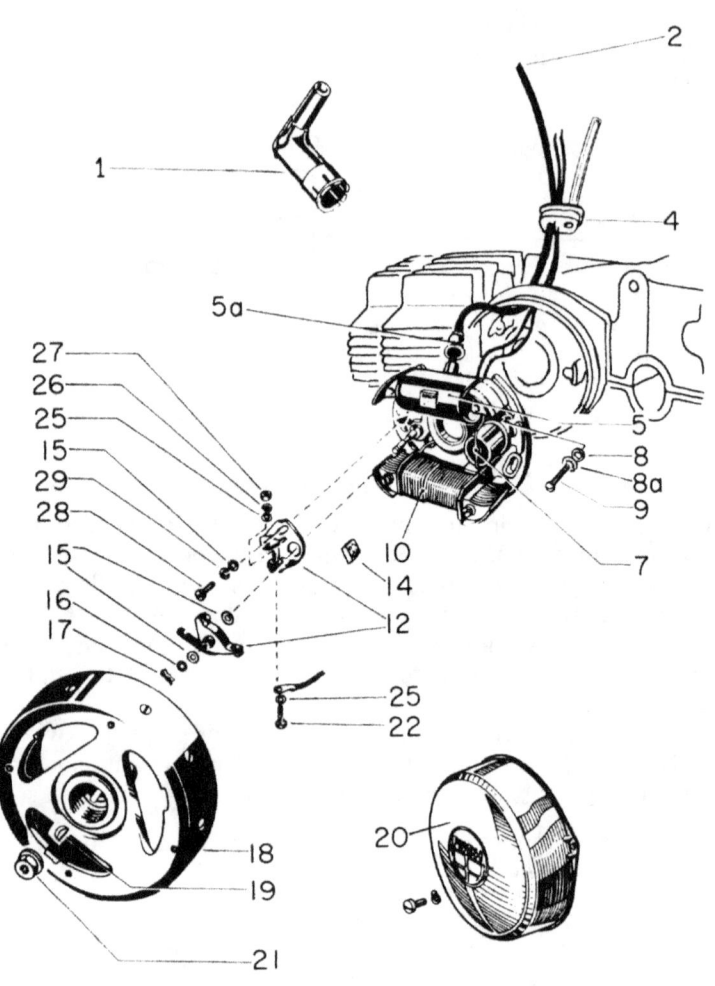

Fig. 11.5 Flywheel magneto-generator components

1 plug connector (with suppressor)
2 plug lead
4 rubber cable socket
5 ignition coil and pole pieces
5a rubber cap
7 condenser
8, 8a, 9 bolt, star washer and nut securing pole pieces
10 lighting coil
12 contact breaker points
14 felt pad lubricator
15 washer
16 shim washer
17 securing clip
18 flywheel
19 key
20 flywheel cover with securing bolt and Belleville washer
21 hexagonal flywheel nut

FLYWHEEL MAGNETO-GENERATOR

Not all flywheels have the OT and VZ marks, in which case the position of the flywheel with the piston exactly at TDC must be marked on the flywheel rim, opposite the crankcase joint line (*see* Fig. 11.4). TDC position can be judged by inserting a pencil or similar probe through the spark plug hole. The correct timing advance position corresponding to VZ can then be measured off around the rim of the flywheel and marked, as shown. This circumferential dimension is 16-18 mm (0·63-0·71 in.)

For best performance the timing of the ignition advance on the Maxi engine is quite critical, i.e. should always be within the 16-18 mm dimension against the direction of revolution, i.e. anti-clockwise, looking at the face of the flywheel.

Removal of Flywheel Generator

Some form of locking device and an extractor are necessary to remove the flywheel (both tools are available as special parts). The former is used to hold the flywheel whilst the retaining nut is unscrewed (and tightened, when replacing the flywheel). The extractor is necessary to pull the flywheel off the crankshaft, to which it is keyed.

Once the flywheel is removed, disassembly of individual components for replacement, etc. is straightforward, after first removing electrical connections if necessary. Figure 11.5 shows the flywheel generator parts in detail. Note that various leads—e.g. contact breaker and coil leads—have soldered connections. If the capacitor is to be changed, this must be pushed out of the baseplate with a wooden dowel. The hole is then cleaned out and a new capacitor pressed in place with new caulking compound.

12 The Electrics

A NOMINAL 6 volt supply for lighting (and horn) is derived from the low tension coil in the flywheel generator, fed directly to the lighting switch via a single (yellow) wire. Lighting and horn circuits are also single wire "earth return". The actual circuit voltage is determined by the air gap between the pole shoes on the magneto generator, the recommended gap being 0·0059–0·0079 in. (0·15–0·20 mm). This gap can be adjusted by loosening the coil fixing screws and gently tapping the laminations with a soft hammer. Increasing the gap will decrease the output voltage, and vice versa.

Three different wiring systems have been used on Maxi models (*see* Figs. 12.1–12.3). The simplest has only a single-filament headlamp, with tail lamp and horn. Other systems are based on a twin-filament headlamp bulb, with main and dipped (dim) switch positions, distinguished by the angular shape of the headlamp (on models imported into Britain). This system may be fitted with either a Merit or C.E.V. switch. A third system is also shown in the accompanying wiring diagrams, it is immediately distinguishable by three wire leads from the flywheel generator.

For models fitted with a circular headlamp, the front of the headlamp can be removed for bulb changing by undoing the screw, turning the contact spring of the reflector one way or the other and withdrawing the bulb and socket. Refit in the reverse order, turning the contact spring to the centre of the bulb to hold in place.

For models with a rectangular headlamp, the front is again held in place by a single screw at the bottom. Removal of this screw allows the front to be detached from its locating slot in the main casing. Turn the contact spring on the back of the reflector unit to release the bulb. Refit new bulb, turn the spring back to contact the centre of the bulb and replace the front unit.

The bulb in the rear light unit is immediately accessible by undoing the screw holding the plastic cover in place and then pulling downwards to detach. This bulb is in a bayonet fitting, released by pressing in, turning clockwise and then withdrawing. A replacement bulb is pressed in place, turned to the right and then pulled back to lock in place. The plastic cover can then be refitted.

Lighting faults are not likely to be common, but if a bulb repeatedly blows the cause may be excessive voltage generated in the lighting circuit.

THE ELECTRICS

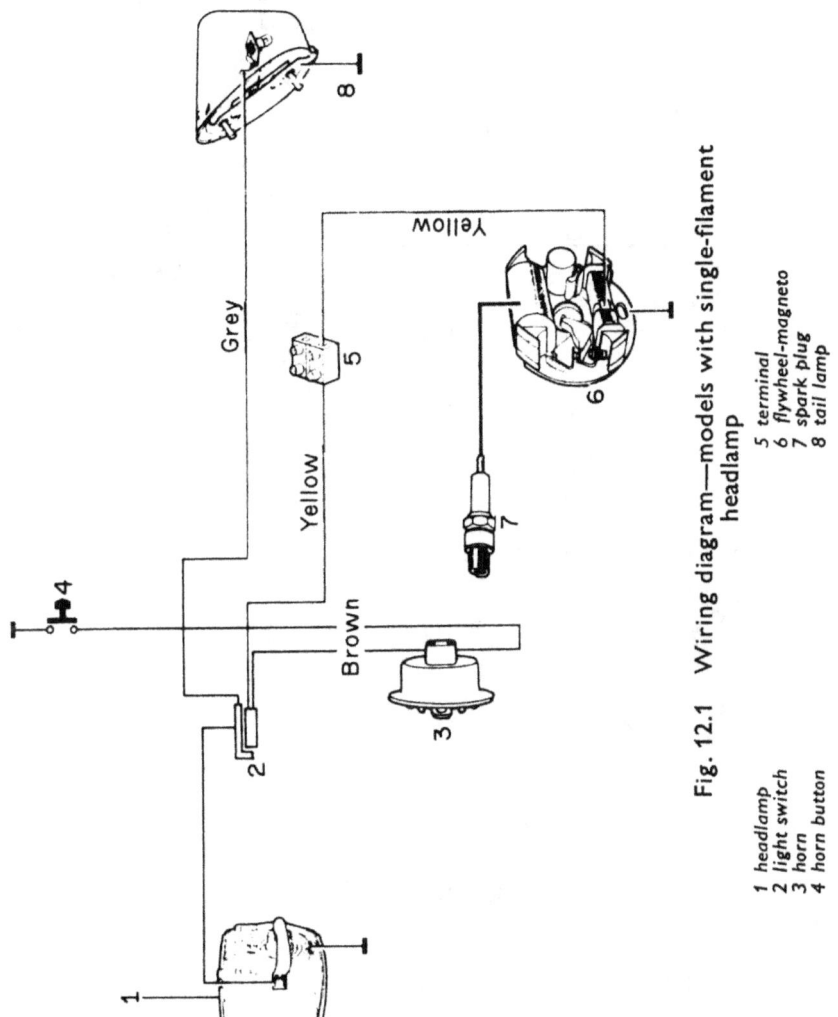

Fig. 12.1 Wiring diagram—models with single-filament headlamp

1 headlamp
2 light switch
3 horn
4 horn button
5 terminal
6 flywheel-magneto
7 spark plug
8 tail lamp

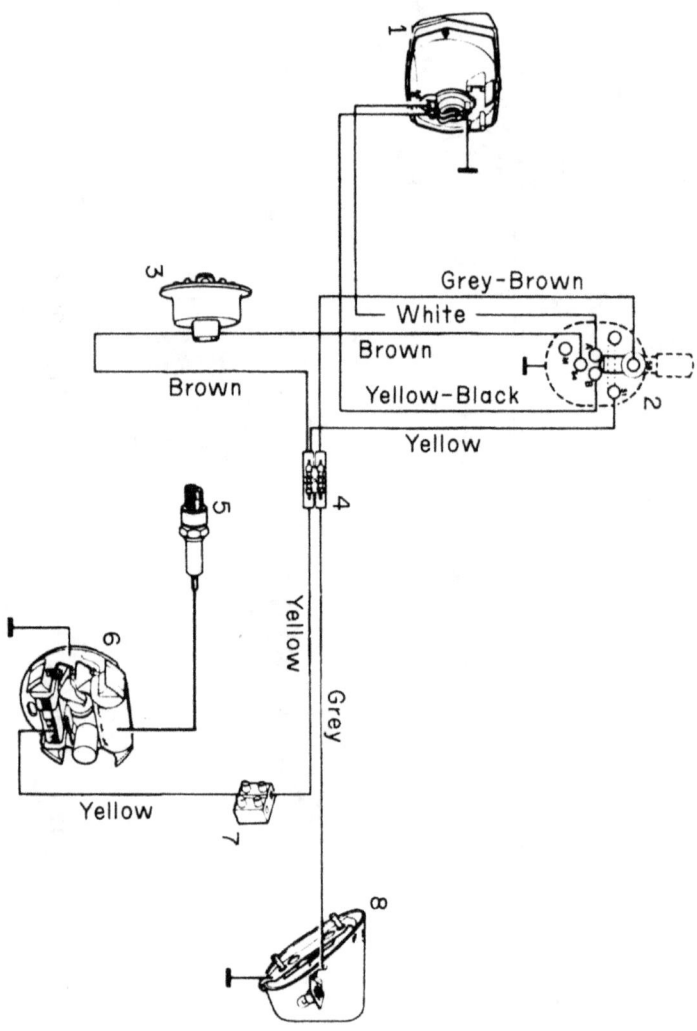

Fig. 12.2 Wiring diagram—models with dipping headlamp and combined switch

1 headlamp
2 light switch and horn press
3 horn
4 terminal block
5 spark plug
6 flywheel magneto
7 rubber terminal block
8 tail lamp

Note: C.E.V. switch shown. Merit switch may also be fitted when switch connections are slightly different (see Fig. 12.2)

INSTRUCTIONS

MAXI

THE ELECTRICS

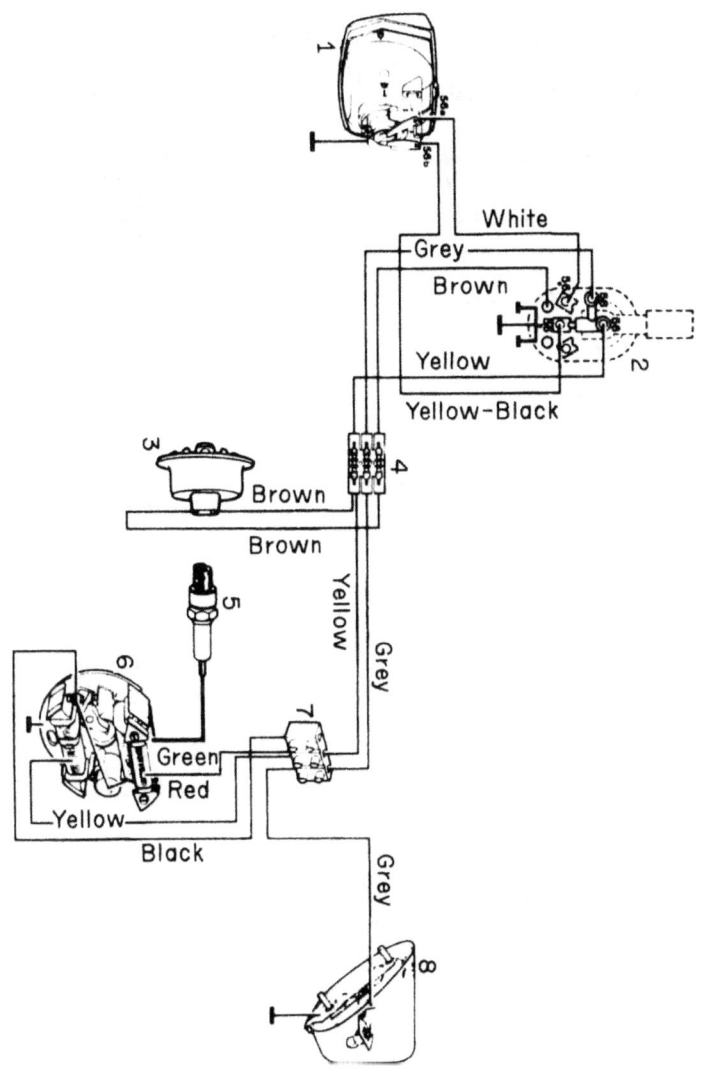

Fig. 12.3 Wiring diagram for third alternative system used

1 headlamp
2 combined switch (Merit)
3 horn
4 rubber terminal
5 spark plug
6 flywheel magneto
7 rubber terminal block
8 tail lamp

This can be reduced by increasing the gap between the pole shoes, as explained in the first paragraph.

PUCH MAXI LIGHTING SYSTEMS

System	Headlamp	Tail lamp	Remarks
6 V 17 W	6 V 15 W	6 V 2 W	Single headlamp
6 V 17 W	6 V 15 W/15 W	6 V 2 W	Continental
		6 V 3 W	England
6 V 21 W	6 V 18 W/18 W	6 V 2 W	Continental
		6 V 3 W	England

Horn in all cases is a buzzer.

Appendix

Importers
Steyr-Daimler-Puch (Great Britain) Limited,
Steyr-Puch House,
211, Lower Parliament Street,
Nottingham NG1 1FZ
(Telephone: 0602-56521)

Puch Distributors and Service Agents

Greater London Area,
East Midlands and Anglia: Glanfield Baldet Ltd.,
70 Wellingborough Road,
Northampton

Oxon and Berkshire: P. Church Limited,
1 Hollow Way,
Cowley,
Oxford
(Telephone: 77094)

Hants, Dorset, Wilts, Somerset, Devon, Cornwall and W. Sussex: Dardani and Large Limited,
137-139 Bournemouth Road,
Parkstone,
Poole,
Dorset
(Telephone: Parkstone 2616)

Bedfordshire, Buckinghamshire and Hertfordshire: J. H. Moore (Watford) Limited,
484 St. Albans Road,
Watford,
Herts
(Telephone: 24001)

North West and West Midlands, East, West and North Ridings of Yorkshire, Northumberland, Cumberland, Westmorland, Durham and Wales:

Alan Taylor (Northern) Limited,
"Elan House",
Manchester Road,
Castleton,
Rochdale,
Lancs.
(Telephone: Rochdale 33221)

Kent:

Chambers of Rochester,
19 High Street and Corporation Street,
Rochester,
Kent
(Telephone: Medway 48326)

Surrey:

Minear and Bruce,
20-22 Bedford Road,
Guildford,
Surrey
(Telephone: 61243/60367)
Central Garage,
Lion Green,
Haslemere
(Telephone: 2168)

Scotland and Northern Ireland:

Harry Fairbairn Limited,
11-13 Montgomery Street,
Irvine,
Ayrshire,
Scotland
(Telephone: Irvine 2793)

Index

ADJUSTERS, chain tension, 29
Adjustment, carburettor, 41
  clutch, 51
  contact breaker, 43, 55
  flux gap, 56
  of idling speed, 39
  timing, 57
Air filter, 41
Alternative wiring diagrams, 61, 62, 63
Armature, 57

BEARINGS, steering head, 35
Big end bearing, 47
Bing-type carburettor, 38
Bore, cylinder, 45
Bosch flywheel magneto generator, 55
  spark plug, 7
Bottom end decarbonizing, 18
Brake efficiency, 25
  lever, 27
  maintenance, 25
  shoe sizes, 27
  shoes, 25
Brakes, 25 et seq.
Braking, 5
Bulb, rear light, 60
Bulbs, 64
  headlamp, 60

CABLE adjusters, 20, 21
  lubrication, 11, 22
  supqort, 21
Cables, 19
Capacitor, 59
Carburation check table, 42
Carburettor, 38 et seq.
  cleaning, 39
  components, 40
  controls, 38
  data, 7

  faults, 42
  tuning, 41
Centre stand, 54
Centrifugal clutch, 1
C.E.V. switch, 60, 62
Chain lubrication, 11, 31
  tension, 12
  adjusters, 29
Chains, 28
  cleaning, 31
  refitting, 31
Changing tyres, 27
Chassis point lubrication, 11
Check table, carburation, 42
Choke, 3, 38
  disengagement, 3
Circuit voltage, 60
Cleaning, carburettor, 39
  chains, 31
  intake silencer, 41
Clearance, clutch, 50, 51, 52
Clutch, 50
  clearance, 50, 51, 52
  drum, 49
  movement, 51
  operation, 1
  wear limits, 50
Components, carburettor, 40
Contact breaker, 55
  adjustment, 43
  gap, 55
  lubrication, 11
Cooling, 1
Countershaft assembly, 52, 53
  gears, 52
Crankcase detail, 48
  group, 49
  plugs, 10
Crankshaft bearing, special tools, 50
  removal, 49

Crankshaft bearing (*contd.*)—
  repair, 50
Cylinder, 45
  and piston groups, 45
  barrel, 18, 45, 53
  bore, 45
  head, 45, 53
  sizes, 45

DAILY maintenance, 12
Decarbonizing, 17 *et seq.*
  bottom end, 18
Decompressor, 3, 4, 47
  cable, 19, 20
Dimensions, 6, 7
Dismantling engine, 44 *et seq.*
Distributors, 65 *et seq.*
Downhill braking, 5
Drain plug, 9
Driving instructions, 4 *et seq.*
Drum diameter, 27

ECONOMIC operation, 4
Efficiency, brakes, 25
Electrical data, 7
Engine, 6
  cooling, 1
  dismantling, 44 *et seq.*
  drive chain, tension, 29
  faults, 14, 15
  group, 1, 43 *et seq.*
  overheating, 15
  removal, 44
  stand, 44
  unit, reassembly, 53
Exhaust cover, detaching, 17

FAULT finding, 13 *et seq.*
Faults, carburettor, 42
500-mile maintenance, 12
Flexible hose, 41
Flooding, 5
Flux gap, 56
Flywheel, 48, 55
  generator, removal, 59
  magneto generator, 48
  magneto generator detail, 58
Fork alignment, 32
Forks & frame, disassembly, 37
Frame components, Maxi N, 36
  components, Maxi S, 35

Front brake, 24
  adjustment, 21
  cable, 19, 20
Front brakes, 3
  fork, 32
  alignment, 32
  detail, 33
  forks, lubrication, 11
  hub, 23, 24
  wheel, 23
Fuel capacity, 6
  consumption, 16
  mixture, 13
  tap, 4

GAP, contact breaker, 55
Gearbox capacity, 6
  lubrication, 11
General specifications, 6
Grease points, 9
Gudgeon pin, 46

HANDLEBAR assembly, 21
  controls, 21, 22
  lock, 4
Handlebars, removing, 22
Headlamp bulbs, 60
  difference, 60
Horn, 60, 64
  button, 22
  circuit, 60 *et seq.*
Hub brakes, 3, 25, 27

IDENTIFICATION numbers, 7
Idler sprocket, 23
Idling adjustment, 39
Importers, 65
Indicator point, timing, 57
Intake silencer, 41

JIG, engine, 44
Jockey wheel, 29

KROMAG wheel, 23

LACK of fuel, 13
Little end bearing, 46
Lighting circuits, 60 *et seq.*
  coil, 56
  faults, 60
  supply, 60

INDEX

Lighting circuits (*contd.*)—
  systems, 64
  voltage, 60
Lock, 4
Lubricants, 9
Lubrication, 9
  cables, 22
  chains, 31

MAGNETO generator, 48
  generator models, 55
Main jet, 39 *et seq.*
  sizes, 39
Maintenance, 500 miles, 12
Marks, timing, 57
Maxi features, 3
  frame, 32
  model differences, 1, 2
    'N', 2
    'S', 2
  models, 1
  N, frame, 36
  S, frame, 35
  S, rear suspension, 34
Merit switch, 60, 61
Misfiring, 14, 15
Mixture adjustment, 38 *et seq.*
Monthly maintenance, 12
Mudguard stays, 23, 37
Mudguards, 37

NEEDLE jet, 41
No spark, 14
Nylon bushes, 29

OIL level, 9
Oiling points, 9
Optimum jet size, 41
Overheating, 15

PARKING, 4
Pedal and chain assembly, 28
  chain tension, 29
  cranks, 28
  removal, 44
  wheel, 28
Pedals, 28
Performance, 7
Petrol-oil mixture, 6
Pinking, 15
Piston, 45
  sizes, 45
  wear, 46
Pivoted fork, 34
Plastic bushes, 32
Points adjustment, 56
Procedure, starting, 4
  stopping, 4
Puch distributors, 65 *et seq.*
  service agents, 65 *et seq.*

REAR brake adjustment, 21
  brake cable, 19, 20
  brake detail, 26
  brakes, 3
  fork, 35 *et seq.*
  hub, 25, 26
  light, 60
  suspension, 2
  suspension, Maxi S, 34
  wheel, 23, 25
Reassembly of engine unit, 53
Refitting chains, 31
Removal, crankcase, 49
  crankshaft, 49
Removing cylinder, 18 *et seq.*
  engine, 44
  handlebars, 22
  front wheel, 23
  rear wheel, 25
Replacing cables, 21
Rim profiles, 23
Routine lubrication, 11
Running in, 6

SCHÜRMANN wheel, 23
Service agents, 65 *et seq.*
Silencer unit, 17, 18
Six-monthly maintenance, 12
Spark plug, 57
  check, 13
  type, 7
Special tools, 7, 47, 50
  crankshaft bearing, 50
Specification, 6
Speedometer head, 22
Standard equipment, 7
Starter clutch cable, 19, 20
  control, 54
Starting lever, 3, 19
  up, 1
Stator, 57

Steering bearing, lubrication, 11
   head, 35
   head bearings, 35
Stopping, 4
Support, cable, 21
Suspension unit, 35

TECHNICAL data, 7
Telescopic forks, 32
Tension, engine drive chain, 29
   pedal chain, 29
Three-monthly maintenance, 12
Throttle, 3
   cable, 19, 20
      adjustment, 21
   control, 5
   grip, 21
   twist grip, 21, 22
Tickler, 3, 14
Tightening torques, 8, 54
Timing, 14, 53
   adjustment, 55 *et seq.*
   marks, 57
Top speed, 4
Transmission fluid, 10
Trouble shooting table, 14 *et seq.*

Tuning, carburettor, 41
Twist grip, 21
   throttle, 3, 4
Tyre pressures, 6
   sizes, 6
Tyres, 27

VOLTAGE output, 56

WEAR, big end bearing, 47
   limits, clutch, 50
   gudgeon pin, 46
   little end bearing, 46
   parts, 35
      forks, 32
   piston, 46
Weekly maintenance, 12
Weights, 6, 7
Wheel bearings, lubrication, 11
   pedal, 28
   rims, 23
   sizes, 23
   types, 23
Wheels, 5
Wiring diagrams, 61, 62, 63
   systems, 60 *et seq.*

INDEX

		page
A)	Machine numbers	5
B)	Operating controls	6
C)	Running-in procedure	9
D)	Riding instructions	10
E)	Lubrication and Maintenance	12
F)	Cleaning the machine	43
G)	Long term storage	44
H)	Lubrication and maintenance chart	45
J)	Trouble shooting	49
K)	Technical data	51

FOREWORD

We are pleased you have decided to purchase this machine and welcome you to the Puch range. We wish you a good start and hope you will enjoy yourself. Please read this book to familiarise yourself with the simple operating, maintenance and service procedures. The references "left" and "right" always refer to the side when seated on the machine.

STEYR - DAIMLER - PUCH
GRAZ   AUSTRIA

A) MACHINE NUMBERS

Position of specification plate, engine number and frame number.

Specification plate,
fixed to right-hand side of
the frame.

Engine number,
stamped on the crankcase
on the right hand side.

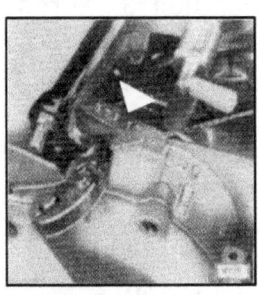

Frame number
stamped on the top
of frame on the right

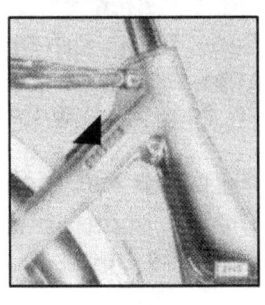

or on the right
hand side of seat post.

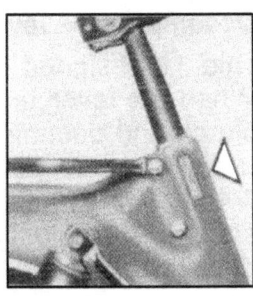

B) CONTROLS

The position of the controls may be seen in the "Technical Data".

Steering lock

To lock, move handlebar to the right. Insert key in to the lock, turn to the left and together with lock cylinder push down, turn to the right and remove key. Unlock by reversed procedure.

Petrol tap (fig. 1)

Position 1 = closed
Position 2 = open
Position 3 = reserve

Carburettor (fig. 2)

1 = tickler
2 = choke: is operated by depressing it (see starting the engine) or choke is operated by means of the lever on the handlebar. See "Technical Data".

Light switch

See "Technical Data".
Fuel tank filler cap
To open, remove cap.

Air pump and tools

The air pump is located under the right hand side engine covering tools in the tool box on the seat.

Decompressor lever and starting lever (fig. 14)

This is designed for starting and stopping the machine. When the lever is fully pulled in for starting, the automatic clutch and decompressor are operated simultaneously.
If the lever is pulled only part way in (by approximately 3/4 in = 2 cm) the decompressor only starts working (for stopping) and only when pulling a further 3/4 in (2 cm) the starting device becomes engaged.

Fig. 1

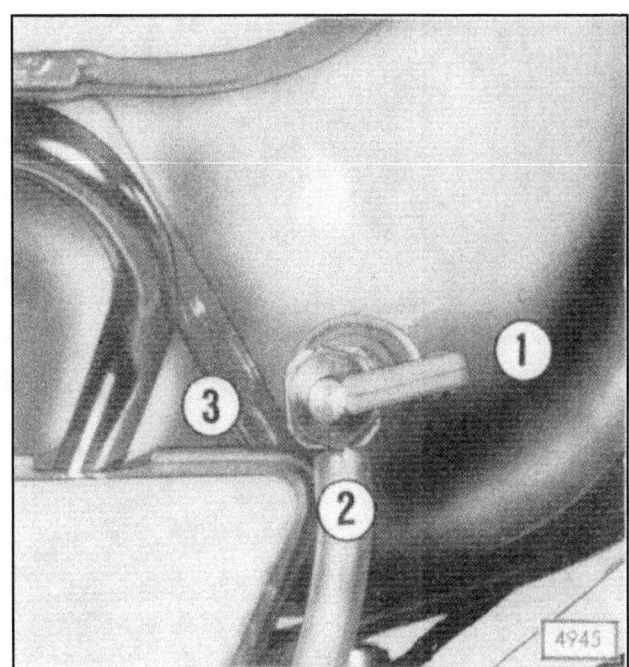

Fig. 2

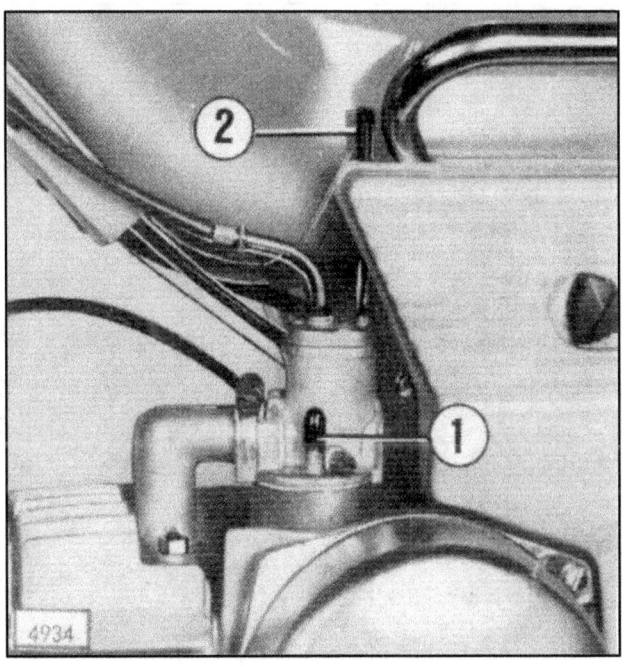

Fig. 3

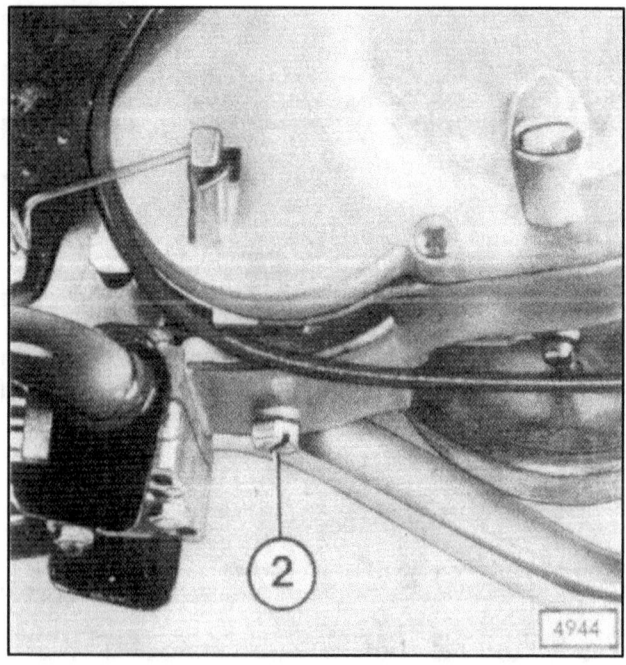

Fig. 4

C) RUNNING-IN PROCEDURE

Checking machine numbers
Prior to using the machine, check that the various numbers (see page 5) correspond with your Registration details.

Checking gearbox oil level
An oil level screw (which also acts as the filler plug) is fitted in the right gearbox cover. The oil level is correct if the oil reaches to the lower edge of the screw hole. If too low, add oil until it overflows. Excess oil must be drained off. For oil quality (Automatic Transmission Fluid — see "Lubricating Chart") and quantily see "Technical Data".

Checking the tyre pressure
Refer to "Technical Data" for correct pressures.

Filling up wih two stroke mixture.

Petroil mixture
All Puch two stroke engines should be run on a petroil mixture, ratio 50 : 1. Use of this mixing ratio reduces formation of exhaust smoke, results in smaller deposits, extends the intervals of cleaning and decreases air pollution.
It is recommended that petrol is mixed only with the oils listed in the "Technical Data" or "Lubricating Chart". Not all filling stations sell these special two stroke oils. When these oils are not available care should be taken when refueling, to adhere to the previously recommended mixing ratio of 25 to 1.

Remember! Never fill up with **pure petrol**.

For U. K. Use only economy petrol (2 star).

Check lights for correct functioning.

D) RIDING INSTRUCTIONS

Starting the engine

Models with pedals

a) Open fuel tap

b) When the engine is cold operate the choke and depress the carburettor tickler to slightly flood the engine.
When the engine is warm, do not operate either the choke or the tickler. Move off in the same way as with a bicycle and, once under way, pull the starting lever (fig. 14) for a short interval and at the same time open the throttle twist grip by approximately ⅓ turn.

Applies only to models with decompressor:
Continuous application of the starting lever means that the decompressor continues operation and the engine will not commence to fire. An alternative starting procedure: Prop machine on stand and start engine by forcefully pedalling and pulling the starting lever for a short interval. If the engine has started, the rear wheel should not touch the ground until the throttle is released, so that the clutch is no longer engaged. If the choke has been operated for a cold start, it should be turned off after the first few hundred yards.

Fully opening the throttle momentarily after a short while will do this automatically.

Riding

The speed of the machine is controlled by the throttle twist grip. After reaching maximum by fully opening the throttle, the twist grip should be turned back to approximately 3/4 open. While the decrease in speed will be hardly noticeable, the fuel consumption will be considerably reduced. Always decrease speed by closing the throttle.

Braking

Close the throttle and apply front and rear brake simultaneously (see controls). On sandy, wet or slippery roads it is recommended to use mainly the rear brake.

Riding downhill

The engine acts as brake if the throttle is closed for downhill riding. Over longer distances, open throttle a few times to ensure that sufficient lubricant reaches the engine. If necessary, reduce speed by braking.
If the speed is reduced to the extent that the clutch becomes disengaged, the engine no longer acts as brake. Engagement or disengagement of the clutch depends purely on engine revolutions. The braking effect of the engine only can be obtained again by reopening the throtlle, which again sets the clutch in operation. However, never increase the speed when going downhill by this method of operation. Reduce speed by applying the brakes with the throttle closed.

Stopping and parking

a) Close the throttle.
b) Apply the brakes, and if required to stop the engine,
c) Pull the decompressor lever (fig. 14) to a position (half way) where the cable will be felt to "jerk" momentarily or push short circuit button (see controls).
d) Close the fuel tap.
e) Lock the machine.

Riding without the engine

(Models with pedals)
Pedal the same way as on ordinary bicycle.

E) LUBRICATION AND MAINTENANCE

Changing gearbox oil.
a) Warm up the engine.
b) Remove the oil filling and level plug (fig. 3/1) and oil drain plug (fig. 4/1).
c) Drain oil by inclining the machine to the right.
d) Refit drain plug.
e) Fill with fresh Automatic Transmission Fluid (approx. 150 cc), see enclosed lubrication chart.
f) Refit oil filling and level plug.

Cleaning and oiling chains

The life of a chain depends to a great extent on care and maintenance. Chains should always be cleaned and greased regularly. When refitting the chains take care that the tension is correct and the connecting links are properly placed — with the closed end pointing in the direction of chain travel (fig. 5).

Greasing cycle parts
By means of lubricating grease

(see lubrication chart)
a) Models with speedometer: At the lubrication nipple (fig. 22/4) for the speedometer drive, one or two strokes of the grease gun.
b) Central bearing (fig. 6)
   Remove the stand spring (fig. 6/2). Undo screws (fig. 6/1). Remove stand. Grease both halves of the stand pivot.
c) Pedal shaft.

Lubricating oil

a) Brake adjusting screw on front wheel (and rear wheel of models with hand brake lever).
b) Adjusting screws for choke cables and decompressor cables (fig. 15/1 and 15/2).
c) Chain tensioning screws.
d) Working surfaces of both brake levers (on models with back pedalling brake, the front wheel brake lever only).
e) Bowden cables.

Fig. 5

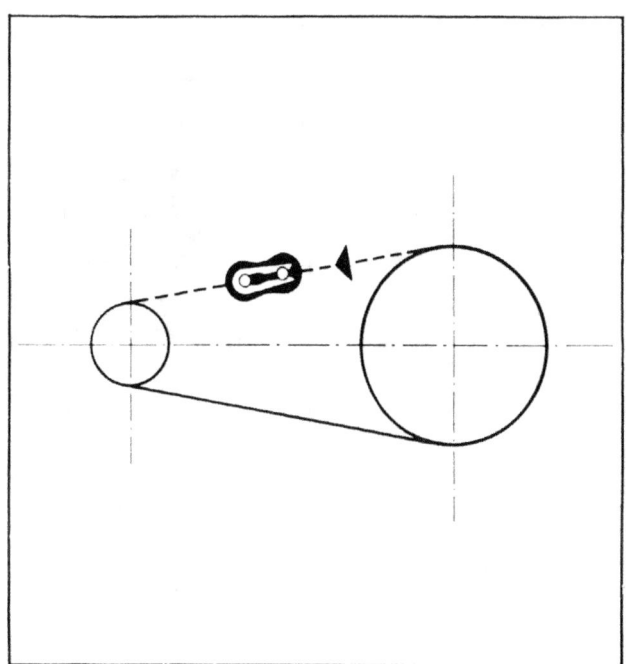

Fig. 6

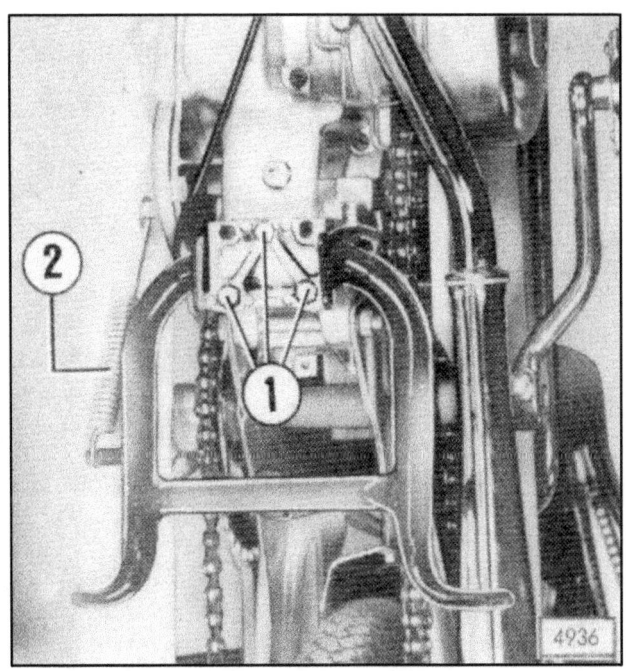

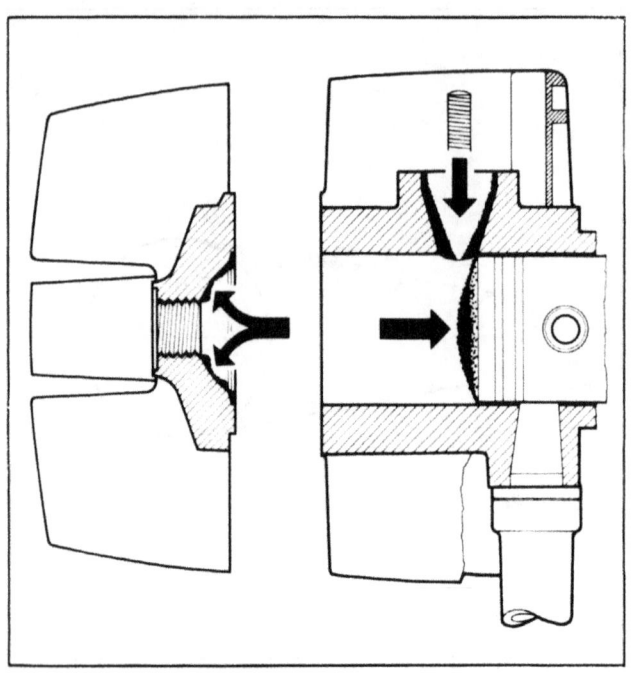

Fig. 7

Lubricating the ignition cam:
Lubricate the grease felt using Bosch grease Ft 1 v 4. The lubricant must not reach the breaker points as this would cause excessive pitting and premature wear of the breaker points.

2. MAINTENANCE

Please contact your Puch agent for any work you do not wish to carry out yourself. The agent will be pleased to advise and help.

Checking sparking plugs

Unscrew sparking plug, connect to H. T. lead and place plug bodyto earth, for instance on the cylinder head. A strong spark must be visible between the sparking plug electrodes when operating the starter. Oiled up plugs or dirty electrodes do not spark and must be cleaned first with a piece of wood or a steel wire brush. Fit only replacement plugs having a heat value in accordance with the enclosed "Technical Data".
The electrode gap should be from (0,016—0,020 in) 0,4 to 0,5 mm, if larger, adjust by bending the earth electrode. When refitting the sparking plug, ensure thread matches properly and the plug can be screwed in easily. Never apply force. Screw in plug by hand for 2 to 3 turns before using the sparking plug spanner. See "Technical Data" for recommended sparking plug.

Engine decoking (fig. 7)

The working principles of internal combustion engines (two stroke) produce deposits on the cylinder head, piston crown and exhaust port affecting proper functioning after a given period. It therefore becomes necessary to remove such oil and carbon deposits from time to time.

Decarbonizing the engine

Carbon deposits on the cylinder head, piston crown and in the exhaust ports are normal with all two-stroke engines and can eventually lead to trouble if not removed in time. Combustion deposits from oil as well as from fuel must therefore be removed regularly.

Cylinder head and piston head (fig. 7)

Carbon deposits on the cylinder head and piston crown should be removed only with a soft, blunt-edged instrument to avoid damage to the light-alloy casting. Scratching should be avoided since every new scratch will harbour more carbon in future use. Only flaking deposits need be removed from the piston crown; there is no need to disturb the piston if it is covered only by a uniform layer of oil carbon. Before refitting the cylinder head thoroughly remove all carbon deposits and scrapings from the cylinder wall with a non-fraying soft cloth and smear the surface lightly with motor oil. Before assembly turn over the engine a few times to make sure it runs easily. Then clean the jointing surfaces with a clean rag and refit with an aluminium gasket. Tighten the four cylinder head nuts crosswise.

Exhaust port

In order to clean the exhaust port remove the exhaust pipe. By cranking turn the engine over (with the sparking plug removed to reduce compression) until the piston reaches its lowest point. Remove the oil carbon from the exhaust port cautiously. Take care not to damage the piston or cylinder working surfaces. When cleaning the exhaust port, it is also a good idea to clean out the silencer.

Cleaning the silencer (fig. 8)

Unscrew and pull off the exhaust endpiece.
Remove oil-carbon deposits from the inside of the silencer using a scraper. Also remove carefully the oily deposits from the fastening device and from the pipes of the exhaust endpiece. Replace the gaskets if necessary.
The machine has been designed to meet legislative requirements with the original silencer fitted. Modification of the silencer is an offence.

Fig. 8

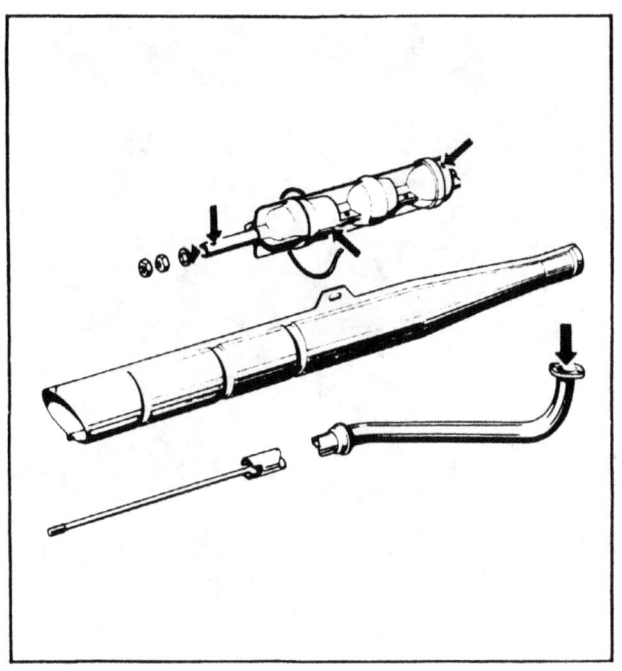

Fig. 9

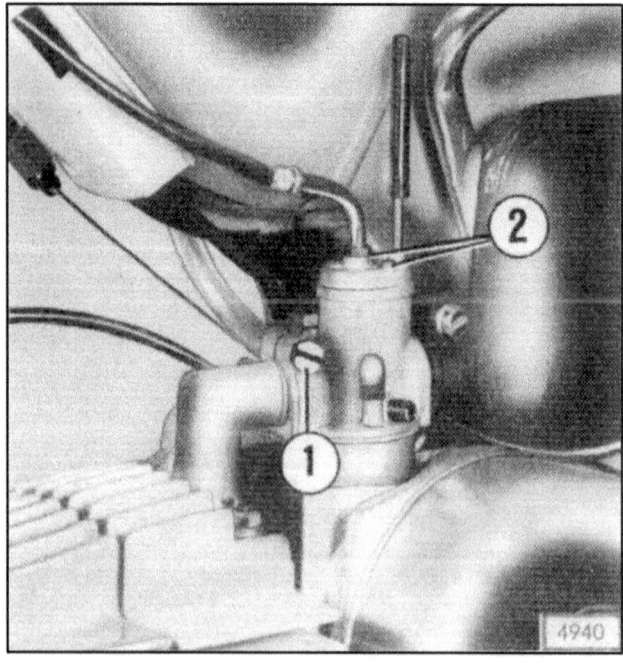

Fig. 10

Cleaning the air filter (fig. 9)

Remove the covering on the left-hand side of the machine (three screws), undo the screw from the intake socket (fig. 9/2), pull the intake silencer with snorkel out from its recess in the frame and pull off the silencer from the carburettor. Pull snorkel off the intake silencer. Wash complete silencer in petrol and dry well. When fitting, see that open end of snorkel does not foul the frame as this prevents air from entering the carburettor.

Cleaning the fuel pipes and lines

Empty the fuel tank.
Pull the fuel pipe from the petrol tap and carburettor and blow it clear. Unscrew the petrol tap.
Use petrol to clean the tap and strainer.

Cleaning the carburettor (fig. 10 and 11)

Maintenance operations on the carburettor need specialized knowledge and should be entrusted to an authorized Puch Service station.

Cleaning the main jet, needle jet and float chamber

a) Close the fuel tap (fig. 1).
b) Remove the left hand side covering.
c) Remove the intake silencer (fig. 9/1).
d) Loosen carburettor clamping screw (fig. 10/1).
e) Pull the fuel pipe from the carburettor.
f) Turn the carburettor with its float chamber (bottom) towards the clutch side and pull off.
g) Undo screws and pull out the top parts with throttle piston and choke (fig. 10/2).

h) Screw off the float chamber.
i) Unscrew the main jet (fig. 11/3) being screwed in the needle jet (fig. 11/4) and clean by blowing through or by using a stiff bristle. Never use a piece of wire. Also unscrew needle jet and clean.
j) Clean the float chamber (fig. 11/2) with petrol.
k) Wash carburettor body and blow through. Make sure that the bores are not clogged with dirt.
l) When refitting the jets tighten them properly.

Adjusting the idling speed
a) Warm up the engine.
b) Completely close the twist grip (throttle down).
c) If the engine threatens to stall, screw in the adjuster (fig. 12/1) until the engine in warm condition regains its even tickover.
Now, with this idling adjustment, adjust the play of the throttle control cable.
a) Loosen the lock nut of the cable adjuster (fig. 12/2).
b) Screw out cable adjuster (fig. 12/3) until there is a play on both the throttle cable and the throttle twist grip. (The cover of the throttle cable can be pulled out from the cable adjuster by appr. 0,0076 in. (2 mm), before the throttle slide is lifted, i. e. before the engine starts running faster.
c) Maintain position of the adjuster and tighten the lock nut.

Fig. 11

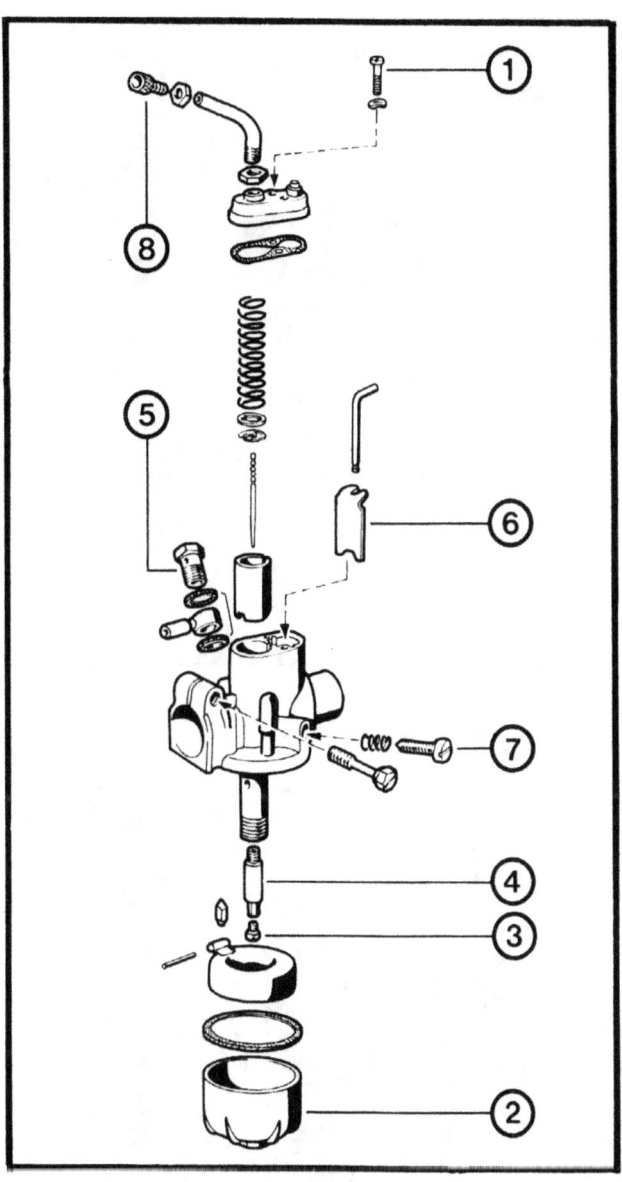

1 Top cover screw
2 Float housing
3 Main jet
4 Needle jet
5 Fixing screw
6 Choke valve
7 Throttle slide stop screw
8 Bowden cable adjusting screw

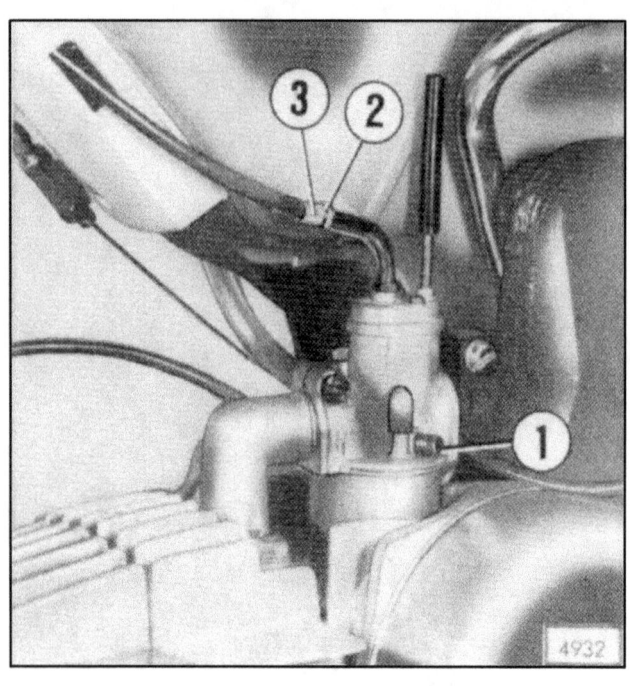

Fig. 12

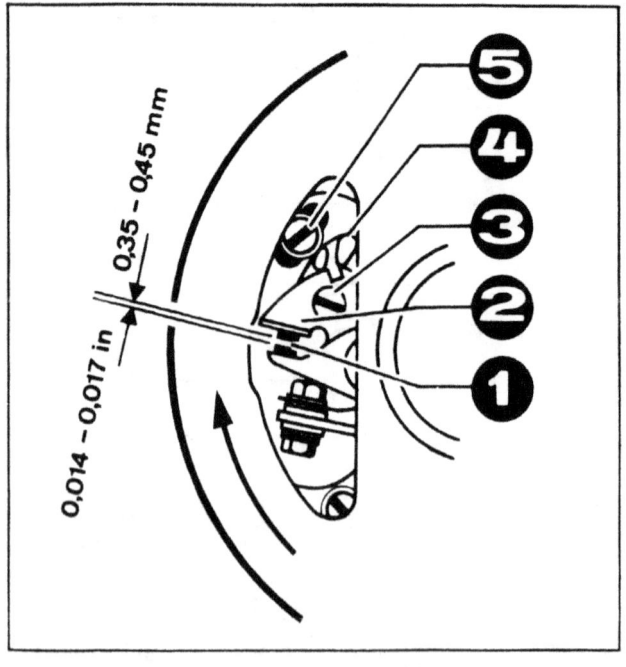

Fig. 13

Checking the ignition system
Ignition timing

The engine will reach maximum output only if the Ignition is correctly adjusted. This is a very specialized operation and should be left to your Puch service station.
For correct ignition timing the following points should be taken into account:
a) Contact breaker points gap.
b) Firing point.
c) Break of magnetic flux.

Contact breaker points gap (For recommended gap see "Technical Data").

Check and adjust the gap through the windows in the flywheel magneto (after removing the cover). When adjusting the breaker gap (fig. 13/1) loosen the fastening screw (fig. 12/3) enabling the anvil (fixed contact) to be moved. For readjusting the position of the anvil insert a screwdriver into the setting seat (fig. 13/4). If the gap has been modified it is necessary to check the ignition point.

Firing point

On the flywheel magneto there is a setting mark. If this coincides with the partition line on the casing, the piston is at top dead centre (TDC). Ignition timing is correct if the distance from the mark on the flywheel to the partition line of the casing is 0,63—0,709 in (16—18 mm) — measured in the direction of rotation of the engine (clockwise) — at the moment when the contact breaker points begin to open. To facilitate checking, it is advisable to mark a mark with a pencil on the flywheel at the specified distance. In order to determine when the contacts begin to open put a cigarette paper between the closed contacts and rotate the flywheel by hand (clockwise) until it is just possible to pull out the paper. This is the point at which the sparking plug fires.

If the contact breaker points open after more than 0,709 in, 18 mm (early ignition spark) turn the magneto base plate in the direction of engine rotation. If the contact breaker points open before 0,63 in./16 mm adjust the magneto base plate against the direction of engine rotation. (OT=TDC; VZ=ignition advance.)

Checking chain tension

The designed slackness of the chain midway between the sprockets should be (½ in) 10 to 15 mm. To readjust the chain loosen both axle nuts and tighten both chain adjusters uniformly. This procedure enables the back wheel to be kept in track. Retighten both axle nuts.

The pedal chain used with machines having pedals need not be tensioned .Correct tension is automatically achieved by the pulley.

Fig. 14

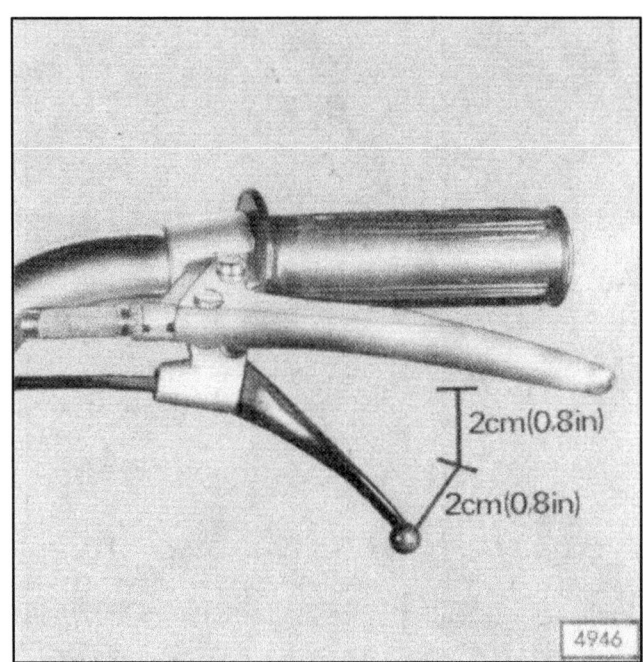

Fig. 15

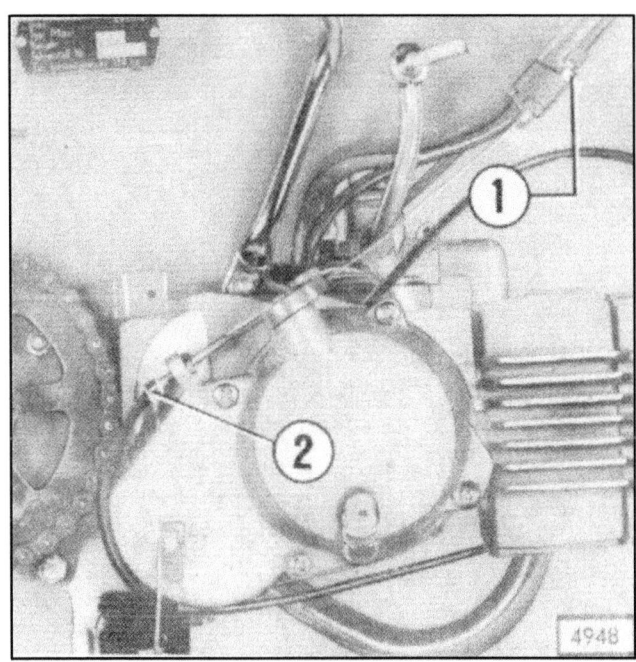

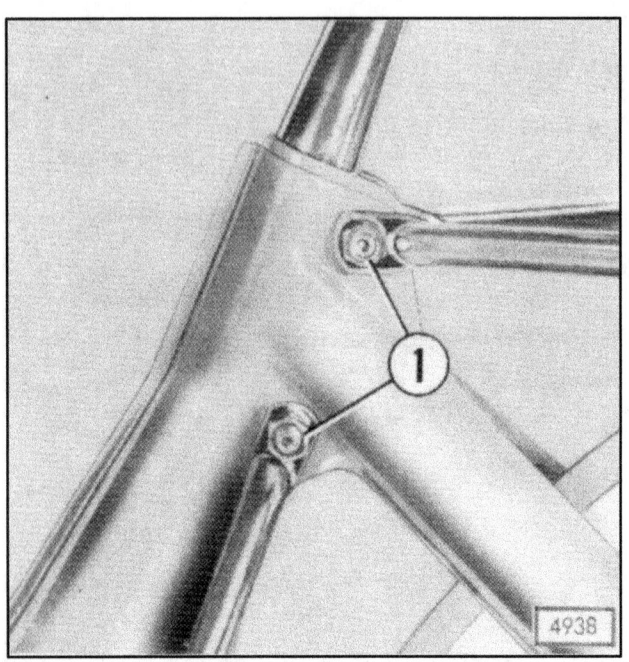

Fig. 16

Adjusting the starting lever and decompressor lever

When newly adjusting or readjusting the control cables, having become necessary due to stretch of the cables, it is expedient to have this done in a Puch Service workshop. For the adjustment use the 2 cable adjusters (fig. 15/1 and 15/2).

Adjust so that the decompressor starts working, when pulling the lever 3/4 in (2 cm), and the starting device is being engaged after pulling a further 3/4 in (2 cm).

When fully pulling the starting and decompressor lever make sure that the decompressor is not opened up to its stop as otherwise the starting function will be impaired.

Adjusting the starter control cable

(Model without decompressor)
The play of the starting device lever (measured at the end of the lever) should be 3/4 in (2 cm). Correct play is achieved by the adjusting screw (fig. 15/1).

Adjusting height of seat

Loosen screws (fig. 16/1) and adjust seat and seat post as required.

Checking the brakes
Front brake.
The correct adjusted travel measured at the end of the handbrake lever is 3/4 in (2 cm) (fig. 17). For readjustment use the adjusting screw (fig. 17/1 or 18/1).

Fig. 17

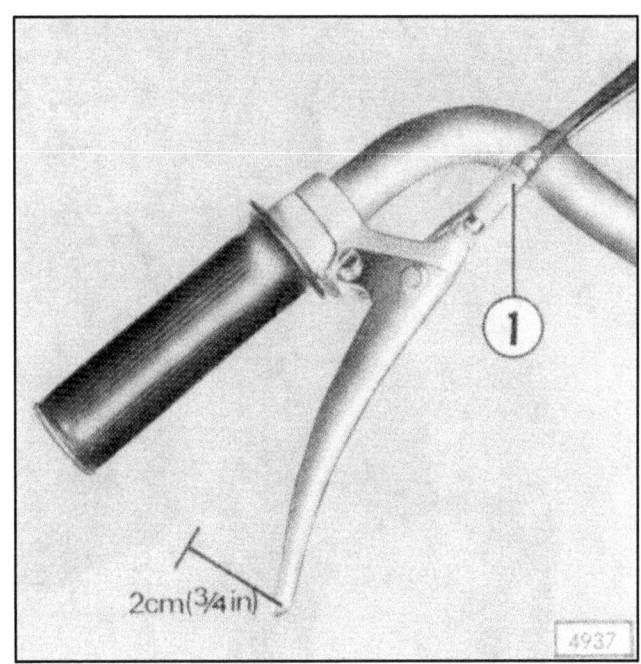

Fig. 18

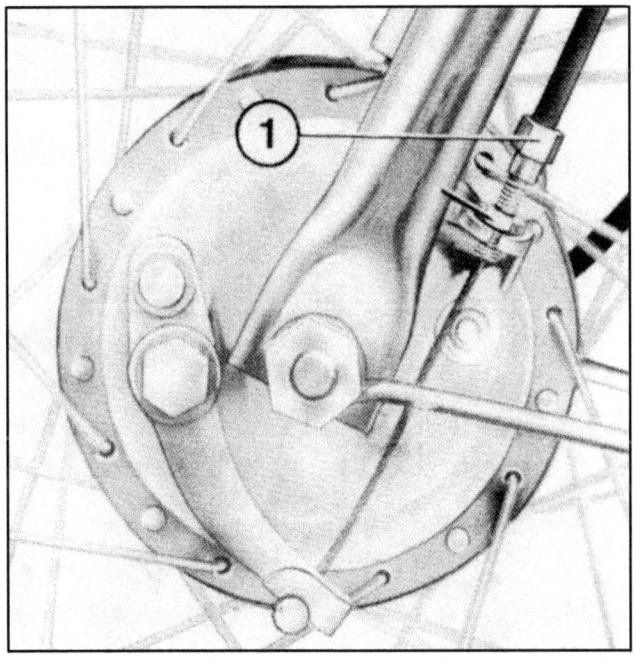

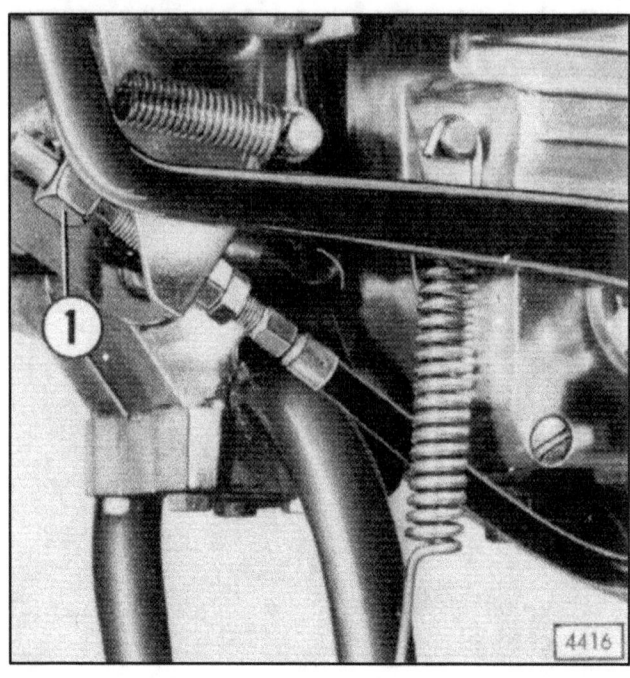

Fig. 19

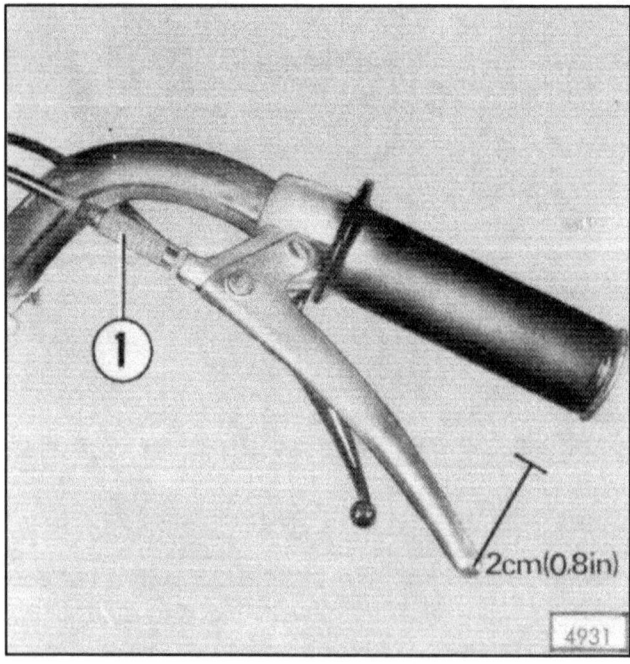

Fig. 20

Rear brake

The play of the brake pedal should be 3/4 in (2 cm). Adjust by means of the adjusting screw (fig. 19/1).

Models with back pedalling brake

The rear brake of these models need be adjusted.

Models with handbrake lever

The correct travel (measured at the end of the handbrake lever is 3/4 in (2 cm). Readjust by means of the adjusting screw (fig. 20/1).

Checking and greasing the hub bearings

As outlined in the workshop manual, remove the hubs. Then clean and check the bearings .Before reassembling grease them with fresh grease (see "Technical Data").

Checking and greasing the steering head bearings

As outlined in the workshop manual, remove the steering bearings, clean and check. Grease with new grease (see "Technical Data").

Retighten nuts and bolts

Check nuts and bolts for tightness. Above all be sure that the engine fixing bolts, the wheel axles and the shock absorber bolts are tight.

Removing the front wheel

Unscrew speedometer drive shaft (fig. 21/3). Disengage brake cable (fig. 22/3). If necessary, loosen the cable adjuster (fig. 22/4 or 17/1). Undo axle nuts (fig. 21/1 and 22/1). Remove mudguard stays from axle (fig. 21/2 and 22/2).

Fig. 21

Fig. 22

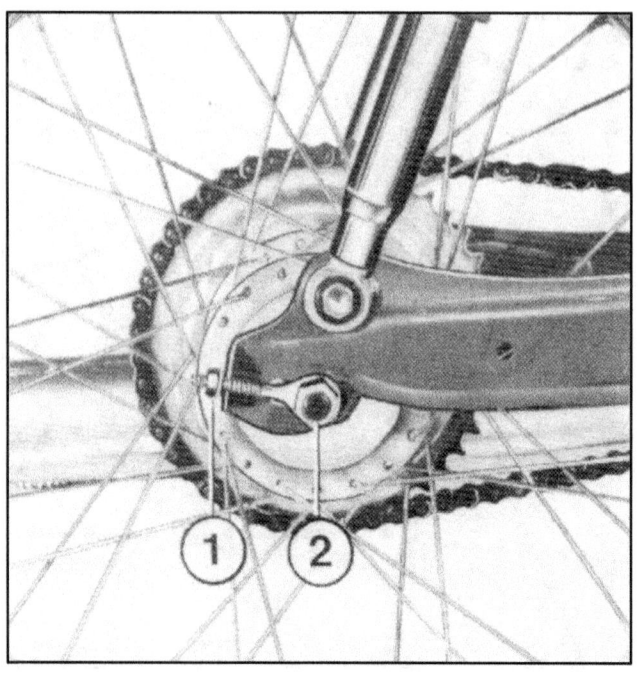

Fig. 23

Fig. 24

Removing the rear wheel

Model with kickstarter:

Loosen chain adjusters (fig. 23/1 and 24/1). Slacken both axle nuts (fig. 23/2 and 24/2). Disengage brake cable from brake lever (fig. 24/3) and from cable sleeve support (fig. 24/4).
Turn cable adjusters out from the grooves.
Push wheel in forward direction. Lift chain outwards from the sprocket. Incline the machine to the left or right and remove the wheel.

Model with back pedalling brake

Loosen chain adjusters (fig. 25/1 and 26/1).. Slacken both axle nuts (fig. 25/2 and fig. 26/2). Turn cable adjusters out of the grooves. Push wheel forward. Remove driving chain (fig. 25/3) and pedal chain (fig. 26/3) from their sprockets. Incline the machine to the left, pull the rear wheel out, pressing the pulley slightly forward.

Model with handbrake lever

Disengage brake cable and continue as detailed above.

Fig. 25

Fig. 26

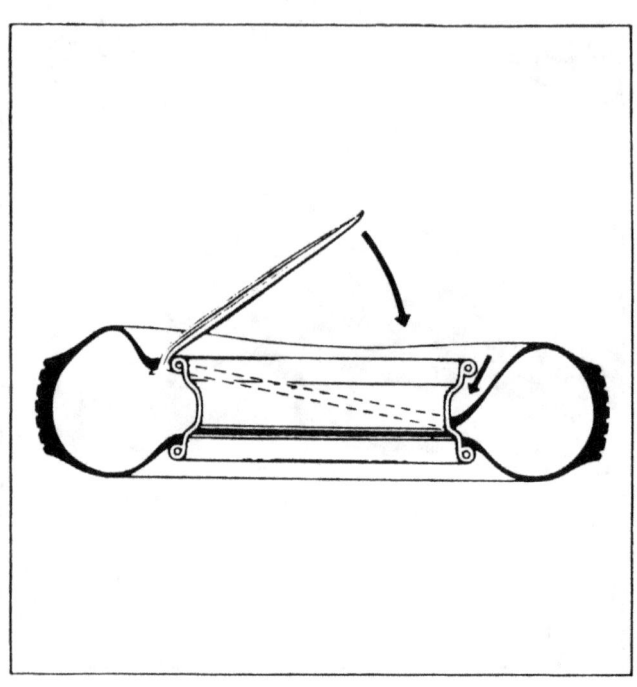

Fig. 27

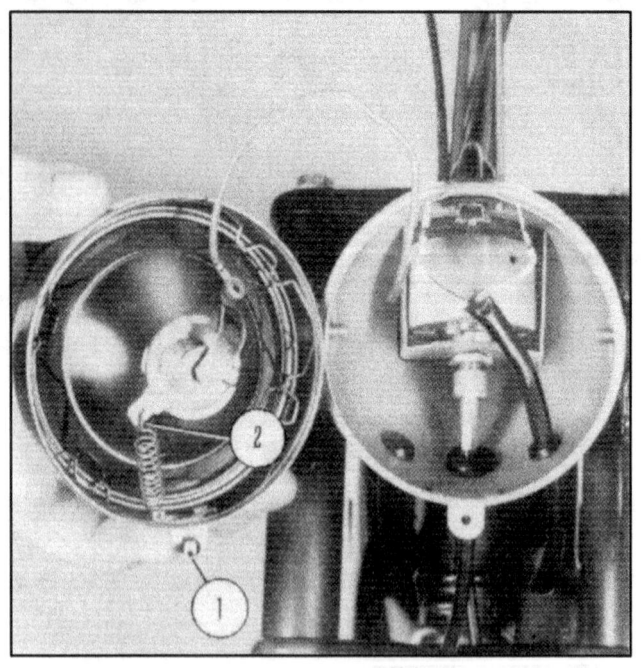

Fig. 28

Changing tyres (fig. 27)

To remove tyre, unscrew valve cap, depress valve needle to let out all the air, unscrew valve lock nut and press back complete valve. Losen the bead tyre section from the rim and press the tyre opposite the valve into the centre groove of the rim. This gives sufficient space to lift the tyre at the valve location over the rim with the tyre lever.

Hold the tyre outside the rim with the tyre lever and work round the rim with the second lever unil the whole circumference of the tyre is outside the rim.

Now remove inner tube. When assembling, fit lightly pumped up inner tube coated with chalk into the tyre, having already fitted the first half of the tyre over the rim. Ensure the tube is not trapped or twisted and make sure that the rim band protecting the tube from the spokes is flat and in the rim centre well.

Changing the headlight bulb

Undo both top headlight screws (fig. 28/1 and 29/1). Lift housing.
By slight pressure remove headlight glass upward.
Depress bulb, turn the left and pull out.

Replacing rear light or stoplight bulb

Unscrew fixing screw (fig. 30/1) and remove housing. Replace bulb and fit in reverse procedure.

Adjusting the headlamp (fig. 31)

Place the machine on level ground at a distance of (20 ft.) 5 m from a vertical wall.

Chalk on the wall a vertical line corresponding to the centre of the machine and a horizontal crossing line at H above ground level (fig. 31).

The main beam should coincide with the adjusting cross. Loosen the handlamp bracket screw to adjust the beam manually as necessary. Retighten the screw. Check the dipped beam after checking the main beam. The dipped beam is correct if the cut-off above the beam is (2 in) 5 cm below the horizontal line of the adjusting cross.

Adjust the headlamp of models with permanent dip beam as mentioned above.

Fig. 29

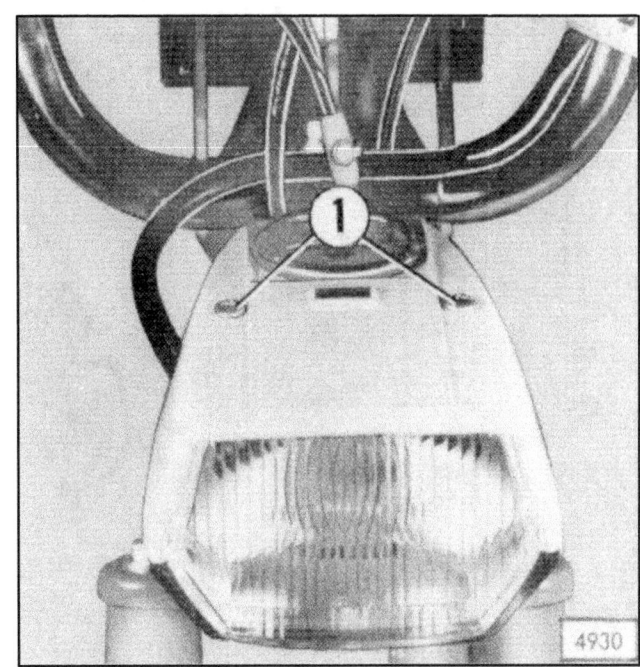

Fig. 30

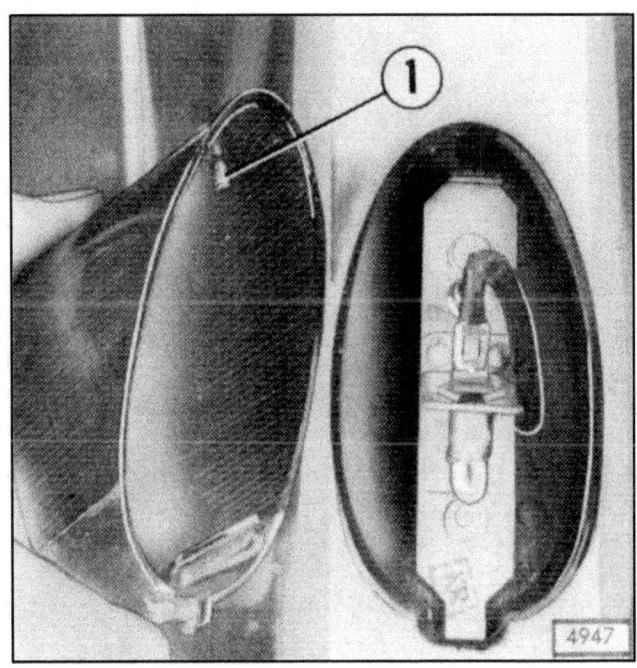

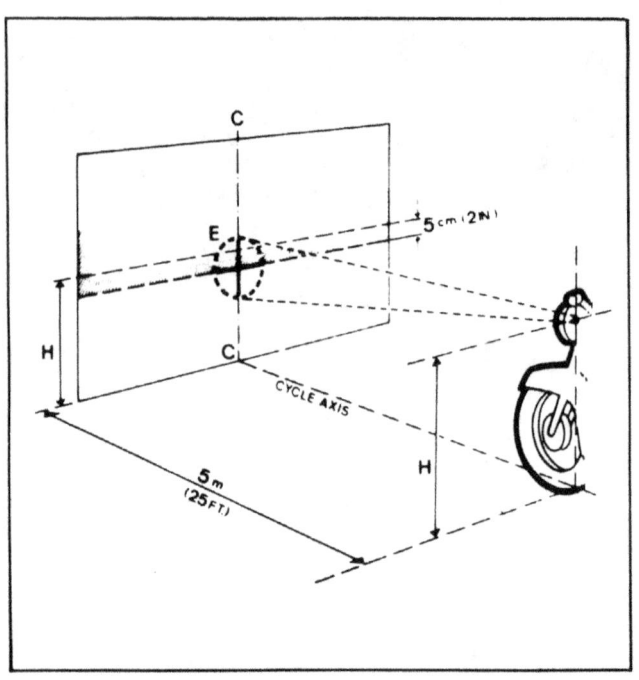

Fig. 31

Fig. 32

F) CLEANING THE MACHINE

Cleaning is advisable before undertaking any maintenance work. Avoid strong water jets which are detrimental to the paintwork and also entail the danger of water penetrating the bearings and brakes or into the carburettor and ignition system where it may cause trouble. A big soft sponge is recommended for external cleaning. Use water liberally for the first cleaning as the dried dirt and sand will scratch the paint surface and cause it to lose its high gloss finish. Use a chamois leather cloth to wipe dry. Application of a mild lacquer preservative is advisable. Chromium parts should be cleaned and greased with a non-acid grease. After the machine has been in use for some time the engine unit will naturally become dirty and it is best cleaned with a good degreasing agent. If petrol is used be careful not to get any on the seat. A dry clean cloth is recommended for cleaning plastic parts. We also recommend cleaning the plastic from time to time with commercial plastic cleaning agents. By applying a good quality compound an excellent glossy, antistatic finish is achieved.

G) LAYING UP

If you wish to lay up your machine or to keep it off the road during winter or at any other time of the year follow these instructions:
Warm up the machine thoroughly, drain oil from the gearbox. Fill with fresh oil.
Clean the machine thoroughly to remove dust, oil and dirt.
Remove all rust.
Treat all bright metalwork with non-acid grease.
Grease all lubricating points.
Clean the chain thoroughly and grease with a high-viscosity oil. Treat all painted parts with lacquer preservative.
In order to prevent the tank from rusting it is recommended that it be filled with petrol. If the garage is not fireproof flush the tank with oil. Close the fuel tap in either case.
Remove the sparking plug, take off the carburettor, put the piston to TDC position, fill the cylinder with 30 cc of motor oil. Screw in the sparking plug and fix the carburettor.
Inflate the tyres to the correct pressure.
Jack up the machine in a dry room. Cover with tarpaulin or wrapping paper. It is very dangerous to let the engine run for a short time only after the machine has been laid up as the engine will not be sufficiently warmed up and acidic water vapor, created inevitably by the combustion process, will condense and cause the bearings to rust.

Using the machine again

Open the breather screw (fig. 32/1) and let the oil drain off. Refit the breather screw, open the fuel tap and start the engine, allowing it to become fully warmed up.

H) LUBRICATION AND MAINTENANCE

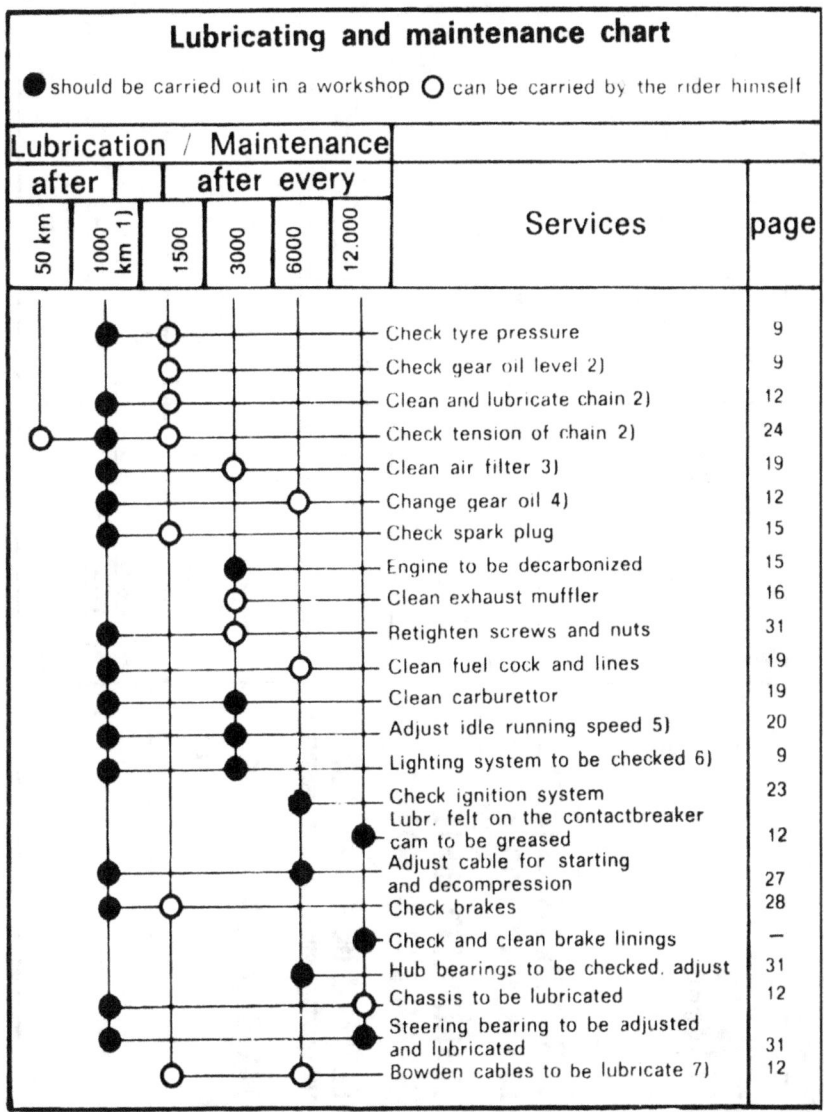

Lubricating and maintenance chart

● should be carried out in a workshop   ○ can be carried by the rider himself

Lubrication after		Maintenance after every			Services	page
50 km	1000 km 1)	1500	3000	6000	12.000		
	●	○				Check tyre pressure	9
		○				Check gear oil level 2)	9
	●	○				Clean and lubricate chain 2)	12
○	●	○				Check tension of chain 2)	24
	●		○			Clean air filter 3)	19
	●			○		Change gear oil 4)	12
	●					Check spark plug	15
			●			Engine to be decarbonized	15
	●		○			Clean exhaust muffler	16
	●		○			Retighten screws and nuts	31
	●			○		Clean fuel cock and lines	19
	●			○		Clean carburettor	19
	●		○			Adjust idle running speed 5)	20
	●					Lighting system to be checked 6)	9
			●			Check ignition system	23
			●			Lubr. felt on the contactbreaker cam to be greased	12
	●		●			Adjust cable for starting and decompression	27
	●	○				Check brakes	28
			●			Check and clean brake linings	—
			●			Hub bearings to be checked. adjust	31
			○			Chassis to be lubricated	12
			●			Steering bearing to be adjusted and lubricated	31
		○	○			Bowden cables to be lubricate 7)	12

1) Mandatory check, 2) from time to time and before any major trips, 3) when used on asphalt roads every 1000 km, on roads that are dusty in parts every 500 km and on tracks that are dusty throughout every 200 km, 4) or at least twice annually, 5) whenever the carburettor has been cleaned, 6) before any trip, 7) if too stiff.

PUCH

SCHMIERMITTELTABELLE
FÜR PUCH-MOTORRÄDER, -ROLLER, -MOPEDS

LUBRICATION TABLE
FOR PUCH-MOTORCYCLES, -SCOOTERS, -MO-PEDS

TABLEAU DE GRAISSAGE
POUR PUCH-MOTOCYCLETTE, -SCOOTER, -CYCLOMOTEUR

TABLA DE LUBRICANTES
PARA PUCH-MOTOCICLETAS, -MOTONETAS Y -MOTOBICICLETAS

	Viskosität / Viscosity / Viscosie / Viscosidad		AGIP	ARAL	BP
Mopeds / Mopeds / Cyclomoteur / Motobicicletas	Für Treibstoffgemisch / For fuel mixture / Pour mélange de carburant / Para mezcla de carburante	SAE 40 oder SAE 50 2)	AGIP F 1 2 TSM	ARAL 2 T Motor Oel 1)	BP TWO STROKE OIL BP SUPER TWO STROKE OIL
Motorräder / Motorcycles / Motocyclette / Motocicletas		SAE 40	AGIP 2 T	ARAL 2 T Motor Oel	BP SUPER TWO STROKE OIL BP SUPER TWO STROKE OIL
		SAE 40	AGIP F 1 WOOM MOTOR OIL HD 40 50	ARAL SPEZIAL Motor Oel SAE 40	BP ENERGOL HD SAE 40 or 50
		SAE 30	AGIP F 1 WOOM MOTOR OIL HD 40	ARAL SPEZIAL Motor Oel SAE 40	BP ENERGOL HD SAE 40
		SAE 20—30	AGIP F 1 WOOM MOTOR OIL HD 30	ARAL SPEZIAL Motor Oel SAE 30	BP ENERGOL HD SAE 30
	AUTOMATIC TRANSMISSION FLUID		AGIP F 1 ROTRA ATF	ARAL Getriebeöl SGF	BP AUTOMATIC TRANSMISSION FLUID Type A. Suffix A
1	Stoßdämpferöl / Shock absorber oil / Huile d'amortisseur / Aceite de amortiguadores		AGIP F 1 Shock Absorber	ARAL 1010	BP ENERGOL HLP 40
2			AGIP F 1 OSO 35	ARAL Oel GFU	BP ENERGOL HLP 65
3			AGIP F 1 OSO 55	ARAL Oel GFX	BP ENERGOL HLP 100
4			AGIP F 1 OSO 85	ARAL Oel GFY	BP ENERGOL HLP 175
	Abschmierfett / Grease / Graisse / Grasa Lubricante		AGIP F 1 Grease 30	ARAL Mehrzweckfett	BP MEHRZWECKFETT L 2
	Lithium-Seifenfett / Lithium base grease / Lithium graisse de savon / Grasa de jabón de litio		AGIP F 1 Grease 30	ARAL Mehrzweckfett	BP MEHRZWECKFETT L 2
		SAE 90	AGIP F 1 ROTRA HYPOID 90	ARAL Getriebeöl SAE 90	HYPOGEAR EP BP SAE 90

STEYR-DAIMLER-PUCH, AG
GRAZ   AUSTRIA

907.1.71.305.6
5. Auflage d e/s

Die Ölmenge und die Qualität für Sommer- und Winterbetrieb) ist der Betriebsanleitung zu entnehmen. The quantity and quality of oil may be quoted from the owner's manual.
Pour quantité et qualité d'huile (été et hiver) voir les instructions d'service. La quantidad y la qualidad del aceite hay que separer de las instrucciones de servicio (para servicio durante el verano el invierno).

Firmenbezeichnung (alphabetisch geordnet). The names of the firms are alphabetically ordered. Définitions des marques par ordre alphabétique. Razon social (en orden alfabético).

CASTROL	ESSO	FILTRATE	MOBIL	PAM	SHELL	SUNOCO	TOTAL	VALVOLINE	VEEDOL
CASTROL two stroke or CASTROL Super two stroke	ESSO 2- MOTOR OIL	FILTRATE SUPER 2 OIL	Mobiloil TT	PAM two stroke OIL	SHELL 2 T two stroke oil	SUNLUBE HD 40	TOTAL 2 TV	VALVOLINE MD 40 or MD 50 HP Super outboard & two cycle Motoroil	VEEDOL SPECIAL
CASTROL two stroke or CASTROL Super two stroke	ESSO 2-T MOTOR OIL	FILTRATE SUPER 2 or Mobiloil 2-stroke Super	Mobiloil TT or Mobiloil 2-stroke Super		SHELL 2 T two stroke oil SHELL SUPER two stroke oil	SUNLUBE HD 40 SUNOCO OUTBOARD MOTOR OIL		VALVOLINE HP SUPER OUTBOARD & TWO CYCLE MOTOR OIL	
CASTROL 50	ESSO MCTOR OIL 40/50	FILTRATE SUPER 2 oder SUPER 50	Mobiloil TT	PAM two stroke OIL	SHELL 2 T two stroke oil	SUNLUBE HD 40	TOTAL SUPER HD 50	VALVOLINE SUPER HPO SAE 40 od 50	VEEDOL SPECIAL two stroke OIL
CASTROL 40	ESSO MOTOR OIL 40	FILTRATE SUPER 2 OIL	Mobiloil TT	PAM two stroke OIL	SHELL 2 T two stroke oil	SUNLUBE HD 40	TOTAL 2 TV TOTAL SUPER 2-STROKE	VALVOLINE MD 40 or MD 50	VEEDOL SPECIAL
CASTROL 30	ESSO MOTOR OIL 20 W/30	FILTRATE MEDIUM 30	Mobiloil 30	PAM HD MOTOR OIL SAE 30	SHELL X-100/30	SUNLUBE HD 30	TOTAL 2 TV TOTAL SUPER 2-STROKE	VALVOLINE SUPER HPO SAE 30	VEEDOL SPECIAL two stroke OIL
CASTROL 30	ESSO MOTOR OIL 20 W/30	FILTRATE MEDIUM 30	Mobiloil 30	PAM HD MOTOR OIL SAE 30	SHELL X-100/30	SUNLUBE HD 30	TOTAL SUPER HD 30	VALVOLINE SUPER HPO SAE 30	VEEDOL ADELBUS M SAE 30
CASTROL TQF	ESSO AUTOMATIC TRANSMISSION FLUID	FILTRATE AUTO TRANSMISSION FLUID F	Mobil ATF 200	PAM TRANSMATIC FLUID	SHELL DONAX T 6	SUNOCO ATF Type A	TOTAL FLUIDE A	VALVOMATIC Automatic Transmission-Fluid Type A, Suffix A	VEEDOL ATF Type A SUFFIX A
CASTROL HYSPIN AWS 10	ESSO OLEOFLUID 40 X	FILTRATE 5 W	Mobil Velocite Oil E	PAM TURCIR 23	SHELL DONAX A 1	SUNVIS 807 HV	TOTAL AZOLA 10	VALVOLINE R 50 TOS	VEEDOL shock absorber OIL
CASTROL HYSPIN AWS 22	ESSO NUTO H 44	FILTRATE 10 W	Mobil D T E 24		SHELL TELLUS 23	SUNVIS 811 HV		VALVOLINE R 100 TOS	
CASTROL HYSPIN AWS 68	ESSO NUTO H 54	FILTRATE ZERO 20 20 W or TELESCOPIC F	Mobil D T E 26		SHELL TELLUS 33	SUNVIS 825 HV		VALVOLINE R 306 TOS	
CASTROL HYSPIN AWS 150	ESSO NUTO H 64	FILTRATE MEDIUM 30	Mobil D T E 28		SHELL TELLUS 41	SUNVIS 851 HV		VALVOLINE R 506 TOS	
CASTROL GREASE CL	ESSO MULTIPURPOSE GREASE H	FILTRATE SUPER Lithium	Mobilgrease MP Mobilgrease Special	PAM Grease 6 PAM Grease 2	SHELL RETTINAX A	SUNAPLEX 992 EP	TOTAL MULTIS 2	VALVOLINE X-5 light	VEEDOL Multipurpose grease VEEDOL VC lube
CASTROL GREASE LM	ESSO MULTIPURPOSE GREASE H	FILTRATE SUPER Lithium	Mobilgrease MP Mobilgrease Special	PAM Grease 6 multipurpose grease	SHELL RETTINAX A	SUNAPLEX 992 EP	TOTAL MULTIS 2	VALVOLINE X-5 light	VEEDOL Multipurpose grease
CASTROL ST 90	ESSO GEAR OIL GP 90 or ESSO GEAR GX 90	FILTRATE EP 90	Mobilube HD 90	PAM multipurpose GEAR OIL SAE 90	SHELL Spirax 90 EP SHELL Spirax HD 90	SUNOCO MPGL 5 90	TOTAL EP Type B SAE 90	VALVOLINE X-18 90	VEEDOL Multigear Lubricant SAE 90

1) Nicht selbstmischend. Not self mixing. Mélange non automatique. No automatico mixto 2) Für Getriebe. For gearbox. Pour boite de vitesses. Para caja de cambios

LUBRICATION AND MAINTENANCE CART (For U. K. only)

Lubricating and maintenance chart

The maintenance jobs, which are due between the compulsory services can be carried out by the rider himself.

Before every ride check:
Fuel reserve, tyre pressure, fitness of brakes, lighting, existence of tools.

Every week check:
Oil level in gearbox, clutch adjustment, clearance of brake lever and brake pedal

- ○ These jobs can be carried out by the rider himself
- ● These jobs should be carried out in a workshop

	Compulsory Service after			Maintenance after every				SERVICES
300 m	1800 m	3600 m	600 m	1800 m	3600 m	7200 m		
		●				●	Decarbonize the cylinder and exhaust assy
	●				●		Decarbonize exhaust
	●				●		Replace air cleaner 1)
	●				●		Check spark plug and clean
●							Clean fuel strainer and fuel lines
	●				●		Clean carburetor, adjust idling air and idle running speed
●							Adjust idling air and idle running speed
●	●	●		○	●	●	Check clutch adjustment and readjust if necessary 2)
●	●	●	○	○	●	●	Check ignition system ignition point and adjust if necessary
●	●	●	○	○	●	●	Check front wheel brake, adjust if necessary
●	●	●	○	○	●	●	Check rear wheel brake, adjust if necessary
		●				●	Check tension of chain and lubricate, check track (adjusting)
		●				●	Check hub bearings and grease
		●				●	Check steering bearings and grease
					●		Change oil of telescopic fork 3)
					●		Change oil of shock absorbers 3)
●	●	●			●	●	Check bolts and nuts for tightness
							Retighten cylinder head bolts (every 600 miles after decoking)
		●				●	Grease chassis
●	●	●			●	●	Lubricate bowden cables
●	●	●			●	●	Check oil level in gearbox
●	●	●			●	●	Change oil in gearbox 4)
●	●	●			●	●	Check electrical equipment
							Check horn
							Check tyre pressure
		●			●	●	Check and grease chain, check sprockets for tightness
		●				●	Grease lubricating felt pad at the breaker cam
	●				●		Check brake linings
●	●	●			●	●	Check gearshift, if necessary adjusting 5)
●	●	●			●	●	Short test ride

1) Cleaning and oiling if model MS, VS and Maxi are concerned
2) Maxi: Do not adjust clutch but cable for starting and decompression
3) Only necessary to models VZ 50 MN and M 125
4) Twice a year at least
5) Only handcontrolled machines

J) TROUBLE SHOOTING

Engine does not start or running engine stops

Cause	Remedy
1. Fuel tap closed	Open fuel tap or switch to "Reserve"
2. Fuel tank is empty	Switch fuel tap over to "Reserve" or fill up with petrol mixture
3. Sparking plug is contaminated	Clean sparking plug
4. Sparking plug is defective	Replace sparking plug
5. Sparking plug gap is not correct	Adjust gap by bending the earth electrode
6. Ignition cable has worked loose or came off	Refit plug cap
7. Too much or too little gas	Open throttle about 1/3
8. a) Carburettor flooded, or vehicle fell over	Start with throttle wide open. If the engine is badly flooded open drain plug of the crankcase (fig. 33/1) and drain fuel
8. b) To aid starting with a hot engine	Remedy as above
9. Fuel pipe is clogged	Blow through the fuel pipe
10. Fuel tap is clogged	Have it cleaned by a Puch workshop
11. Main jet is clogged	Clean main jet
12. Impurities at the valve seat of the float needle	Clean valve seat
13. Float needle not fixed in its notch	Remove float needle, and re-engage it

— 49 —

Engines runs unevenly or misfires

Cause	Remedy
1. There is not enough fuel in the tank	Open fuel tap to "Reserve", refuel with petroil mixture
2. Carburettor is loose	Retighten carburettor fixing screw
3. Float leaks	Replace float
4. Ignition cable is not properly connected	Refit plug cap
5. Sparking plug is defective	Replace sparking plug
6. Jet needle is loose	Clamp needle in its notch. Correct notch see "Technical Data"
7. Fuel mixture is not correct	Drain fuel tank, refuel with correct petroil mixture (see "Technical Data")

Poor performance

Cause	Remedy
1. Choke working all the time	Push choke back (or "snap-open" throttle)
2. Exhaust is clogged	Remove oily deposits from the exhaust
3. Carburettor is loose	Retighten carburettor fixing screws
4. Sparking plug is defective	Replace sparking plug
5. Brakes catch	Adjust brakes
6. Clutch slips	Readjust clutch
7. Exhaust port is clogged	Decoke exhaust port
8. Float leaks, float needle deformed (jams)	Check all parts of the float chamber and replace if necessary
9. Float needle is loose	Clamp needle in its notch. Correct needle position see "Technical Data"
10. Air filter is clogged	Clean air filter
11. Fuel mixture is not correct	Drain fuel tank, refuel with correct mixture

 TECHNICAL DATA **MAXI N/S**

CONTROLS

- Speedometer
- Steering lock
- Rear brake lever
- Decompressor lever
- Light switch
- Choke
- Pedal crank
- Frame number
- Hand brake lever
- Throttle twist grip
- Filler cap
- Carburettor tickler
- Engine number
- Fuel cock
- Model detail plate

ENGINE

Maximum output	2,2 hp at 4500 r.p.m.
Maximum torque	0,38 mkp at 3600 r.p.m.
Compression ratio	11
Bore	38 mm
Stroke	43 mm
Displacement	48,8 cc
Cooling	air cooled
Lubrication	petroil lubrication
Carburettor	Bing 1/14
Main jet	64
Needle jet	2,20
Needle position	2nd notch from top
Ignition	magneto ignition
Breaker point gap	0,35—0,45 mm
Ignition timing	0,8 —1,2 mm in advance of TDC (14—17,5°crank angle)
Spark plug	Bosch W 175 T 1 or Champion L 86
Spark gap	0,4—0,5 mm
Dynamo	flywheel magneto Bosch 6 V, 22 W

POWER TRANSMISSION

Gearbox	single speed automatic
Clutch	centrifugal
Primary transmission	helical gears
Secondary transmission	chain 1/2" x 3/16"
Pedalling chain	chain 1/2" x 1/8"

GEAR RATIOS

Engine gear	106 : 21; i = 5,05
Gear-rear wheel	45 : 16; i = 2,81
Pedalling transmission	37 : 20; i = 1,85

CHASSIS

Frame	shell type frame
Front wheel suspension	telescopic fork; 50 mm spring travel
Rear wheel suspension	shock absorbers 50 mm spring travel } Maxi „S" only
Brakes	Internal expanding shoe brakes
Dia. of brake drum	80 mm
Width of brake lining	20 mm
Total effective braking surface	52 cm²
Tire size front and rear	21 x 2,00
Tire pressure front/rear	25/32 psi (1,8/2,25 kg/cm²)
Fuel tank	3,2 litres

DIMENSIONS AND WEIGHTS

Wheelbase . . . . 1120 mm
Overall length . . . . 1700 mm
Overall width . . . .   690 mm
Overall height . . . . 1000 mm
Ground clearence . . . . . .   100 mm
Dry weight . . . .   42 kg

ELECTRICAL EQUIPMENT

Headlamp bulb . . . . 6 V, 18/18 W
Rearlamp bulb . . . . 6 V, 3 W
Warning device . . . . buzzer

PERFORMANCE AND CONSUMPTION

Top speed . . . . 28 mph (45 km/h)
Hill climbing ability 15%
Standard fuel consumption
(DIN 70030) . . . . 177 m/Imp. gal. (1,6 litres/100 km)

Test commences on a flat track in top gear at 2/3 top speed. The track length of 6,2 m (10 km) is used either way and may have very short upward and downward gradients of a maximum of 1,5%. The vehicle must be adjusted to specification and and tyres must have correct pressure. The rider must not weight more than 143,32 lb (65 kg). The measured consumption is increased by 10% take into account unfavourable conditions.

CAPACITY AND QUALITY OF LUBRICANTS

(see bypacked lubrication table)

ENGINE	Mixture of economy petrol 1 or 2 star with a branded motor oil of SAE 40—50. Mixture ratio 25 : 1 (= 4%) or 50 : 1 with special two stroke oil.
GEARBOX	170 cc Automatic-Transmission-Fluid
GREASE NIPPLES, CABLES	Summer and winter grease. For lubrication of the grease nipples also SAE 90 can be used. For lubrication of the cables also SAE 30 can be used.
WHEEL BEARING	Summer und winter Lithium base grease.
CHAIN	Summer und winter SAE 90.

WIRING DIAGRAM AND LIGHT SWITCH

907.1.71.318.2 1276

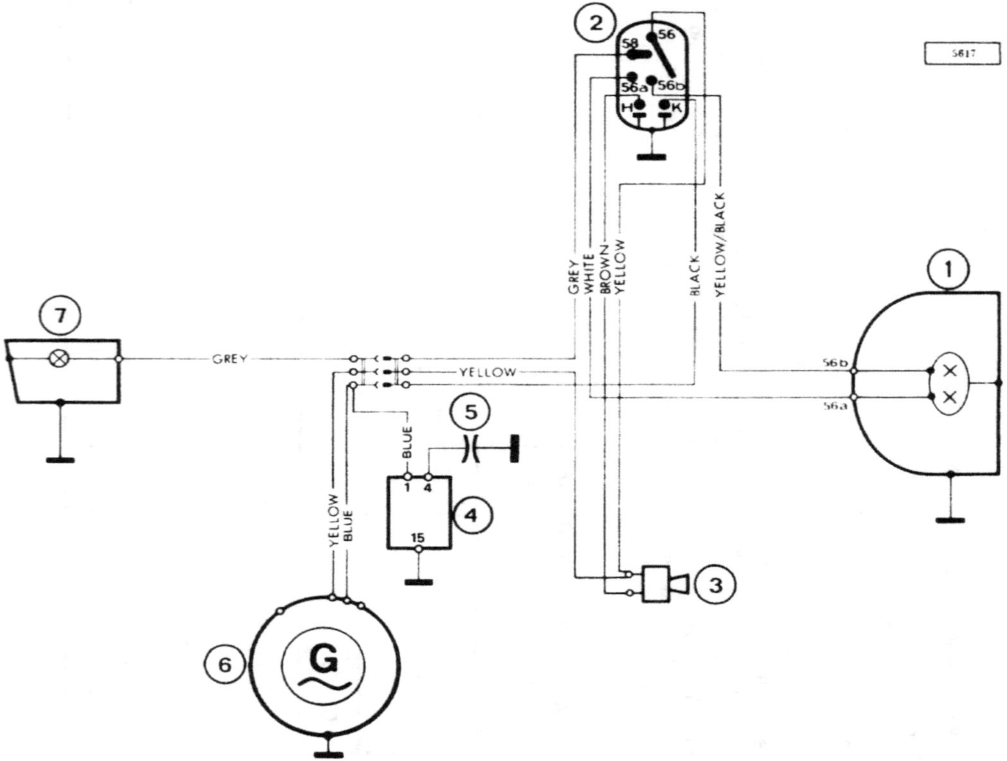

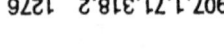

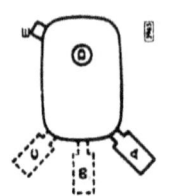

A = Switched off
B = dimmed light
C = main beam
D = Buzzer
E = no function

1 Headlamp
2 Light switch
3 Buzzer
4 Ignition coil
5 Spark plug
6 Flywheel magneto
7 Tail light

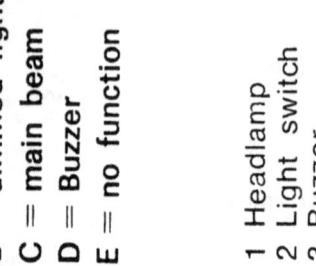

Steyr-Daimler-Puch

of America Corporation
P. Box 7777
Greenwich, Connecticut 06830

Single-Speed-Automatic

USA   Models: **RIGID**
                         MAXI
                         MAXI-S
                         NEWPORT

Spare-Parts Catalogue
Edition October 1976

MAXI/USA

907.1.71.577.4

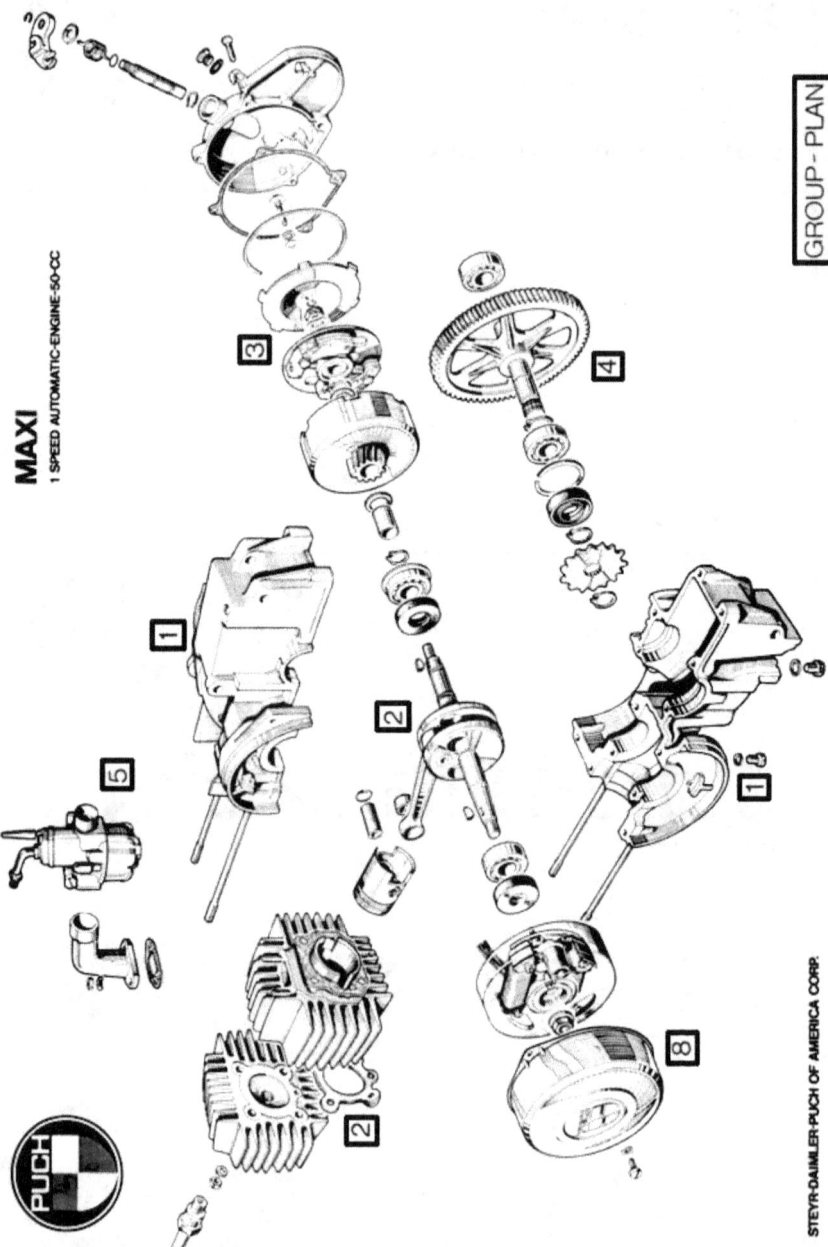

Puch 1-speed Maxi USA

CONTENTS

ENGINE
1. CRANKCASE
2. CYLINDER, PISTON, CRANKSHAFT
3. CLUTCH
4. GEARBOX
5. CARBURETOR
6. INTAKE SILENCER
7. EXHAUST
8. MAGNETO GENERATOR

CHASSIS
11. FRAME, FUEL TAB, SADDLE
11a. SINGLE SEAT, LUGGAGE CARRIER AND 2nd LOCK FOR MAXI-S
12. MUDGUARD, LUGGAGE CARRIER
13. CHAIN GUARD (fairings)
14. PROP STAND
15. PEDALS, CHAINS, CHAIN TENSIONER
15a. REAR WHEEL SUSPENSION (Pivoted fork, Suspension unit)

FRONT FORK
16. FRONT FORK WITH STEERING
17. HANDLEBAR AND CONTROLS
18. CABLES

ROAD WHEELS
19. FRONT WHEEL for RIGID, MAXI and NEWPORT
19a. FRONT WHEEL for MAXI-S
20. REAR WHEEL for RIGID, MAXI and NEWPORT
20a. REAR WHEEL for MAXI-S

ELECTRICAL EQUIPMENT
21. HEADLAMP, TAIL-STOP-LIGHT, RATTLE, HARNESS
21a. SPEEDOMETER WITH SPEEDOMETER DRIVE

ACCESSORIES
22. TOOLS, PUMP

To convert millimeters to inches, multiply by 0,03937

Puch 1-speed Maxi USA

MODEL **RIGID**   VIEW l.h.

MODEL MAXI   VIEW r.h.

Edition October 1976   SPARE PARTS   PAGE 4

Puch 1-speed Maxi USA

MODEL MAXI-S   VIEW l.h.

MODEL NEWPORT   VIEW r.h.

Puch 1-speed Maxi USA

USA SINGLE-SPEED-AUTOMATIC MODELS **RIGID**, **MAXI**, **MAXI-S** and **NEWPORT** are available in the following colors:

poppy red	RAL	3002	Color-code-number	49
yellow	Puch	1060	Color-code-number	67
white	RAL	9002	Color-code-number	19
purple	Puch	4054 M	Color-code-number	47
silver	RAL	9006	Color-code-number	90
green	Puch	6064	Color-code-number	55
red	Puch	3052 T	Color-code-number	45
blue	Puch	5051 T	Color-code-number	73
champagne	Puch	1063	Color-code-number	14
metalic brown	RAL	8017	Color-code-number	37
black	RAL	9005	Color-code-number	30

In ordering laquered parts, please do not forget to state the matching color-code-number along with the spare-part-number

e.g. 349.2.20.800.0/ + color code from above list

Puch 1-speed Maxi USA

IMPORTANT

To get a quick and correct settlement of your spare parts orders following statements are necessary:

1. Exact statement of vehicle
2. Engine no.
3. Spare parts no.
4. Description
5. Colour
6. Required quantity
7. Wanted way of delivery

Beside this our general terms of sale and delivery are valuable.

Please direct your orders to: place for stamp

GENERAL EXPLANATIONS

Statements as "left", "right", "front", "rear" at the description of spare parts are referring to the moving direction of vehicle. The given dimensions (in mm) for particular parts have to be considered as standards. (To convert millimeters to inches, multiply by 0,03937).

A reference number bracketed on the illustrated page means that this number appears several times on the illustrated page.

A ref.no. within brackets before a spare part means, that the said part is only similar to the illustration.

A "N" before the statement of requd. quantity is marking a standard part. The abbreviation "as requd." means "as required"; the abbreviation "p.m." means "per meter".

The content of the present manual is not obliging for delivery and quipment of vehicle.

Edition October 1976 SPARE PARTS   PAGE 7

Puch 1-speed Maxi USA

EXPLANATION OF THE SPARE PARTS CLASSIFICATION NUMBERS

To facilitate the systematic arrangement of the various spare parts in your spares depot, the system of classification by numbers is explained below.

Types of numbers:

A E.g.   900.1028   a so-called "900-number" given to standard parts, commercial parts and electrical equipement parts.

B E.g.   24865   a 2-5 figure number. (Such numbers used to be given to the spares of models manufactured in the past. Insofar as such parts are used in currently produced machines, these numbers will still appear in the spares lists.)

C E.g.   349.1.40.802.0
                       .1
                      etc.

a 7 - 10 figure number. From the composition of this number the following information can be deduced:

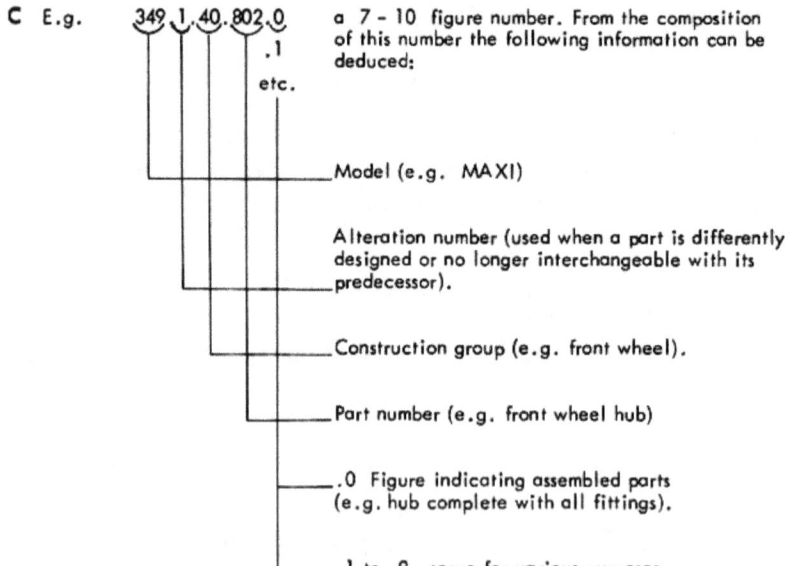

Model (e.g. MAXI)

Alteration number (used when a part is differently designed or no longer interchangeable with its predecessor).

Construction group (e.g. front wheel).

Part number (e.g. front wheel hub)

.0 Figure indicating assembled parts (e.g. hub complete with all fittings).

.1 to .9 serve for various purposes

TYPE NUMBER FOR MAXI IS **349**

Edition October 1976   SPARE PARTS   PAGE 7a

Puch 1-speed Maxi USA

LIST OF CONSTRUCTIONS GROUPS

10	CRANKCASE, CYLINDER, ENGINE PARTS
12	CLUTCH
13	GEARBOX
15	CARBURETTOR, INTAKE SILENCER
16	EXHAUST
20	FRAME
21	REAR SUSPENSION
22	FUEL TANK, FUEL TAP
23	SADDLE
24	STANDS
27	MUDGUARDS
28	DRIVING CHAIN, CHAIN GUARDS
29	LUGGAGE CARRIER
30	FRONT FORK
31	STEERING
32	HANDLEBAR
40	FRONT WHEEL
41	REAR WHEEL
42	CRANKS
50 to 59	ELECTRICAL EQUIPMENT
70	TOOLS
72	EQUIPMENT, REAR MIRROR
—	CONTROL CABLES 910 = TYPNUMMER

DETERMINED BY LAW AS FROM 1977!

349.1.72.810.0   REAR MIRROR

349.1.72.311.0   CLIP compl.

Edition October 1976   SPARE PARTS   PAGE 7b

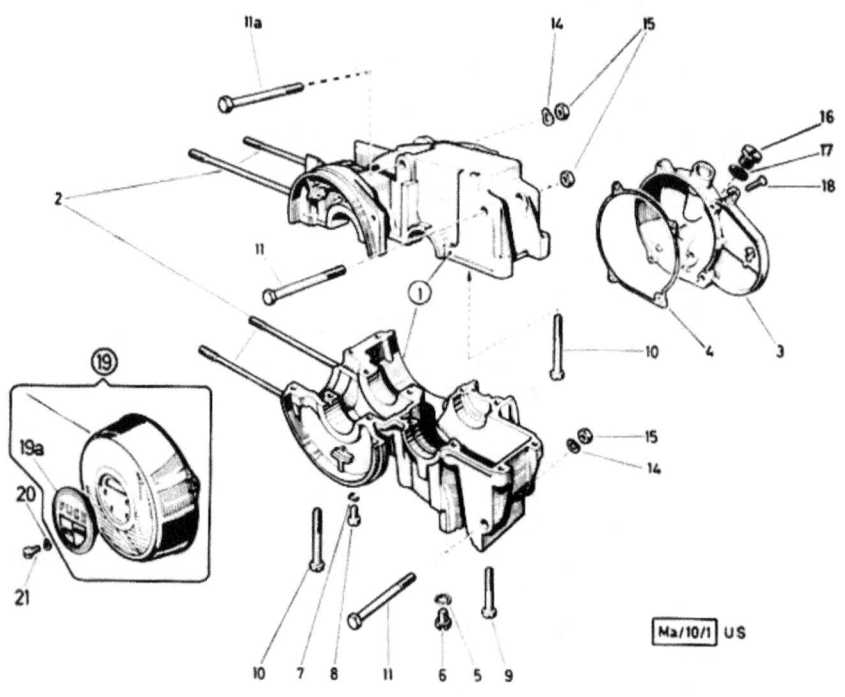

Puch 1-speed Maxi USA

1. CRANKCASE

Ref.-No.	Part-No.	Description		Model Rigid	Model Maxi, Maxi-S	Model Newport
1	349.1.10.832.0	CRANKCASE compl.		1	1	1
2	360.1.10.034.1	STUD BOLT M6, 103 long		4	4	4
3	349.5.10.335.1	COVER		1	1	1
4	349.1.10.349.1	COVER GASKET		1	1	1
5	26482	SEAL WASHER A8x14 DIN 7603	for oil drain	N1	1	1
6	901.1053	HEXAGON BOLT M8x10 Sz DIN 933		N1	1	1
7	24365	SEAL WASHER A6x12 DIN 7603	for oil control and crankcase bleeding	N2	2	2
8	900.1305	CHEESE HEAD SCREW M6x8 DIN 84		N2	2	2
9	900.1216	CHEESE HEAD SCREW M6x30 DIN 84-8.8	for crankcase assembly	N8	8	8
10	901.1308	CHEESE HEAD SCREW CM6x50 DIN 84-8.8		N5	5	5
11	900.1162	HEXAGON BOLT M8x1x80 DIN 960-8.8		N2	-	-
11	901.1001	HEXAGON BOLT M8x1x75 DIN 960-8.8		N-	2	2
11a	901.1002	HEXAGON BOLT M8x1x90 DIN 960-8.8	for engine suspension	N1	1	1
14	900.3211	SPRING WASHER B8 DIN 137		N2	2	2
15	900.2021	HEXAGON NUT M8x1 DIN 934-8		N2	2	2
15	902.2914	HEXAGON NUT M8x1 DIN 985-8		N1	1	1
16	364.1.10.660.1	OIL FILLER PLUG (M10)		1	1	1
17	27071	SEAL WASHER A10x14 DIN 7603		N1	1	1
18	900.9460	LENS HEAD SCREW for cover fixing M6x25 DIN 966		N4	4	4

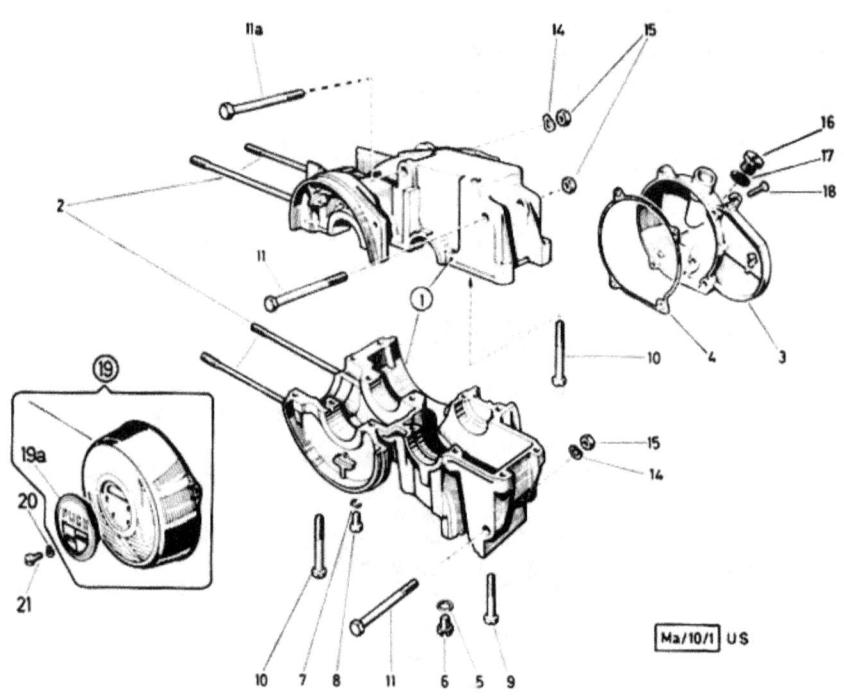

Puch 1-speed Maxi USA

1. CRANKCASE (cont.)

Ref.-No.	Part-No.	Description	Model Rigid	Model Maxi, Maxi-S	Model Newport
19	349.2.10.034.2	GENERATOR COVER (with part 19a)	1	1	-
19	349.4.10.034.2	GENERATOR COVER (with part 19a) (black)	-	-	1
19a	349.1.10.036.1	PLASTIC PANEL	1	1	-
19a	349.2.10.036.1	PLASTIC PANEL (green-gold)	-	-	1
20	900.3202	SPRING WASHER A4 DIN 137 } for generator cover fastening	N 2	2	2
21	900.1509	LENS HEAD SCREW AM4x10 DIN 85	N 2	2	2

Edition October 1976 SPARE PARTS PAGE 11

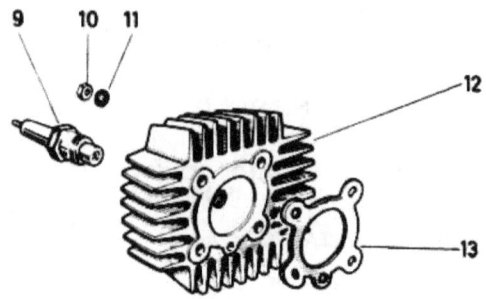
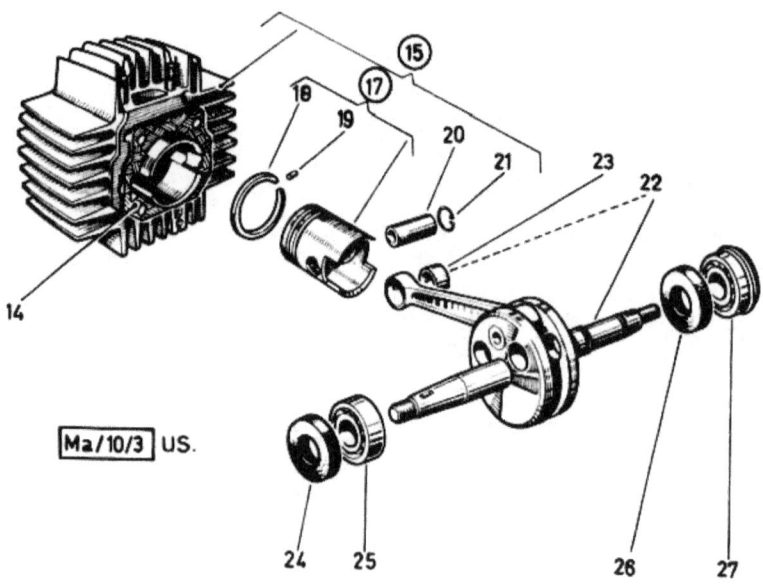

Ma/10/3 US.

Puch 1-speed Maxi USA

2. CYLINDER, PISTON, CRANKSHAFT

Reqd. No.

Ref.-No.	Part-No.	Description	Model Rigid	Model Maxi, Maxi-S	Model Newport
9	902.0728	SPARK PLUG (Bosch W95 T1)	1	(1HP)	
9	902.0726	SPARK PLUG (Bosch W145 T1)	1	(1,5 HP)	
9	902.0724	SPARK PLUG (Bosch W175 T1)	1	(2 HP)	
10	900.2014	HEXAGON NUT M6 DIN 934	N 4		
11	24804	WASHER 6,4 DIN 433	N 4		
12	349.4.10.001.1	CYLINDER COVER	1		
13	328.1.10.804.1	CYLINDER COVER GASKET (Alu-plate, 1,5mm thick)	1	(1 HP)	
13	349.1.10.004.1	CYLINDER COVER GASKET (Alu-foil 4-rows, 0,4mm thick)	1	(1,5 HP and 2 HP)	
14	349.3.10.013.1	CYLINDER BASE FLANGE GASKET (0,5mm thick)	1	(1 HP)	
14	349.1.10.013.1	CYLINDER BASE FLANGE GASKET (1mm thick)	1	(1,5 HP and 2 HP)	
15	349.8.10.005.0	CYLINDER compl. (with piston, wrist pin and wire retaining ring)	1	(1 HP)	
15	349.1.10.005.0	CYLINDER compl. (with piston, wrist pin and wire retaining ring)	1	(1,5 HP and 2 HP)	
17	349.1.10.006.0/21	PISTON compl. ⌀38, sort.1	1		
17	349.1.10.006.0/22	PISTON compl. ⌀38, sort.2	1		
17	349.1.10.006.0/23	PISTON compl. ⌀38, sort.3 as req.	1	(1 HP)	
17	349.1.10.006.0/24	PISTON compl. ⌀38, sort.4	1		
17	349.1.10.006.0/25	PISTON compl. ⌀38, sort.5	1		
17	349.1.10.106.0/21	PISTON compl. ⌀38, sort.1	1		
17	349.1.10.106.0/22	PISTON compl. ⌀38, sort.2	1		
17	349.1.10.106.0/23	PISTON compl. ⌀38, sort.3 as req.	1	(1,5 HP and 2 HP)	
17	349.1.10.106.0/24	PISTON compl. ⌀38, sort.4	1		
17	349.1.10.106.0/25	PISTON compl. ⌀38, sort.5	1		
18	331.1.10.160.1	PISTON RING (square ring FS 2-38/35x2 fz ka ki DIN 24919 with rounded edges for Alu-cylinder)	N 2		
19	900.4855	NOTCHED LOCKING PIN 2x6 DIN 1473	N 2		

Edition October 1976

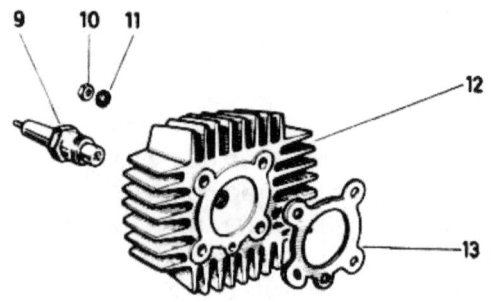

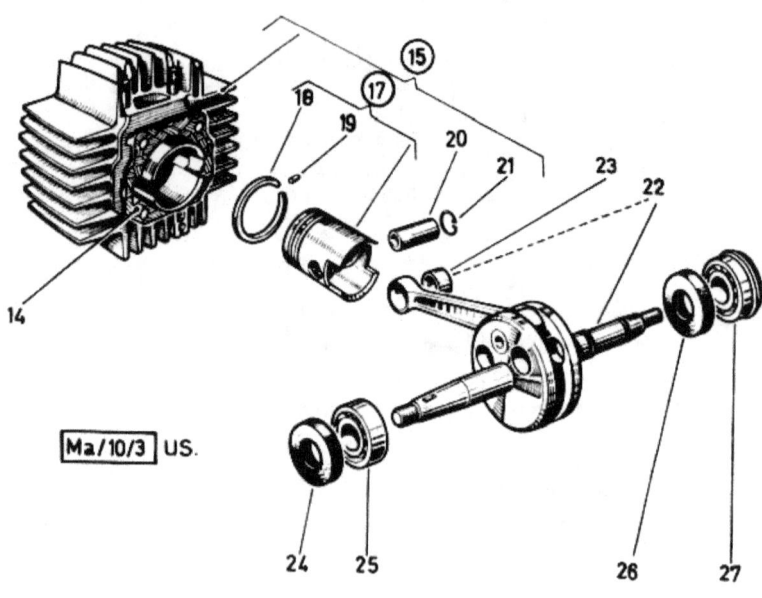

Ma/10/3 US.

Puch 1-speed Maxi USA   Reqd. No.

2. CYLINDER, PISTON, CRANKSHAFT (cont.)

Ref.-No.	Part-No.	Description	Model Rigid	Model Maxi, Maxi-S	Model Newport
20	331.1.10.011.1/12	GUDGEON PIN Ø12x31, sort.2	1		as required
20	331.1.10.011.1/13	GUDGEON PIN Ø12x31, sort.3	1		
21	901.4701	WIRE RETAINING RING B12 DIN 73123		N 2	
22	349.1.10.115.0	CRANKSHAFT compl. with connecting rod, Ø12, with bevel 1:5		1	
23	349.1.10.021.1	BUSH for connecting rod 14/11,6/12		1	
23	349.1.10.021.3	BUSH for connecting rod (for repair)		as req.	
24	901.3801	SEAL RING A17/40/7 NB N05043 } for crankshaft mounting l.h.s.		1	
25	900.6203	DEEP ROW BALL BEARING 40/17/12 6203 DIN 625		N 1	
26	902.3835	SEAL RING A22/40/7 FP N05043 } for crankshaft mounting r.h.s.		N 1	
27	900.6233	DEEP ROW BALL BEARING 40/17/12 Steyr 6203 ZNR		1	

Edition October 1976   SPARE PARTS   PAGE 15

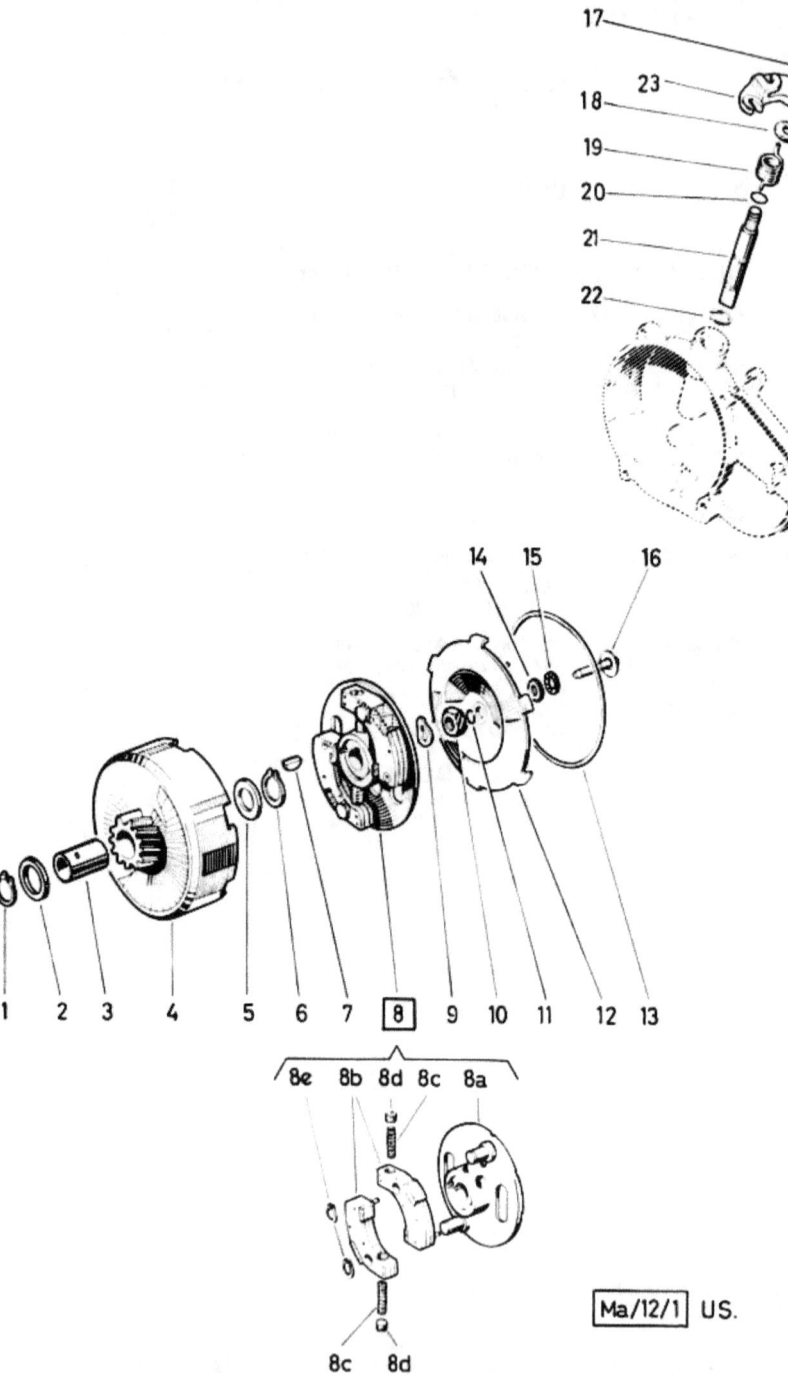

Ma/12/1 US.

Puch 1-speed Maxi USA

3. CLUTCH

Ref.-No.	Part-No.	Description		Reqd. No. Model Rigid / Model Maxi, Maxi-S / Model Newport
1	900.4617	CIRCLIP Sg 17x1 DIN 471		N 1
2	901.3943	WASHER 24/17/1,1	as required	1
	901.3927	WASHER 24/17/1,3		1
	901.3923	WASHER 24/17/1,5		1
	901.3928	WASHER 24/17/1,7		1
3	349.2.12.011.1	BEARING BUSHING 17/15/21,5		1
4	349.3.12.102.2	CLUTCH DRUM (21 teeth)		1
5	901.3929	WASHER 22/15/1,3	as required	1
	901.3924	WASHER 22/15/1,5		1
	901.3930	WASHER 22/15/1,7		1
	900.3028	WASHER 22/15/1,8		1
	901.3942	WASHER 22/15/1,9		1
	901.3949	WASHER 22/15/2,1		1
6	900.4619	CIRCLIP Sg 15x1 DIN 471		N 1
7	23340	WOODRUFF KEY 3x5 DIN 6888		N 1
8	349.1.12.504.0	CLUTCH HUB compl.		1
8a	349.1.12.504.2[x]	CLUTCH HUB loose		1
8b	349.1.12.505.0[x]	PAIR OF CLUTCH SHOE		1
8c	349.1.12.006.1[x]	THRUST SPRING for clutch hub		2
8d	349.1.12.007.1[x]	ADJUSTING SCREW (M10x1x7,5)		2
8e	900.4610	SNAP RING Sg10x1 DIN 471		N 2
9	900.3210	SPRING WASHER B10 DIN 137		N 1
10	900.2011	HEXAGON NUT M10x1 DIN 934-8		N 1

[x] It is only possible to use special tools by adjusting the clutch shoes. By missing the special tools please use only the stated clutch hub compl. under Ref-No. 8.

Edition October 1976 SPARE PARTS   PAGE 17

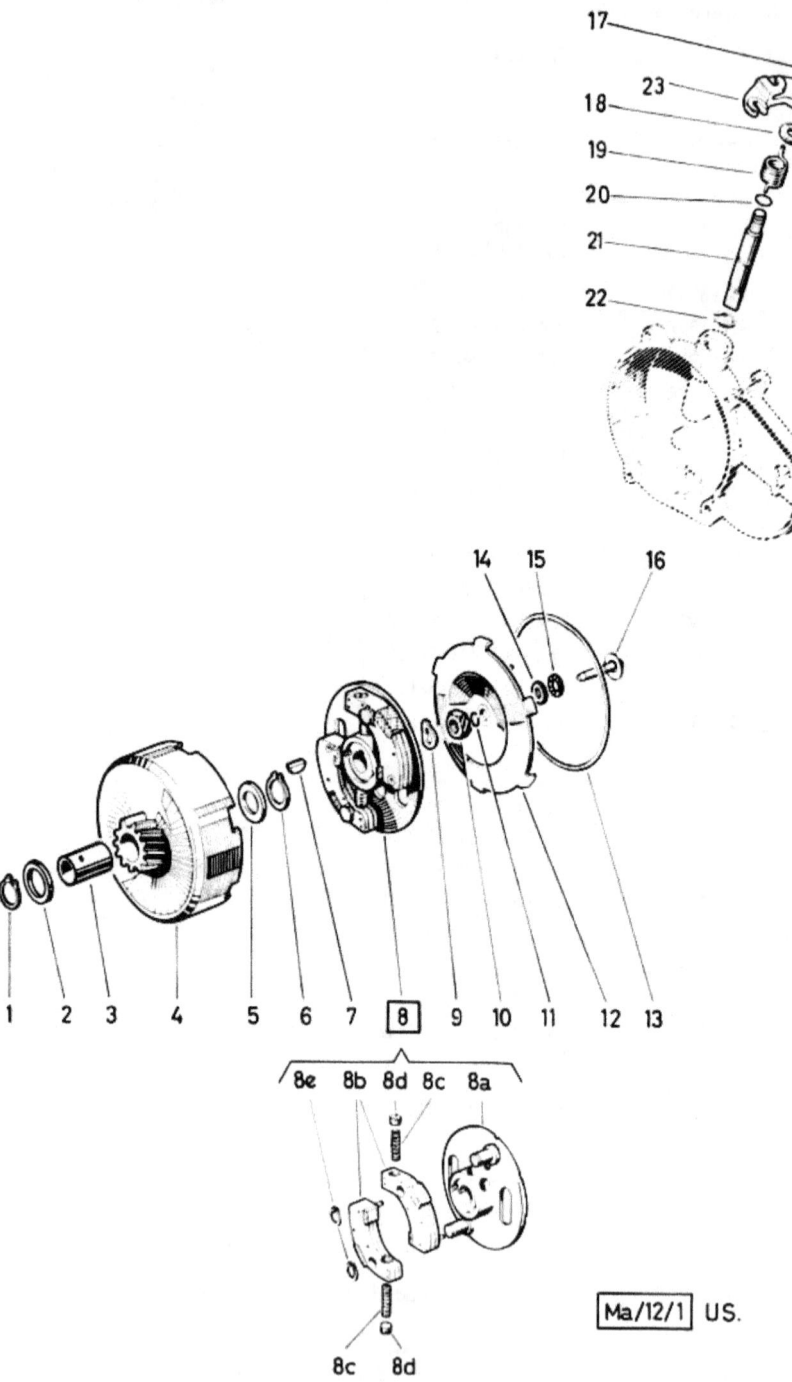

Ma/12/1 US.

Puch 1-speed Maxi USA

3. CLUTCH (cont.)

Ref.-No.	Part-No.	Description	Requd. No. Model Rigid	Model Maxi, Maxi-S	Model Newport
11	900.4635	SPRING RING 5 DIN 9045	N	1	
12	349.1.12.008.1	CLUTCH COVER		1	
13	349.1.12.009.1	RETAINING SPRING		1	
14	349.1.12.015.1	THRUST WASHER 15/5/1		1	
15	900.6840	AXIAL NEEDLE BEARING 6,4x17,2x1,984		1	
16	349.1.12.014.1	THRUST BOLT, 25 long		1	
16	349.5.12.014.1	THRUST BOLT, 24,5 long		as req.	
16	349.6.12.014.1	THRUST BOLT, 23,4 long		as req.	
17	900.4606	BZ-CIRCLIP 6 DIN 6799		1	
18	050.1221	RUBBER WASHER 20/7,8/2		1	
19	349.3.12.022.1	RETURN SPRING		1	
20	900.3793	RUBBER SEAL RDR 9,3x3,4 DIN 3770	N	1	
21	349.3.12.028.1	DECLUTCHING SHAFT, Ø14		1	
22	900.4766	C-RING H14x1		1	
23	349.1.12.331.1	DECLUTCHING LEVER		1	

Edition October 1976 SPARE PARTS PAGE 19

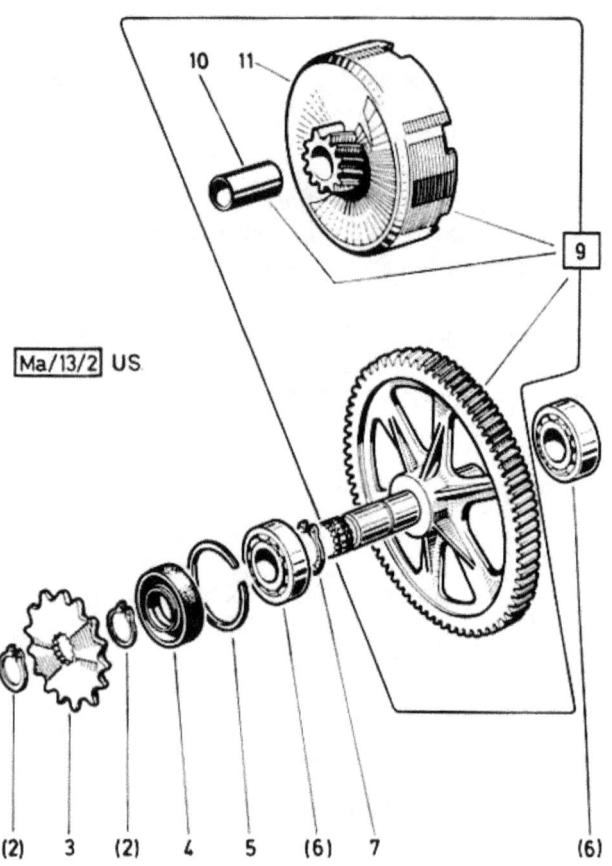

Puch 1-speed Maxi USA

4. GEARBOX

Ref.-No.	Part-No.	Description	Requd. No. Model Rigid / Model Maxi, Maxi-S / Model Newport
2	900.4616	SNAP RING Sg 16x1 DIN 471	N 2
3	050.1316	GEARBOX CHAIN SPROCKET (11 teeth)	1 (1 HP) as required
3	56.1.1322	GEARBOX CHAIN SPROCKET (13 teeth)	1 (1 HP)
3	349.1.13.014.1	GEARBOX CHAIN SPROCKET (14 teeth)	1 (1,5 HP)
3	349.1.13.016.1	GEARBOX CHAIN SPROCKET (16 teeth)	1 (2 HP)
4	901.3801	SEAL RING BA 40/17/7 DIN 3760	N 1
5	901.4656	RETAINING RING SP 40 DIN 5417	N 1
6	900.6203	DEEP ROW BALL BEARING 40/17/12 6203 DIN 625	N 2
7	900.4617	SNAP RING Sg 17x1 DIN 471	N 1
9	349.3.13.120.0	PRIMARY DRIVE compl. (21, 106 teeth) (consisting of clutch drum, bearing bush and gearshaft with pressed-on gear wheel)	1
10 11	--------------	see group 3. CLUTCH	-

Edition October 1976

SPARE PARTS PAGE 21

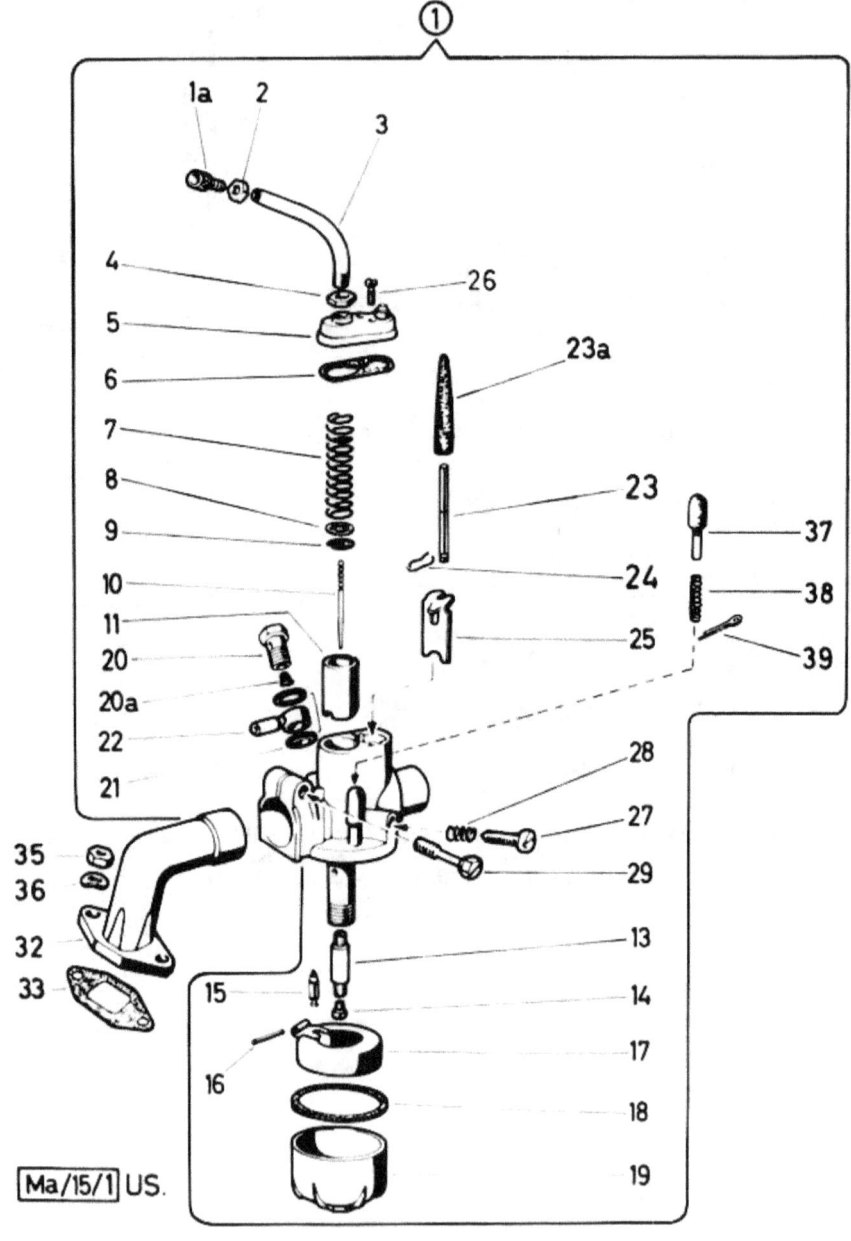

Puch 1-speed Maxi USA

5. CARBURETTOR

Reqnd. No.
- Model Rigid
- Model Maxi, Maxi-S
- Model Newport

Ref.-No.	Part-No.	Description	Reqd. No.	
1	349.4.15.400.0	CARBURETTOR, compl (Bing 1/12/294)	1	(1HP, 17mph)
1	349.2.15.400.0	CARBURETTOR, compl (Bing 1/12/292)	1	(1 HP)
1	349.3.15.400.0	CARBURETTOR, compl (Bing 1/12/293)	1	(1,5HP)
1	349.8.15.500.0	CARBURETTOR, compl (Bing 1/14/160)	1	(2 HP)
1a	050.1520	BOWDEN CABLE ADJUSTING SCREW (M5)	1	
2	900.2115	NUT BM5 DIN 439 for bowden cable adjusting screw	N 1	
3	349.1.15.018.1	PIPE ELBOW	1	
4	26779	NUT BM6x0,75 similar DIN 934 for pipe elbow	1	
5	349.1.15.019.1	CARBURETTOR COVER	1	
6	349.1.15.029.1	GASKET for carburetor cover	1	
7	362.2.15.031.1	THRUST SPRING for throttle slide (reinforced)	1	
8	362.1.15.014.1	DISC Ø13x0,5	1	
9	362.1.15.013.1	CLAMP SPRING	1	
10	330.1.15.016.1	JET NEEDLE (36,5 long, with 2 grooves)	1	(1 HP and 1,5 HP)
10	364.4.15.516.1	JET NEEDLE (36,5 long)	1	(2 HP)
11	349.1.15.015.1	THROTTLE SLIDE No. 24	1	
13	349.1.15.008.1/22	NEEDLE JET No. 2,22	1	
14	362.1.15.009.1/54	MAIN JET No. 54	1	(1 HP)
14	362.1.15.009.1/52	MAIN JET No. 52	1	(1 HP, 17mph)
14	362.1.15.009.1/60	MAIN JET No. 60	1	(1,5 HP)
14	362.1.15.009.1/58	MAIN JET No. 58	1	(1,5 HP) as required
14	362.1.15.009.1/64	MAIN JET No. 64	1	(2 HP)
14	362.1.15.009.1/62	MAIN JET No. 62	1	(2 HP) as required
14	362.1.15.009.1/..[x]	MAIN JET No. ..[x]	-	
15	362.2.15.026.2	FLOAT NEEDLE (with point of Viton)	1	
16	362.1.15.027.1	PIN for ring float (Ø1,5x17)	1	
17	362.2.15.025.2	RING FLOAT	1	

[x] Please indicate engraved number

Edition October 1976

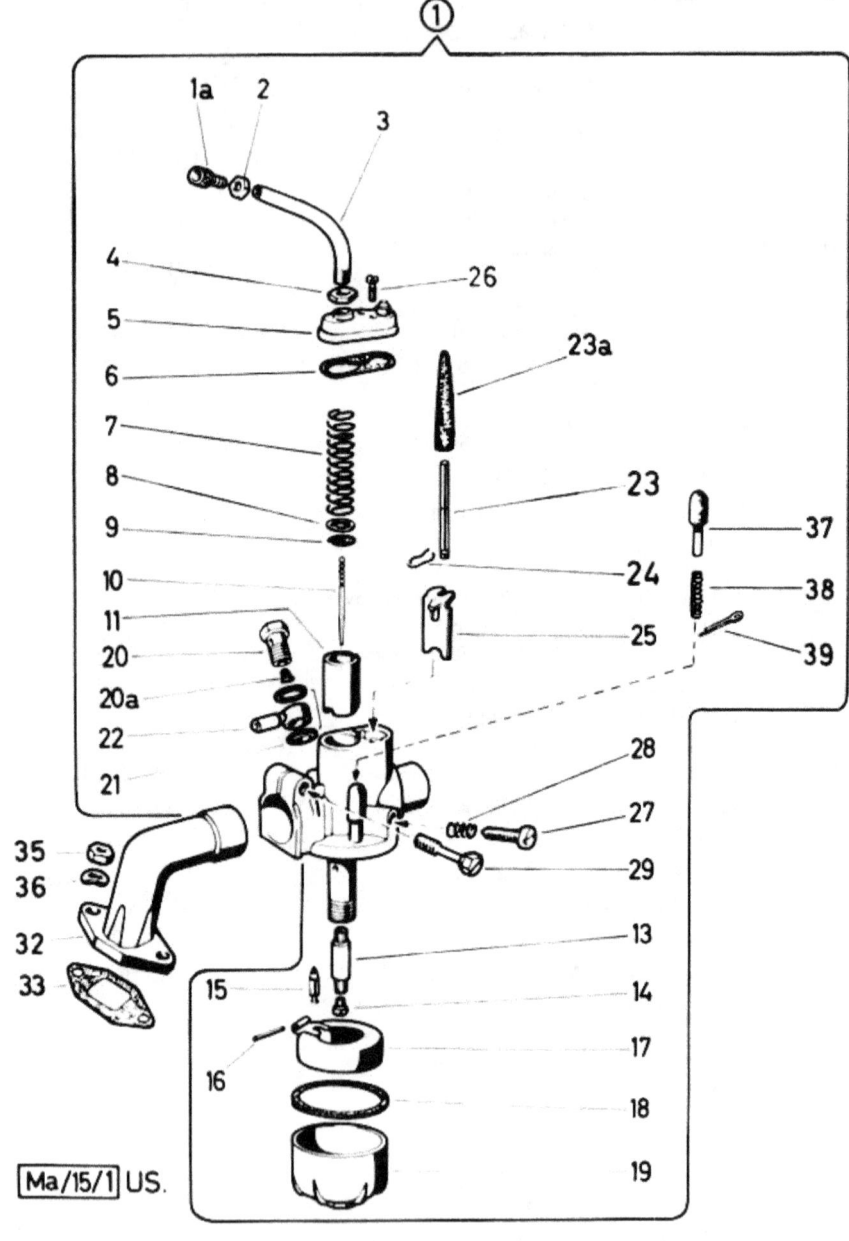

Puch 1-speed Maxi USA

5. CARBURETTOR (cont.)

Reqd. No.
- Model Rigid
- Model Maxi, Maxi-S
- Model New Port

Ref.-No.	Part-No.	Description	Rigid	Maxi/Maxi-S	New Port	Notes
18	362.1.15.028.1	GASKET 45/41/1,5 for float		1		
19	362.1.15.024.1	FLOAT		1		
20	320.1.15.039.1	FIXING SCREW		1		
20a	362.1.15.037.2	SIEVE		as req.		
21	900.3702	FIBRE WASHER A8x12 DIN 7603		N 2		
22	320.1.15.038.1	HOSE SWIVEL CONNECTOR		1		
23	349.2.15.063.1	THRUST PIN for start slide		1		(1 HP and 1,5 HP)
23	349.1.15.063.1	THRUST PIN for start slide		1		(2 HP)
23a	349.1.15.047.1	LENGTHENING		1		
24	362.1.15.064.1	CLAMP SPRING for pressure pin		1		
25	349.1.15.065.1	START SLIDE		1		
26	050.1535	HEAD SCREW (for carburettor cover)		2		
27	349.1.15.011.1	ADJUSTING SCREW for throttle slide		1		
28	349.1.15.012.1	THRUST SPRING for adjusting screw		1		
29	349.1.15.013.1	CLAMP SCREW (M6)		1		
32	349.2.15.130.1	CARBURETTOR CONNECTING SLEEVE		1		(1 HP and 1,5 HP)
32	349.1.15.130.1	CARBURETTOR CONNECTING SLEEVE		1		(2 HP)
33	349.1.15.122.1	PAPER GASKET (hard paper 0,5mm thick)		1		
35	24773	HEXAGON NUT M6 DIN 934		N 2		
36	900.3212	CURVED WASHER A6 DIN 137		N 2		
37	328.1.15.036.2	PRESSURE (with plastic-cap)		1		as req.
37	364.1.15.036.2	PRESSURE (with metal-cap)		1		as req.
38	364.1.15.033.1	SPRING FOR PRESSURE		1		
39	364.1.15.034.1	SPLIT PIN		1		

Edition October 1976   SPARE PARTS   PAGE 25

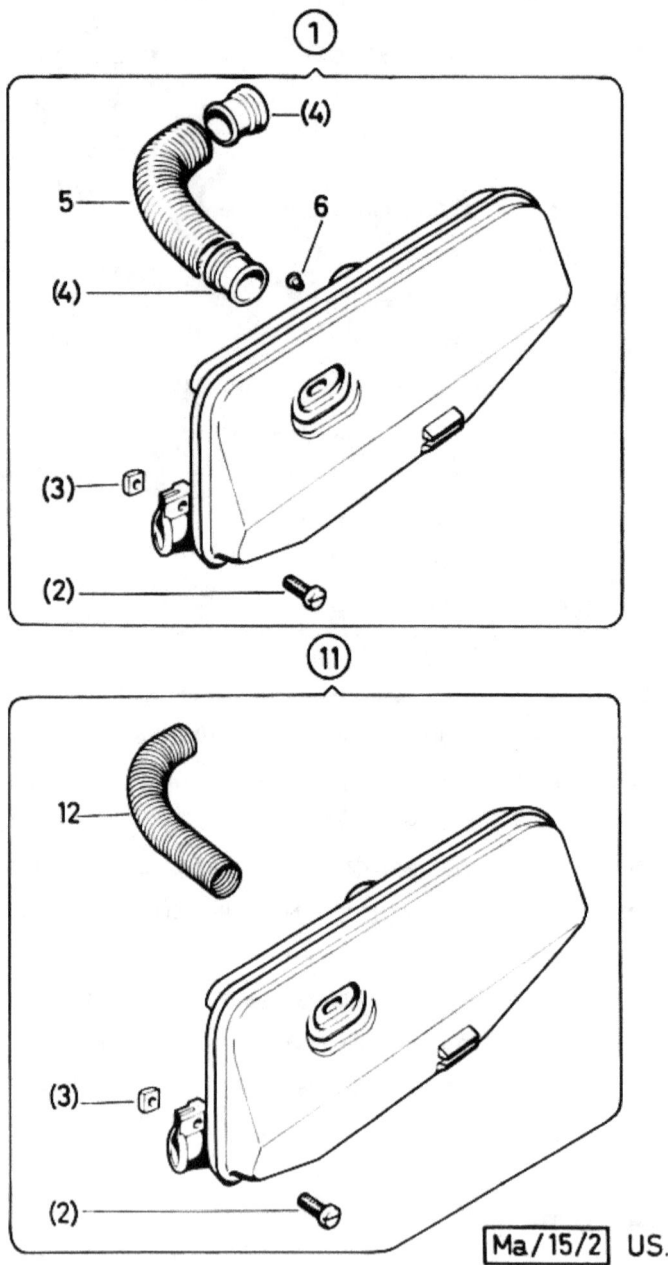

Ma/15/2 US.

Puch 1-speed Maxi USA

6. INTAKE SILENCER

Ref.-No.	Part-No.	Description	Model Rigid	Model Maxi, Maxi-S	Model Newport	Requd. No.
1	349.3.15.070.0	INTAKE SILENCER compl. (with parts 2÷6)			1	(1 HP)
2	900.1320	CHEESE HEAD SCREW M6x20 DIN 84		N 1		
3	900.2206	SQUARE NUT M6 DIN 557		N 1		
4	349.1.15.074.1	ORFICE for intake silencer			2	(1 HP)
5	349.3.15.073.1	INTAKE TUBE (Ø28,5/24x130)			1	(1 HP)
6	367.1.30.004.1	PLUG			1	(1 HP)
11	349.1.15.070.0	INTAKE SILENCER compl. (with parts 2,3 and 12)			1	(1,5 HP and 2 HP)
12	349.1.15.073.1	INTAKE TUBE (Ø19/15x80)			1	(1,5 HP and 2 HP)

Edition October 1976   SPARE PARTS   PAGE 27

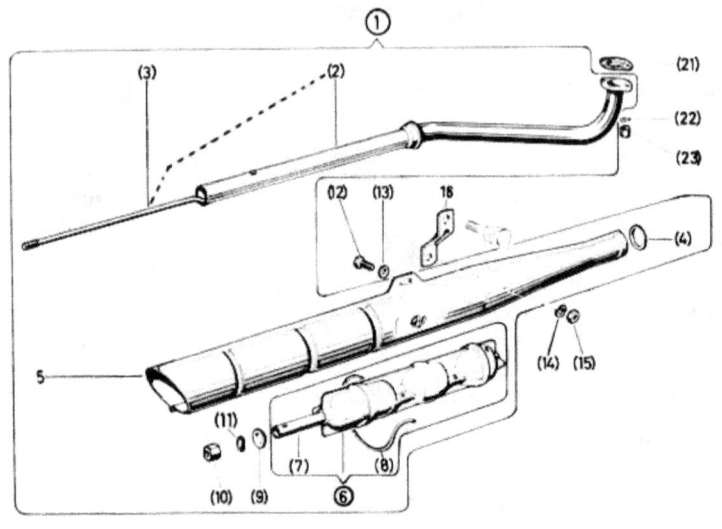
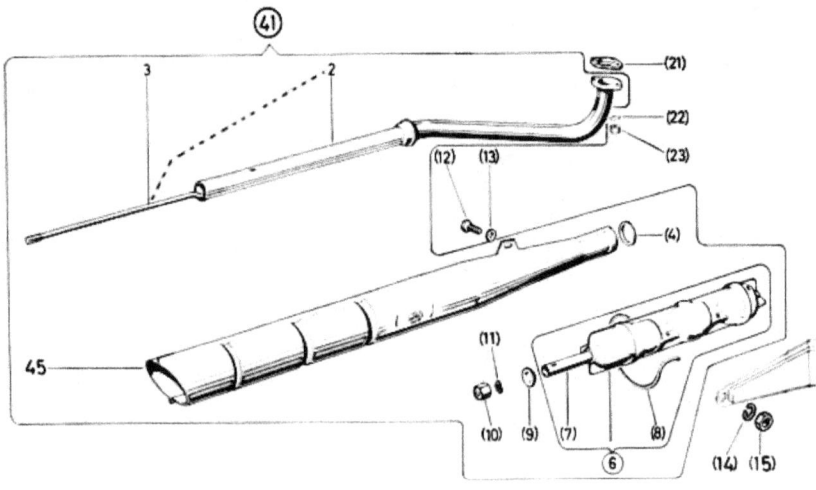

Ma/16/2 US.

Puch 1-speed Maxi USA

7. EXHAUST

Ref.-No.	Part-No.	Description	Model Rigid	Model Maxi, Maxi-S Model Newport	
1	349.4.16.000.0	EXHAUST compl. (with parts 2÷11)	1	-	(1 HP)
1	349.1.16.800.0	EXHAUST compl. (with parts 2÷11)	1	-	(1,5 HP)
1	349.6.16.000.0	EXHAUST compl. (with parts 2+11)	1	-	(2 HP)
2	349.4.16.001.2	EXHAUST PIPE (with part 3)	1	1	(1 HP)
2	349.1.16.801.2	EXHAUST PIPE (with part 3)	1	1	(1,5 HP)
2	349.6.16.001.2	EXHAUST PIPE (with part 3)	1	1	(2 HP)
3	349.3.16.014.1	PULL ROD (M7, 295 long)	1	1	
4	349.1.16.019.1	GASKET 34/26/2	1	1	
5	349.1.16.000.2	SILENCER COVER	1	-	
6	349.1.16.011.9	DAMPING INSERT compl. (with parts 7 and 8)	1	1	
7	349.1.16.013.1	END PIPE	1	1	
8	253.1635/07	ASBESTOS CORD Ø3x165 per meter	-	-	
9	349.1.16.018.1	WASHER 16/7,5/3	1	1	
10	900.2975	HEXAGON NUT M7 (self-locking)	1	1	
11	900.3207	SPRING WASHER A7 DIN 137	N 1	1	
12	26422	HEXAGON HEAD SCREW M7x16 DIN 933-8.8	N 1	1	
13	24796	PLAIN WASHER 7,4 DIN 125	N 1	1	
14	29189	SPRING WASHER B7 DIN 127	N 1	1	
15	24774	HEXAGON NUT M7 DIN 934	N 1	1	
16	349.1.16.015.1	FIXING BRACKET	1	-	
21	050.1615	EXHAUST-FLANGE GASKET	1	1	
22	900.3213	SPRING WASHER B6 DIN 137	N 2	2	
23	902.2919	HEXAGON NUT (M6, BRASS)	2	2	
41	349.2.16.500.0	EXHAUST compl. (with parts 2÷4, 6÷11 and 45)	-	1	(1 HP)
41	349.2.16.800.0	EXHAUST compl. (with parts 2÷4, 6÷11 and 45)	-	1	(1,5 HP)
41	349.6.16.500.0	EXHAUST compl. (with parts 2÷4, 6÷11 and 45)	-	1	(2 HP)
45	349.1.16.500.2	SILENCER COVER	-	1	

Edition October 1976   SPARE PARTS

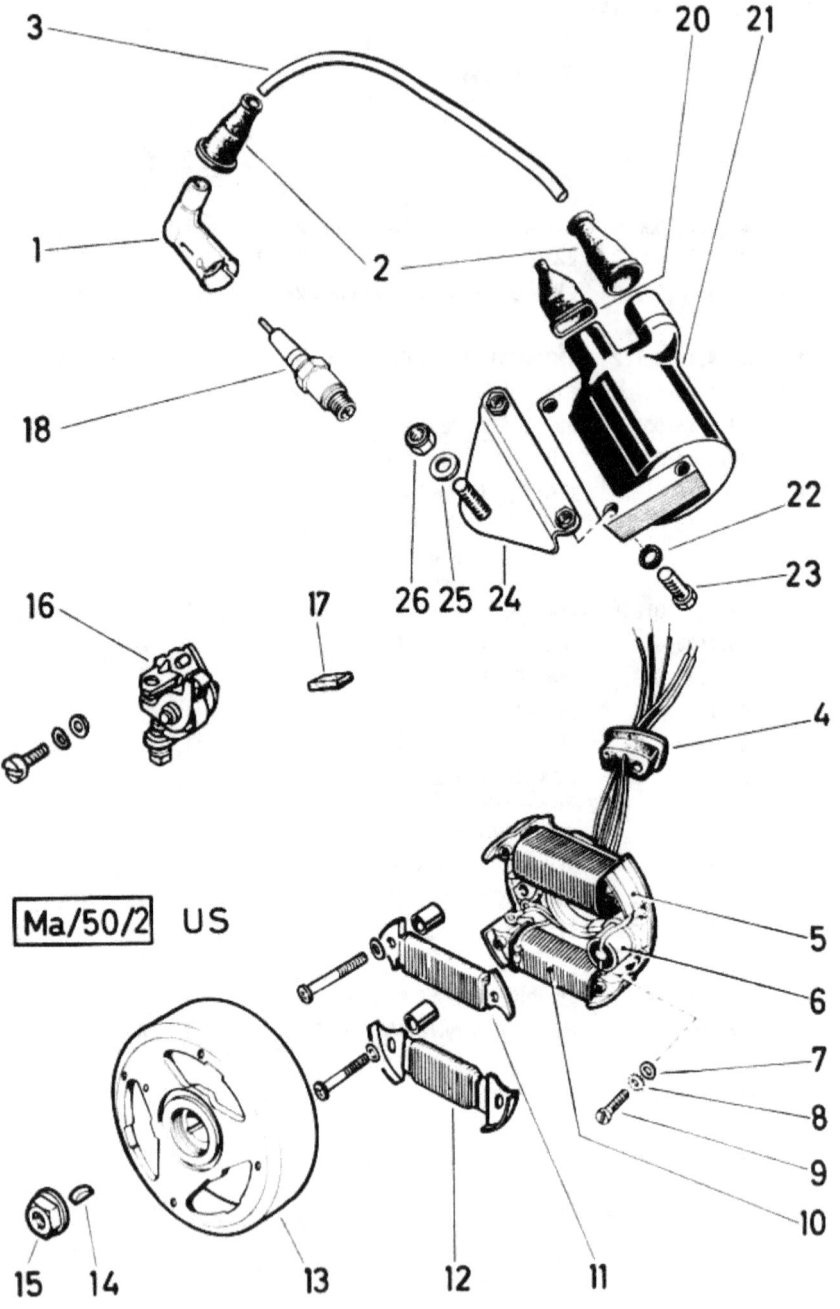

Ma/50/2 US

Puch 1-speed Maxi USA

B. MAGNETO GENERATOR

Ref.-No.	Part-No.	Description	Requd. No. Model Rigid / Model Maxi, Maxi-S / Model Newport
--	349.2.50.800.0	MAGNETO GENERATOR ASS'Y (Bosch 0 212 124 042 RDP 1 (R) 6V 22-5/10W)	1
1	325.1.52.005.0	SPARK PLUG PROTECTOR	1
2	700.1.09.006.1	PROTECTION CAP (Bosch 1 230 522 011)	2
3	900.0717/07	IGNITION CABLE (220mm)	per meter
4	349.2.10.810.1	RUBBER SOCKET	1
5	366.1.50.012.2	IGNITION ARMATURE (Bosch 1 214 210 069)	1
6	500.2.50.013.2	CONDENSER (Bosch 1 237 330 037)	1
7	901.3941	WASHER 8/4,2/1	3
8	900.3253	SERRATED LOCK WASHER J4,3 DIN 6798	N 3
9	27458	LENS HEAD SCREW AM4x15 DIN 85	N 3
10	349.2.50.811.2	GENERATOR ARMATURE, 22W (Bosch 1 214 210 064)	1
11	349.2.50.814.2	GENERATOR ARMATURE, 10W (Bosch 1 214 210 492)	1
12	349.2.50.819.2	GENERATOR ARMATURE 5W (Bosch 1 214 210 490)	1
13	349.2.50.810.2	FLYWHEEL (Bosch 1 215 254 635)	1
14	900.4503	WOODRUFF-KEY 3x3,7 DIN 6888	N 1
15	901.2943	HEXAGON NUT with band M10x1-8	1
16	302.3.50.015.0	CONTACT-SET (Bosch 1 217 013 021)	1

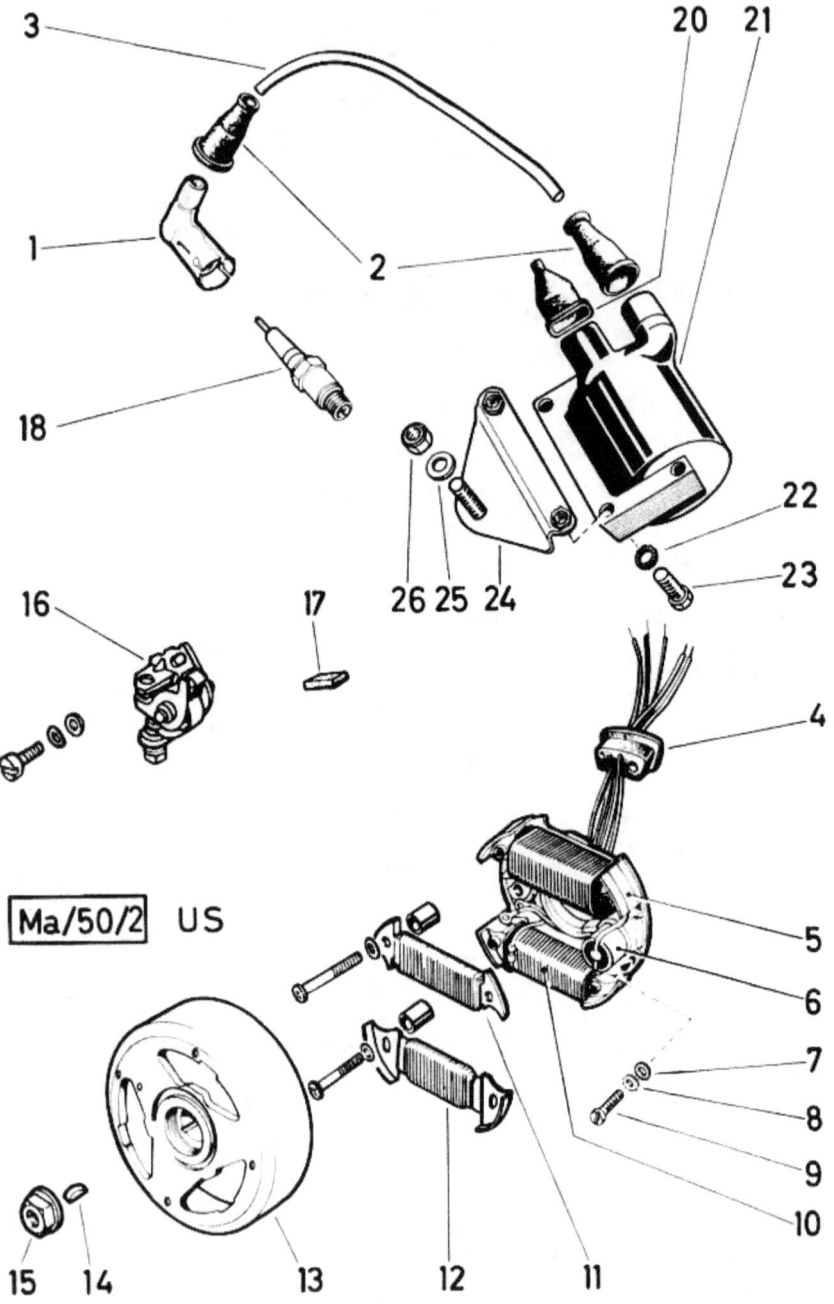

Puch 1-speed Maxi USA

8. MAGNETO GENERATOR (cont.)

Ref.-No.	Part-No.	Description	Model Rigid	Model Maxi, Maxi-S	Model Newport
17	364.4.50.618.1	LUBRICATOR FELT PAD (Bosch 2 201 005 007)		1	
18	--------------	PLUG - please see group CYLINDER, ENGINE PARTS		-	
20	902.0745	PROTECTION CAP (Bosch 2 200 522 002)		2	
21	904.0759	IGNITION COIL (Bosch 0 212 940 003)		1	
22	900.3257	SERRATED WASHER J5,3 DIN 6798		N 2	
23	900.1043	HEXAGON HEAD SCREW M5x20 DIN 931		N 2	
24	349.1.52.853.2	BRACKET		1	
25	24795	WASHER 6,4 DIN 125		N 1	
26	900.2966	HEXAGON NUT M6 DIN 985		N 1	

Parts not identified by a number are not available singly from Messrs. Bosch.

Edition October 1976   SPARE PARTS

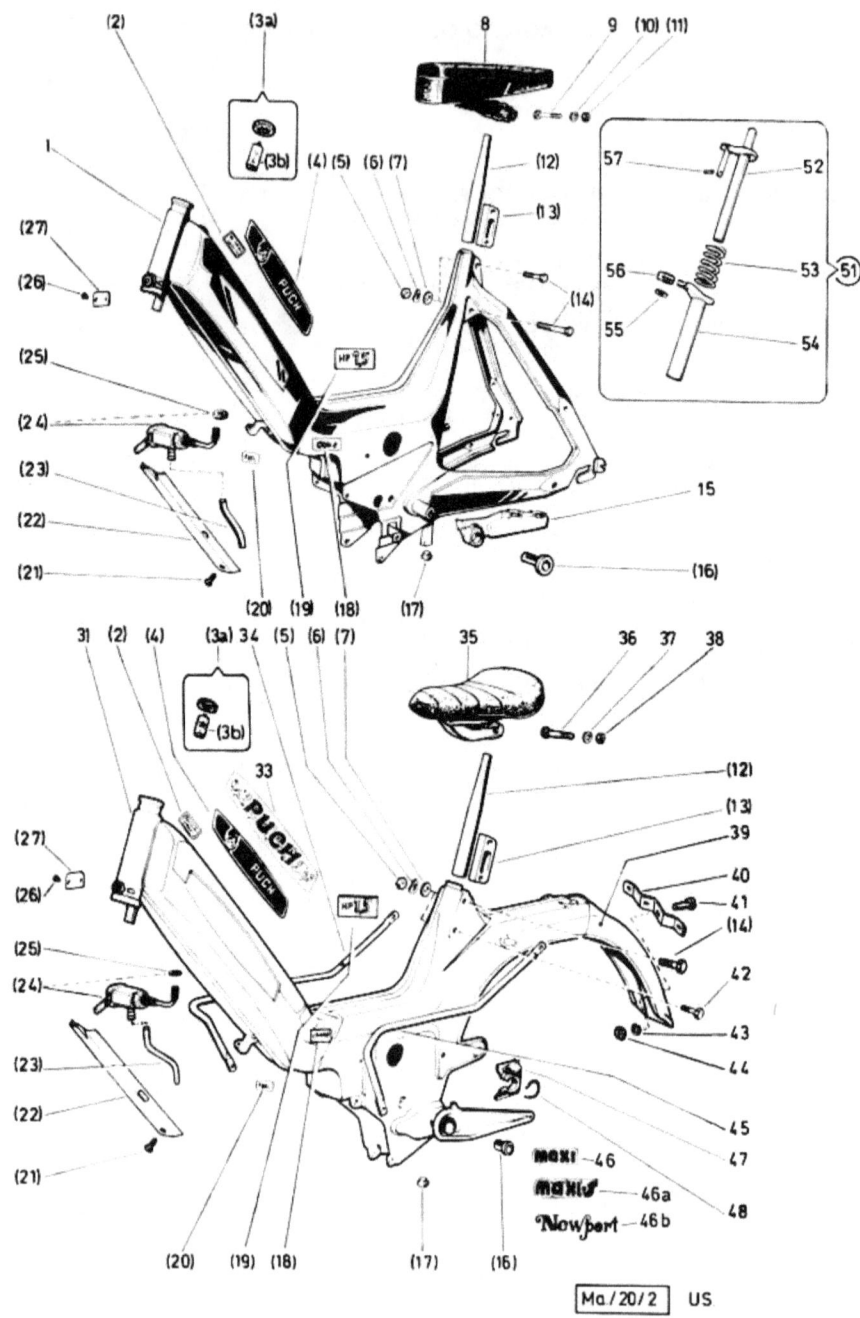

Ma/20/2 US

Puch 1-speed Maxi USA

11. FRAME, FUEL TAB, SADDLE

Ref.-No.	Part-No.	Description	Model Rigid	Model Maxi	Model Maxi-S	Model Newport
1	349.6.20.100.0	FRAME compl. (with bearing shells and bearing bushings)	1	-	-	-
2	349.2.22.834.1	TRANSFER PICTURE (do not use unleaded gasoline) black	1	1	1	1
2	349.3.22.834.1	TRANSFER PICTURE (do not use unleaded gasoline) white	-	1	-	1
3a	349.1.22.820.0	FILLER CAP	1	1	1	1
3b	349.1.22.821.1	MEASURE CUP	as required			
4	349.2.20.837.0	TRANSFER PICTURE l.h. and r.h. (Puch)	per pair -			
5	900.2016	HEXAGON NUT M8 DIN 934	N 2	2	2	2
6	900.3211	SPRING WASHER B8 DIN 137	N 2	2	2	2
7	24806	WASHER 8,4 DIN 433	N 2	2	2	2
8	349.1.23.500.0	SADDLE compl. (Messrs. Giuliari)	1	-	-	-
9	902.1987	CUP SQUARE BOLT M8x60 DIN 603	N 1	-	-	-
10	501.1.8405	WASHER 25/8,5/2,5	1	-	-	-
11	900.2016	HEXAGON NUT M8 DIN 934	N 1	-	-	-
12	349.1.23.008.1	BRACKET for saddle	1	1	-	1
13	349.1.20.028.1	CLAMPING PIECE	1	1	1	1
14	27397	HEXAGON HEAD SCREW M8x40 DIN 931-8.8	N 2	1	1	1
15	349.1.20.035.1	CHAIN GUIDE	1	-	-	-
16	349.1.42.005.1	BEARING BUSHING 20/16/19 for pedal spindle	2	2	2	2
17	050.1.2123	RUBBER BUFFER for stand stop	1	1	1	1
18	349.2.20.835.1	INDICATION PLATE (choke) black	1	1	1	1
18	349.3.20.835.1	INDICATION PLATE (choke) white	-	1	-	1
19	349.2.20.843.1	TRANSFER PICTURE (1 HP)	1	1	1	1
19	349.2.20.844.1	TRANSFER PICTURE (1,5 HP)	1	1	1	1
19	349.2.20.845.1	TRANSFER PICTURE (2 HP)	1	1	1	1
20	349.3.20.836.1	TRANSFER PICTURE (fuel) black	1	1	1	1
20	349.4.20.836.1	TRANSFER PICTURE (fuel) white	-	1	-	1
21	900.1437	COUNTERSUNK SCREW M5x12 DIN 963	N 1	1	1	1
22	349.1.20.029.1	FAIRING for bowden cables (grey)	1	1	-	-
22	349.2.20.029.1	FAIRING for bowden cables (black)	-	-	1	1
23	900.0902/07	FUEL HOSE Ø9/5x120	per meter			
24	349.1.22.830.0	FUEL TAP compl. (with reserve)	1	1	1	1
25	349.1.22.031.1	SEAL RING 10,5/8,5/1	1	1	1	1

Edition October 1976

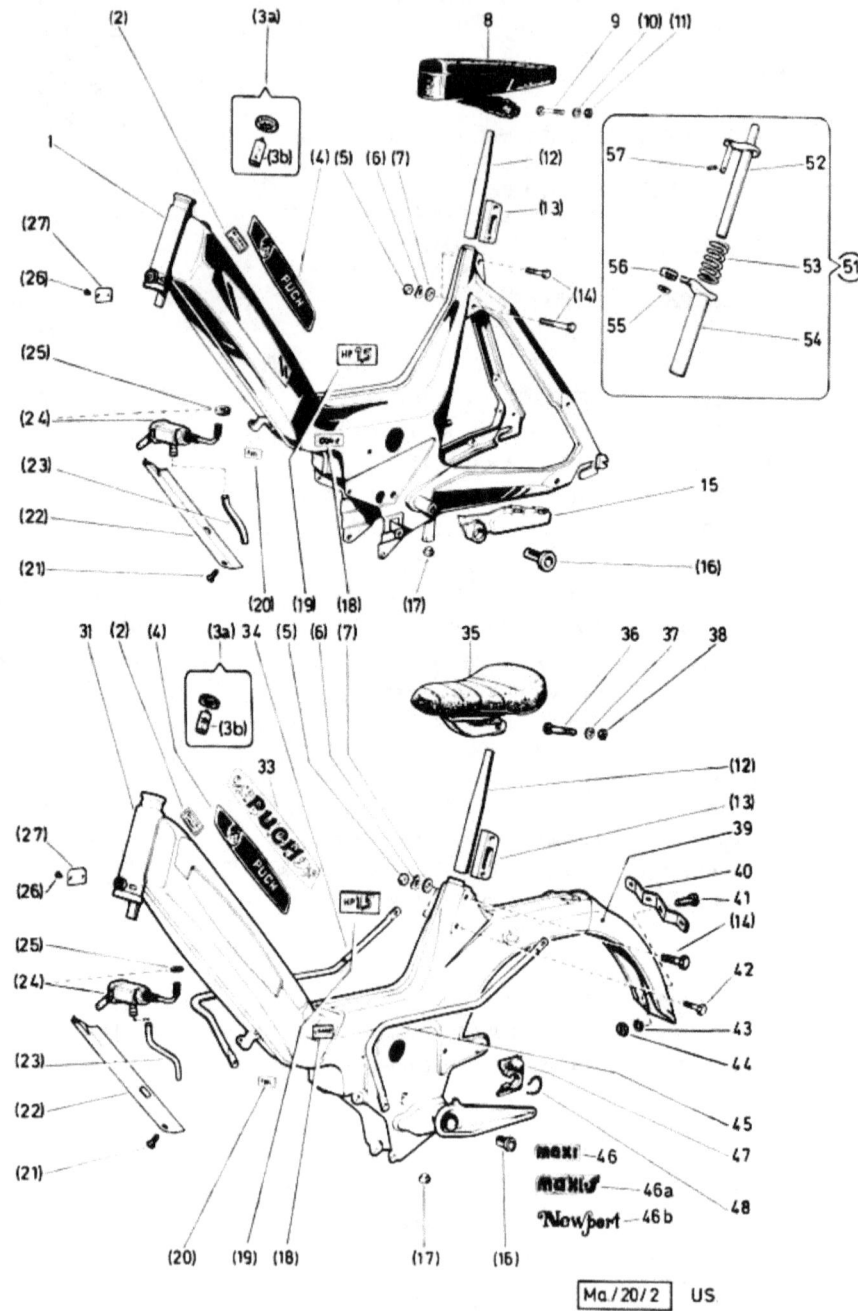

Puch 1-speed Maxi USA

11. FRAME, FUEL TAB, SADDLE (cont.)

Ref.-No.	Part-No.	Description	Model Rigid	Model Maxi	Model Maxi-S	Model Newport
26	900.4191	POP-RIVET Ø2,4x4	2	2	2	2
27	349.1.20.833.1	MARKING PLATE	1	1	1	1
31	349.2.20.800.0	FRAME compl. (with bearing shells and bearing bushings)	-	1	1	1
33	349.4.20.547.0	TRANSFER PICTURE l.h. and r.h. (Puch)	-	-	-	per pair
34	349.1.20.826.1	CARRYING HANDLE r.h.	-	1	1	1
35	349.5.23.000.0 x	SADDLE compl. (Messrs. Centin) black	-	1	-	-
35	349.7.23.000.0	SADDLE compl. (Messrs. Centin) brown	-	-	-	1
36	901.1034	HEXAGON BOLT M10x60 DIN 931-8.8	-	1	-	1
37	24807	WASHER 10,5 DIN 433	N	1	-	1
38	24776	HEXAGON NUT M10 DIN 934	N	1	-	1
39	349.3.20.510.2	REAR FENDER (Primer)	-	1	1	1
40	349.1.27.820.1	LICENSE PLATE BRACKET	-	as req.		
41	900.1312	CHEESE HEAD SCREW M5x10 DIN 84	N	2	2	2
42	900.1048	HEXAGON BOLT M8x35 DIN 931-8.8	N	1	1	1
43	29190	SPRING RING B5 DIN 127	N	2	2	2
44	900.2105	HEXAGON NUT M5 DIN 555	N	2	2	2
45	349.1.20.525.1	CARRYING HANDLE l.h.	-	1	1	1
46	349.1.20.847.1	TRANSFER PICTURE (MAXI)	-	2	-	-
46a	349.1.53.857.1	TRANSFER PICTURE (MAXI-S)	-	-	2	-
46b	349.1.20.846.1	TRANSFER PICTURE (Newport)	-	-	-	2
47	349.1.20.535.1	CHAIN GUIDE	-	1	1	1
48	349.1.20.536.1	RETAINING RING for chain guide	-	1	1	1
51	349.1.23.108.0	SUSPENDED SADDLE SUPPORT compl. (with parts 52÷57)	1	-	-	-
52	349.1.23.108.2	SADDLE SUPPORT loose	1	-	-	-
53	349.1.23.109.1	TENSION SPRING	as requd. 1	-	-	-
54	349.1.23.107.2	CONDUIT TUBE	1	-	-	-
55	900.3915	PLAIN WASHER 20/10,1/1,5	1	-	-	-
56	349.1.23.110.1	SLIDE BUSH	1	-	-	-
57	900.4841	SLOTTED HOLLOW PIN 3x20 DIN 1481	N 1	-	-	-

x SINGLE SEAT FOR MAXI-S SEE GROUP 11a.

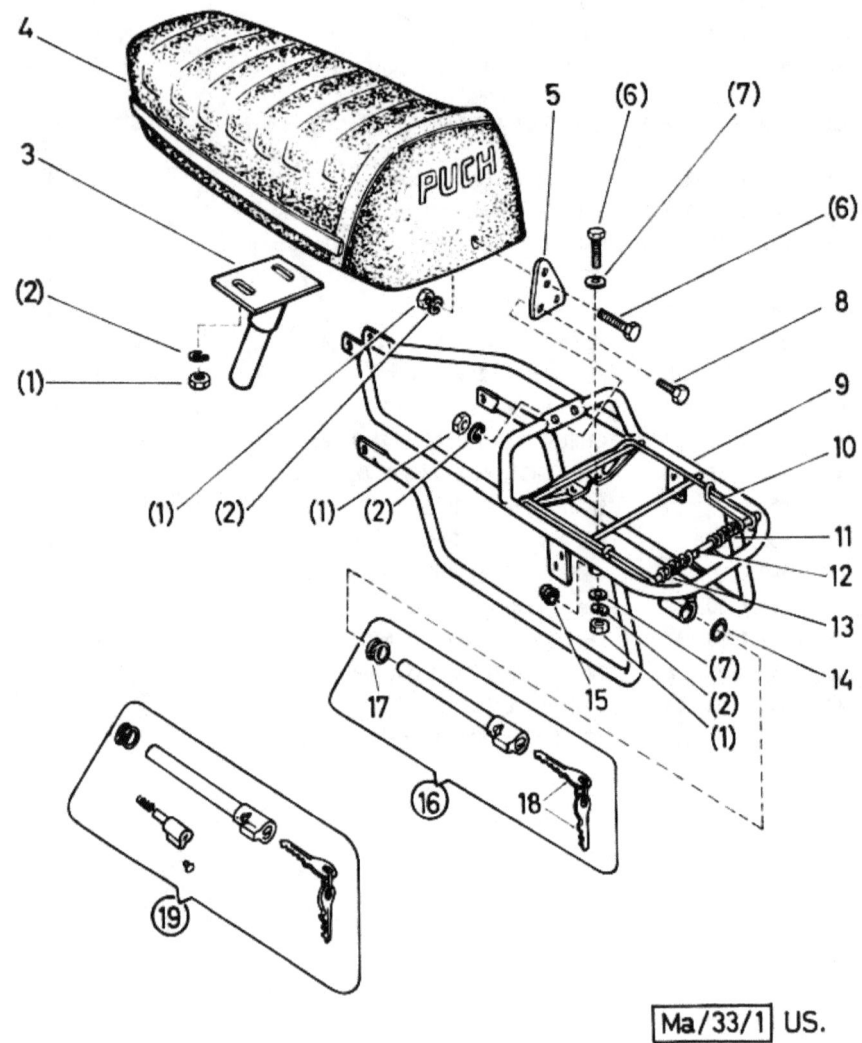

Ma/33/1 US.

Puch 1-speed Maxi USA

11a. SINGLE SEAT, LUGGAGE CARRIER AND 2nd LOCK

Ref.-No.	Part-No.	Description	Requd. No. Model Maxi-S
1	24773	HEXAGON NUT M6 DIN 934	N 7
2	26834	SPRING WASHER B6 DIN 127	N 7
3	349.1.33.507.2	SEAT BRACKET	1
4	349.1.33.600.0	SINGLE SEAT	1
5	349.1.33.608.1	SHAKLE	1
6	24928	HEXAGON SCREW M6x16 DIN 933	N 3
7	24804	WASHER 6,4 DIN 433	N 4
8	24927	HEXAGON SCREW M6x12 DIN 933	N 2
9	349.6.29.600.0	LUGGAGE CARRIER compl.	1
10	349.2.29.627.1	LUGGAGE HOLDER	1
11	349.2.29.626.1	SPRING r.h.	1
12	349.2.29.624.1	SPRING AXLE Ø6x142	1
13	349.2.29.625.1	SPRING l.h.	1
14	359.1.21.323.1	STOP RING	1
15	359.1.55.020.1	GROMMET	1
16	349.1.21.522.0	LOCK compl.(with parts 17 and 18)	1
17	359.1.21.359.1	THRUST SPRING	1
18	350.2.30.023.1	SPARE KEY (please state key-number)	2
19	349.1.20.522.9	SET OF LOCKS (consistet of front and rear lock)	1

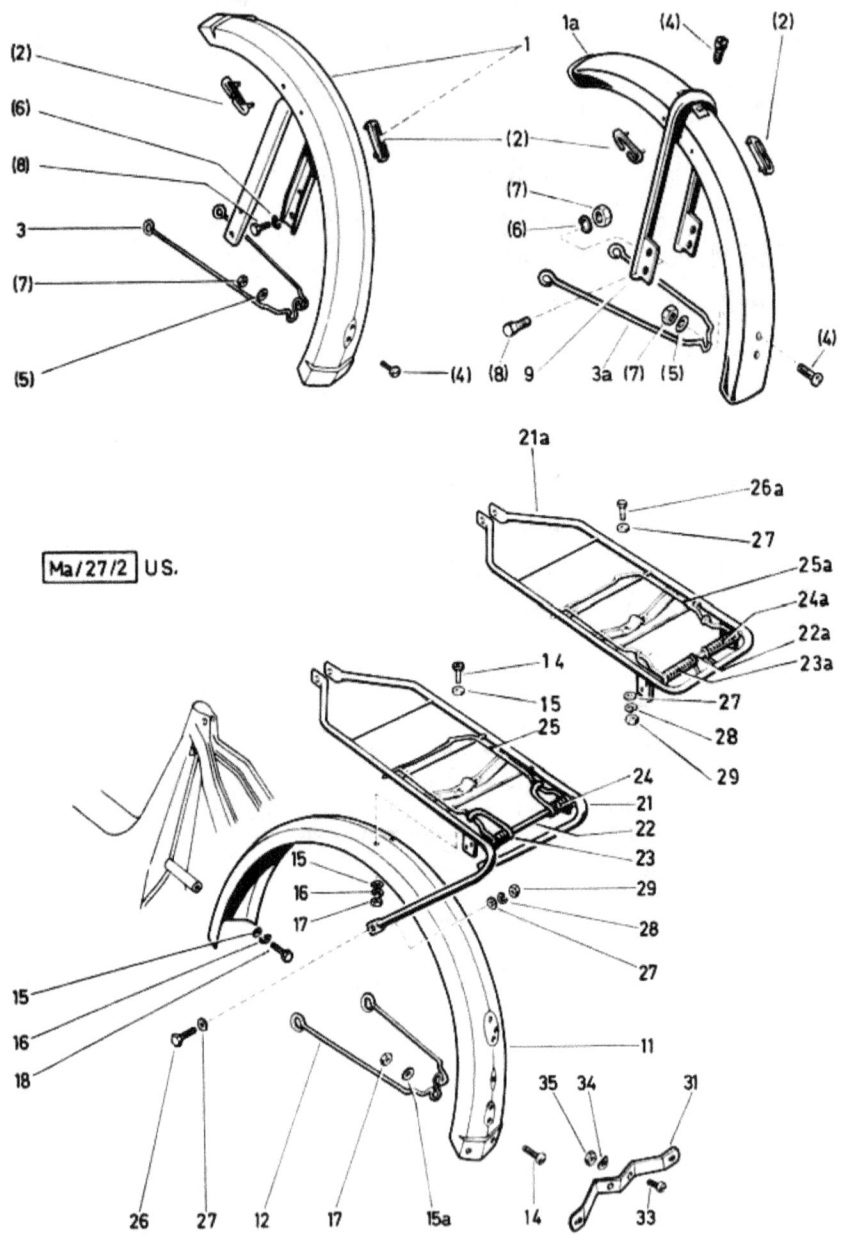

Ma/27/2 US.

Puch 1-speed Maxi USA

12. MUDGUARD, LUGGAGE CARRIER

Requd. No.

Ref.-No.	Part-No.	Description	Model Rigid	Model Maxi	Model Maxi-S	Model Newport
1	349.2.27.100.0	FRONT MUDGUARD compl. (with part 2)	1	1	-	1
1a	321.2.27.100.1	FRONT MUDGUARD (INOX)	-	-	1	-
2	350.2.27.003.1	CABLE GUIDE	2	2	2	2
3	349.2.27.003.1	MUDGUARD BRACE front (295mm long)	1	1	-	1
3a	321.1.27.002.1	MUDGUARD BRACE front (310mm long)	-	-	1	-
4	25429	LENS HEAD SCREW AM5x12 DIN 85	N 2	2	4	2
5	900.3455	SECURING WASHER JZC 5	2	2	2	2
6	29190	SPRING WASHER B5 DIN 127	N 4	4	6	4
7	24772	HEXAGON NUT M5 DIN 934	N 2	2	4	2
8	26509	HEXAGON HEAD SCREW M5x10 DIN 933	N 4	4	4	4
9	321.1.27.009.2	MUDGUARD HOLDER	-	-	1	-
11	349.2.27.810.2	REAR MUDGUARD	1	-	-	-
12	349.2.27.012.1	MUDGUARD BRACE rear	1	-	-	-
14	25429	LENS HEAD SCREW AM5x12 DIN 85	N 4	-	-	-
15	24803	PLAIN WASHER 5,3 DIN 433	N 5	-	-	-
15a	900.3455	SECURING WASHER JZC 5	2	-	-	-
16	29190	SPRING WASHER B5 DIN 127	N 3	-	-	-
17	24772	HEXAGON NUT M5 DIN 934	N 4	-	-	-
18	902.1008	HEXAGON BOLT M5x10 (brass)	1	-	-	-
21	349.4.29.800.0	LUGGAGE CARRIER compl.	1	-	-	-
21a	349.2.29.800.0^x	LUGGAGE CARRIER compl.	-	1	-	1
22	349.4.29.024.1	SPRING AXLE Ø6x165	1	-	-	-
22a	349.2.29.624.1	SPRING AXLE Ø6x142	-	1	-	1
23	349.4.29.025.1	SPRING l.h.	1	-	-	-
23a	349.2.29.625.1	SPRING l.h.	-	1	-	1
24	349.4.29.026.1	SPRING r.h.	1	-	-	-
24a	349.2.29.626.1	SPRING r.h.	-	1	-	1
25	349.4.29.027.1	LUGGAGE HOLDER	1	-	-	-
25a	349.1.29.527.1	LUGGAGE HOLDER	-	1	-	1
26	900.1108	HEXAGON SCREW M6x20 DIN 933	N 2	-	-	-
26a	24928	HEXAGON SCREW M6x16 DIN 933	N -	2	-	2
27	24804	PLAIN WASHER 6,4 DIN 433	N 4	4	-	4

^xLUGGAGE CARRIER FOR MAXI-S SEE GROUP 11a.

Edition October 1976

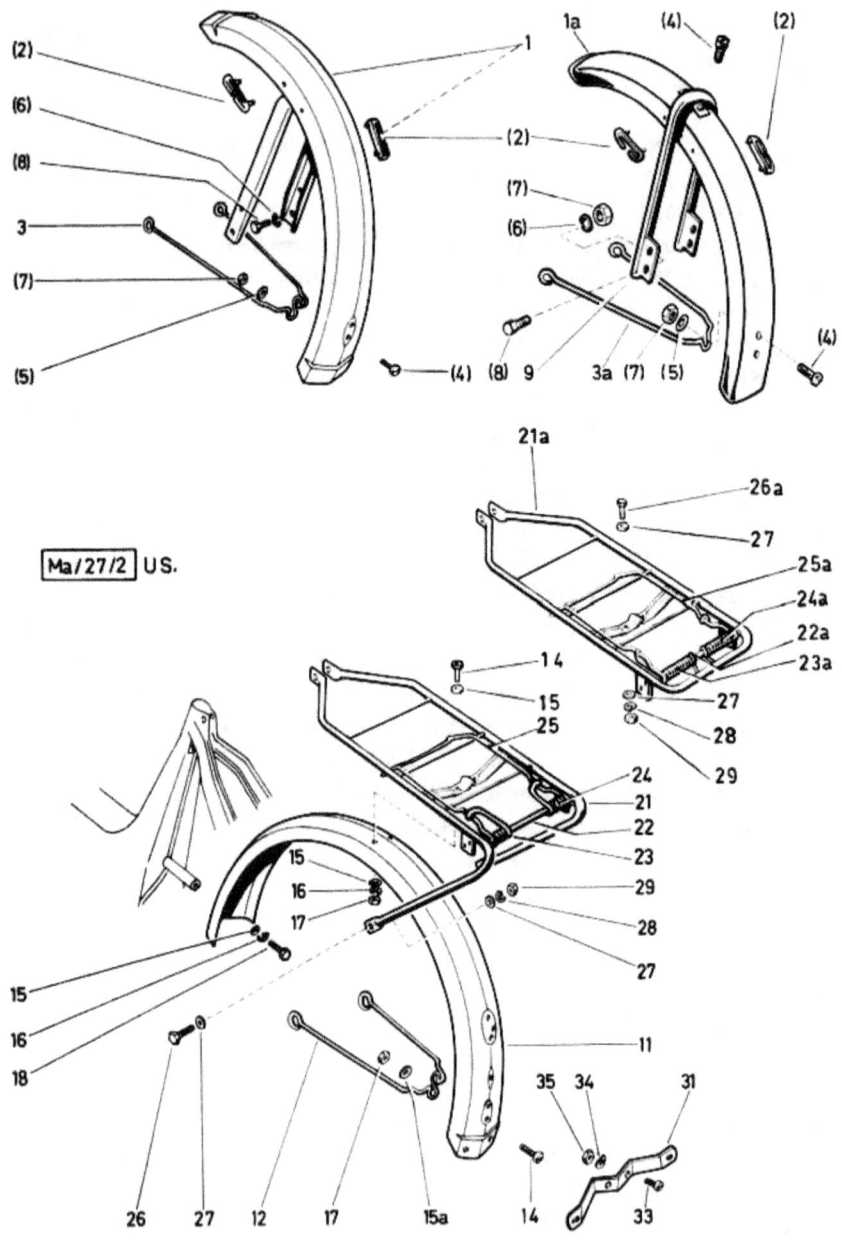

Ma/27/2 US.

Puch 1-speed Maxi USA

12. MUDGUARD, LUGGAGE CARRIER (cont.)

Ref.-No.	Part-No.	Description	Requd. No. Model Rigid	Model Maxi	Model Maxi-S	Model Newport
28	26834	SPRING RING B6 DIN 127	N 2	2	-	2
29	24773	HEXAGON NUT M6 DIN 934	N 2	2	-	2
31	349.1.27.820.1	LICENSE PLATE BRACKET	as req.	-	-	-
33	900.1312	CHEESE HEAD SCREW M5x10 DIN 84	N 2	-	-	-
34	900.3217	CRINKLE WASHER B5 DIN 137	N 2	-	-	-
35	900.2105	HEXAGON NUT M5 DIN 555	N 2	-	-	-

Edition October 1976   SPARE PARTS   PAGE 41

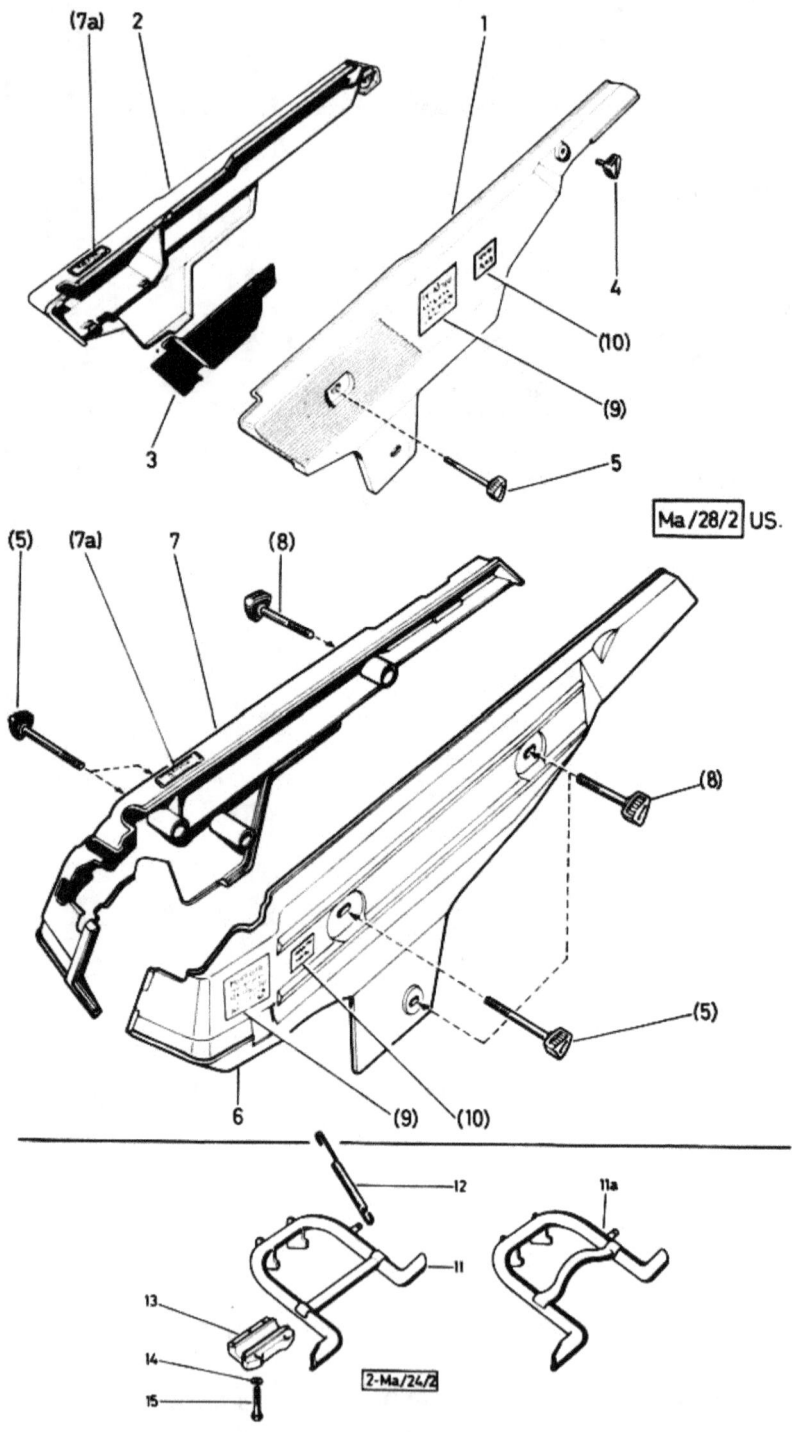

Puch 1-speed Maxi USA

13. CHAIN GUARD (fairings)

Ref.-No.	Part-No.	Description	Model Rigid	Model Maxi, Maxi-S Model Newport
1	349.1.28.002.2	CHAIN GUARD l.h. (grey)	1	-
2	349.1.28.003.1	CHAIN GUARD r.h. (grey)	1	-
3	349.1.28.004.1	COVER for chain guard r.h.s.	1	-
4	349.2.28.006.2	CLAMPING SCREW (M5, 13 long) black	4	-
5	349.2.28.007.2	CLAMPING SCREW (M5, 47 long) black	1	3
6	349.2.28.502.1	CHAIN GUARD l.h. (grey)	-	1
6	349.3.28.502.1	CHAIN GUARD l.h. (black)	-	1
7	349.4.28.503.1	CHAIN GUARD r.h. (grey)	-	1
7	349.5.28.503.1	CHAIN GUARD r.h. (black)	-	1
7a	413.1.10.079.1	INDICATION PLATE (attention, before starting oil is to be filled in engine)	1	1
8	349.2.28.506.2	CLAMPING SCREW (M5, 36,5 long) black	-	3
9	349.2.20.834.1	INDICATION PLATE (black)	1	1
9	349.3.20.834.1	INDICATION PLATE (white)	-	1
10	349.1.20.840.1	INDICATION PLATE (SPARK PLUG) black (1 HP)	1	1
10	349.2.20.840.1	INDICATION PLATE (SPARK PLUG) white (1 HP)	-	1
10	349.1.20.841.1	INDICATION PLATE (SPARK PLUG) black (1,5 HP)	1	1
10	349.2.20.841.1	INDICATION PLATE (SPARK PLUG) white (1,5 HP)	-	1
10	349.1.20.839.1	INDICATION PLATE (SPARK PLUG) black (2 HP)	1	1
10	349.2.20.839.1	INDICATION PLATE (SPARK PLUG) white (2 HP)	-	1

14. PROP STAND

11	349.5.24.000.2	PROP STAND	1	-
11a	349.3.24.500.2	PROP STAND	-	1
12	128.2410	PROP STAND SPRING	1	1
13	349.3.24.006.1	PROP STAND BEARING CUP	1	1
14	900.3212	SPRING WASHER A6 DIN 137	N 3	3
15	26427	HEXAGON BOLT M6x35 DIN 931	N 3	3

Edition October 1976   SPARE PARTS   PAGE 43

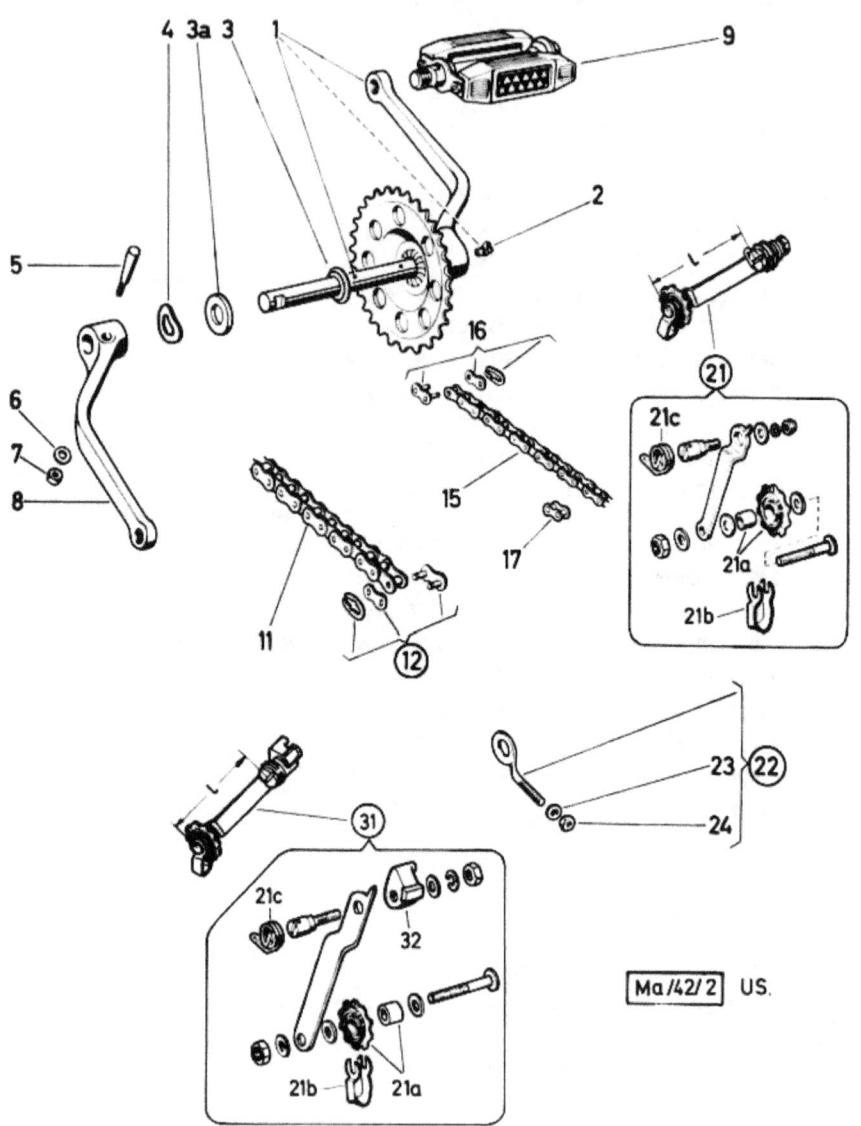

Ma/42/2 US.

Puch 1-speed Maxi USA

15. PEDALS, CHAINS, CHAIN TENSIONER

Ref.-No.	Part-No.	Description	Model Rigid	Model Maxi, Maxi-S Model Newport
1	349.4.42.103.0	CRANK r.h. compl. (28 teeth, with pedal spindle welded and part 2)	1	1
2	360.1.40.011.1	GREASE NIPPLE	1	1
3	349.1.42.105.1	SPACER 33/16/5	1	1
3a	900.3017	SPACER 30/17/3	1	1
4	900.3994	SPRING WASHER 30/17/0,5	1	1
5	605.1313	COTTER	1	1
6	900.3926	WASHER 14/6,5/2	1	1
7	900.2909	HEXAGON NUT 1/4" (26Gg/inch)	1	1
8	349.2.42.102.1	CRANK l.h.	1	1
9	600.1.18.067.0	PEDAL compl. (with rear reflector)	per pair	
11	907.1.28.105.0	DRIVING CHAIN compl. (1/2"x3/16"x7,75) 105 rollers	1	-
11	907.1.28.100.0	DRIVING CHAIN compl. (1/2"x3/16"x7,75) 100 rollers	-	1
12	907.1.28.001.0	CHAIN MASTER LINK compl.	1	1
15	600.1.15.085.0	CHAIN for pedals (1/2"x1/8") 85 rollers	1	-
or	600.6.15.085.0	CHAIN for pedals (1/2"x1/8") 85 rollers	1	-
15	600.1.15.078.0	CHAIN for pedals (1/2"x1/8") 78 rollers	-	1
or	600.6.15.078.0	CHAIN for pedals (1/2"x1/8") 78 rollers	-	1
16	1140.0	CHAIN MASTER LINK compl.	1	1
17	1141	BLOCK (for lengthen the chain for pedals)	as req.	
21	349.1.28.020.0	CHAIN TENSIONER compl. 70mm chain (1HP and 1,5HP)	1	-
21	349.3.28.020.0	CHAIN TENSIONER compl. 80mm chain (2HP)	1	-
21a	349.1.28.021.0	CHAIN TENSIONER ROLLER compl.	1	1
21b	349.1.28.022.1	CHAIN GUIDE CLIP	1	1
21c	349.1.28.023.1	TORSION SPRING for chain tensioner	1	1

Edition October 1976   SPARE PARTS

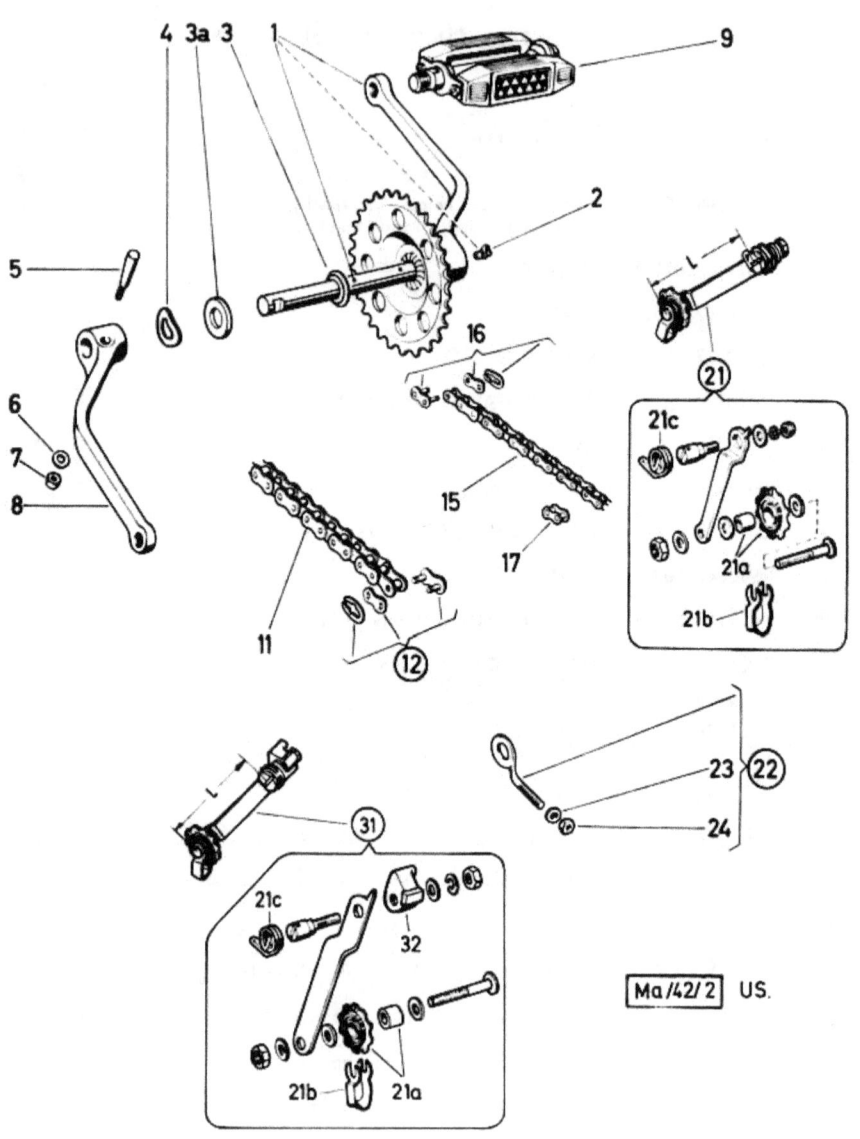

Ma/42/2 US.

Puch 1-speed Maxi USA

15. PEDALS, CHAINS, CHAIN TENSIONER (cont.)

Ref.-No.	Part-No.	Description	Model Rigid	Model Maxi, Maxi-S / Model Newport
22	349.1.41.011.0	CHAIN TENSIONER compl. (with parts 23 and 24)	2	2
23	24804	PLAIN WASHER 6,4 DIN 433	N 2	2
24	900.2014	HEXAGON NUT M6 DIN 934	N 2	2
31	349.3.28.520.0	CHAIN TENSIONER compl. for pedal chain (with parts 21a, 21b, 21c and 32) (l=110mm)	-	1
32	349.1.28.527.1	ADAPTOR	-	1

Edition October 1976   SPARE PARTS   PAGE 47

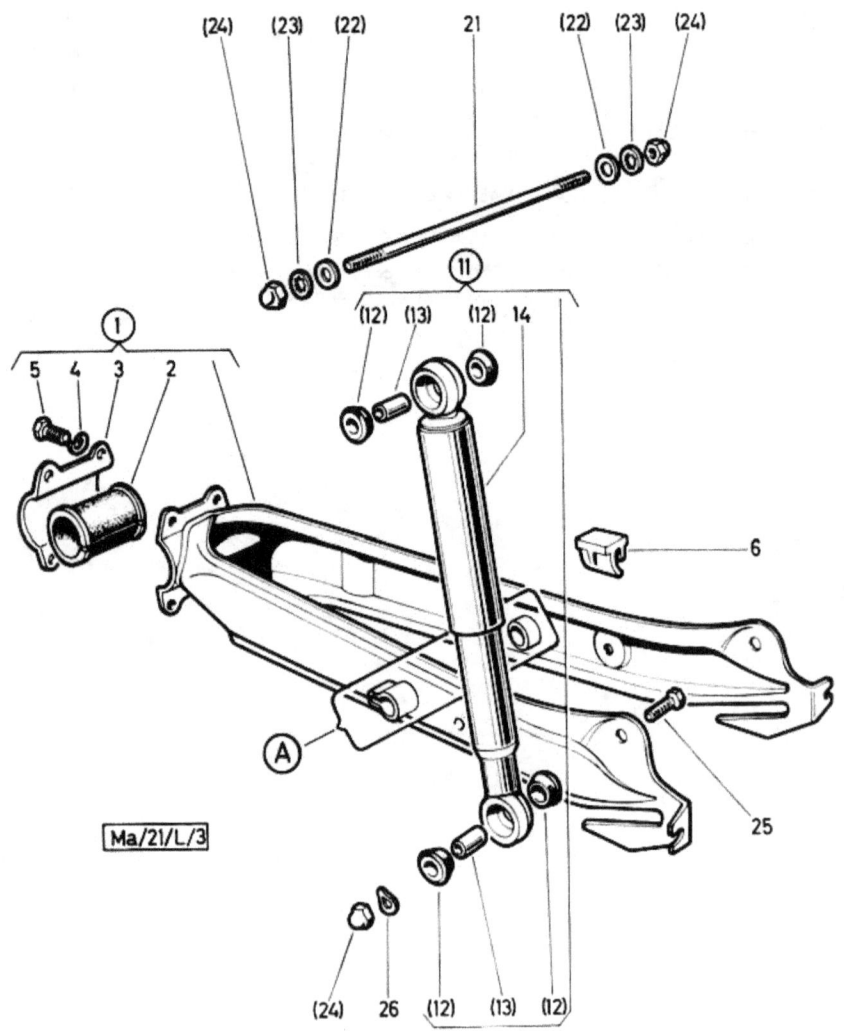

Puch 1-speed Maxi USA

15a. REAR WHEEL SUSPENSION
(Pivoted Fork, Suspension Unit)

Ref.-No.	Part-No.	Description	Model Maxi	Model Maxi S	Model Newport
1	349.1.21.500.0	PIVOTED FORK compl. without detail "A"	1	-	1
1	349.3.21.500.0	PIVOTED FORK compl. with detail "A"	-	1	-
2	349.1.21.509.1	RUBBER BEARING for pivoted fork	1	1	1
3	349.1.21.504.1	BEARING BUSH	1	1	1
4	26819	SPRING RING B8 DIN 127	N 4	4	4
5	900.1144	HEXAGON SCREW M8x16 DIN 933-8.8	N 4	4	4
6	----------------	Not for these models	-	-	-
11	349.2.21.550.0	SUSPENSION UNIT compl. (Sebac, grey)	2	-	-
11	349.3.21.550.0	SUSPENSION UNIT compl. (Sebac, black)	-	2	2
12	349.1.21.551.1	RUBBER BEARING for suspension unit	8	8	8
13	349.1.21.552.1	SLEEVE 12/8,3/19	4	4	4
14	349.2.21.553.1	SLIDING TUBE (Ø40mm, plastic) grey	2	-	-
14	349.3.21.553.1	SLIDING TUBE (Ø40mm, plastic) black	-	2	2
21	349.1.21.513.1	BOLT (M 8, 191 long)	1	1	1
22	126.3025	WASHER 20/8,5/1	2	2	2
23	22805	TOOTHED LOCK WASHER J8,4 DIN 6797	N 2	2	2
24	900.2935	DOMED NUT M8 DIN 1587	N 4	4	4
25	900.1020	HEXAGON SCREW M8x30 DIN 931-8.8	N 2	2	2
26	900.3211	SPRING WASHER B8 DIN 137	N 2	2	2

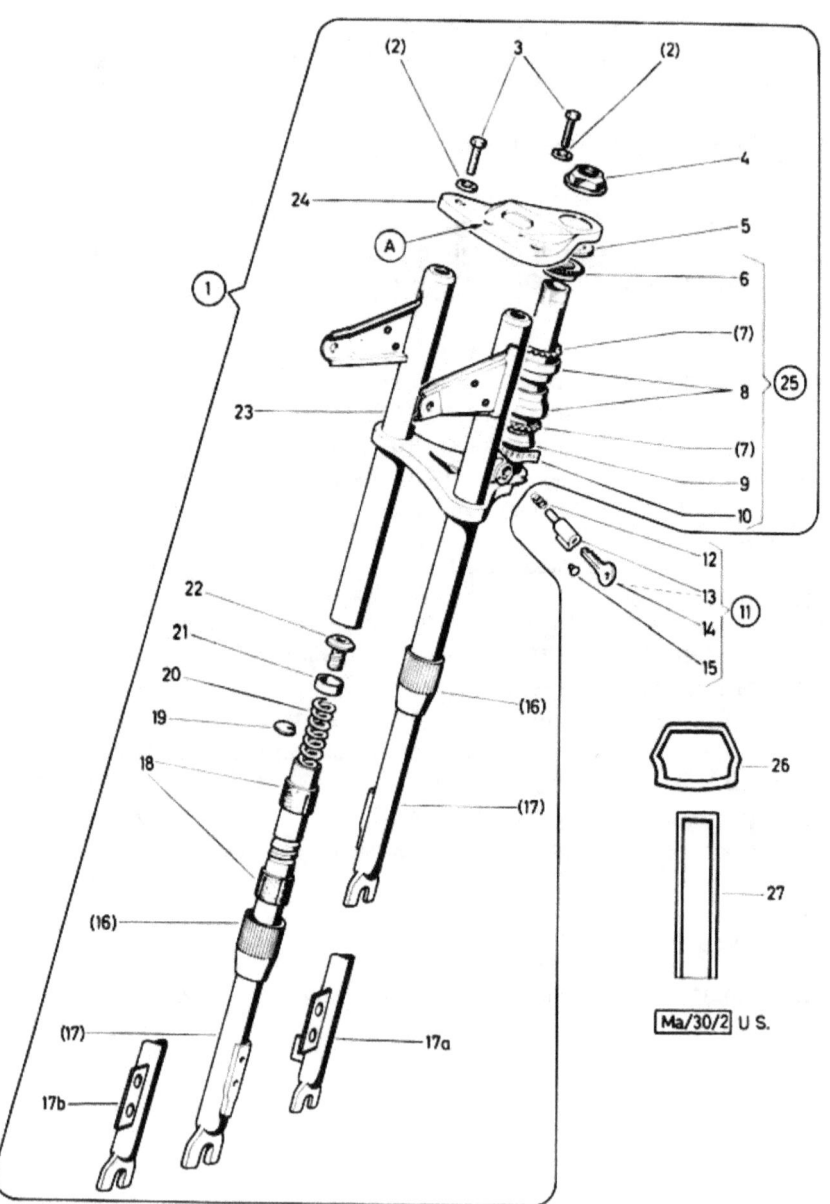

Puch 1-speed Maxi USA   **16. FRONT FORK WITH STEERING**

Ref.-No.	Part-No.	Description	Model Rigid Maxi	Model Maxi-S	Model Newport
1	349.1.30.800.0	FRONT FORK compl (with parts 2÷10 and 16,17,18÷24)	1	-	1
1	321.3.30.200.0	FRONT FORK compl (with parts 2÷10 and 16,17a,17b,18÷24)	-	1	-
2	126.2.30.025.1	WASHER 20/8,5/2	2	2	2
3	900.1104	HEXAGON HEAD SCREW M8x25 DIN 933	N 2	2	2
4	349.1.30.018.1	FORK SHAFT NUT	1	-	1
(4)	349.1.30.518.1	FORK SHAFT NUT	-	1	-
5	901.3935	WASHER 32/26,2/2,5	1	1	1
6	600.1.33.007.1	TOP GUIDE BUSHING	1	1	1
7	3298	BALL RETAINER	2	2	2
8	600.2.33.005.1	BEARING CUP	2	2	2
9	600.2.33.006.1	BOTTOM GUIDE BUSHING	1	1	1
10	349.1.30.015.1	SPRING STRAP	1	1	1
11	330.1.20.052.9	LOCK cpl. version "Neimann" (with parts 12÷15)	1	1	1
12	330.1.20.059.1	THRUST SPRING	1	1	1
13	330.1.20.052.0	LOCK compl. (with 2 keys)	1	1	1
14	350.2.30.023.1	SPARE KEY (please state key-number)	-	-	-
15	330.1.20.060.1	AL-NOTCHED RIVET	1	1	1
16	349.1.30.137.1	GROOVED SHELL	2	2	2
17	349.1.30.115.2	SLIDING TUBE	2	-	2
17a	321.1.30.215.2	SLIDING TUBE l.h.	-	1	-
17b	321.1.30.016.2	SLIDING TUBE r.h.	-	1	-
18	349.1.30.126.1	GUIDE BUSHING 27/22, 8/30	4	4	4
19	367.1.30.031.1	WASHER for thrust spring	4	4	4
20	349.2.30.134.1	THRUST SPRING Ø19x184, thickness of wire Ø3	2	2	2
21	349.1.30.117.1	DAMPING STOP 27/19,2/10	2	2	2
22	349.1.30.135.1	THREADING COUPLING	2	2	2
23	349.1.30.806.2	BOTTOM BRIDGE FOR FORK	1	1	1
24	349.1.30.007.1	TOP BRIDGE FOR FORK (with hole by "A")	1	-	1
(24)	349.2.30.507.2	TOP BRIDGE FOR FORK (with hole by "A")	-	1	-
25	349.1.31.000.0	STEERING SET compl	as required		
26	349.1.30.144.1[x]	TRANSFER PICTURE	-	-	1
26	349.2.30.144.1[xx]	TRANSFER PICTURE	-	-	1
27	349.1.30.143.1[x]	TRANSFER PICTURE	-	-	2
27	349.2.30.143.1[xx]	TRANSFER PICTURE	-	-	2

[x] for model Newport laquered in color metalic brown
[xx] for model Newport laquered in color champagne

Edition April 1977 SPARE PARTS   PAGE 51

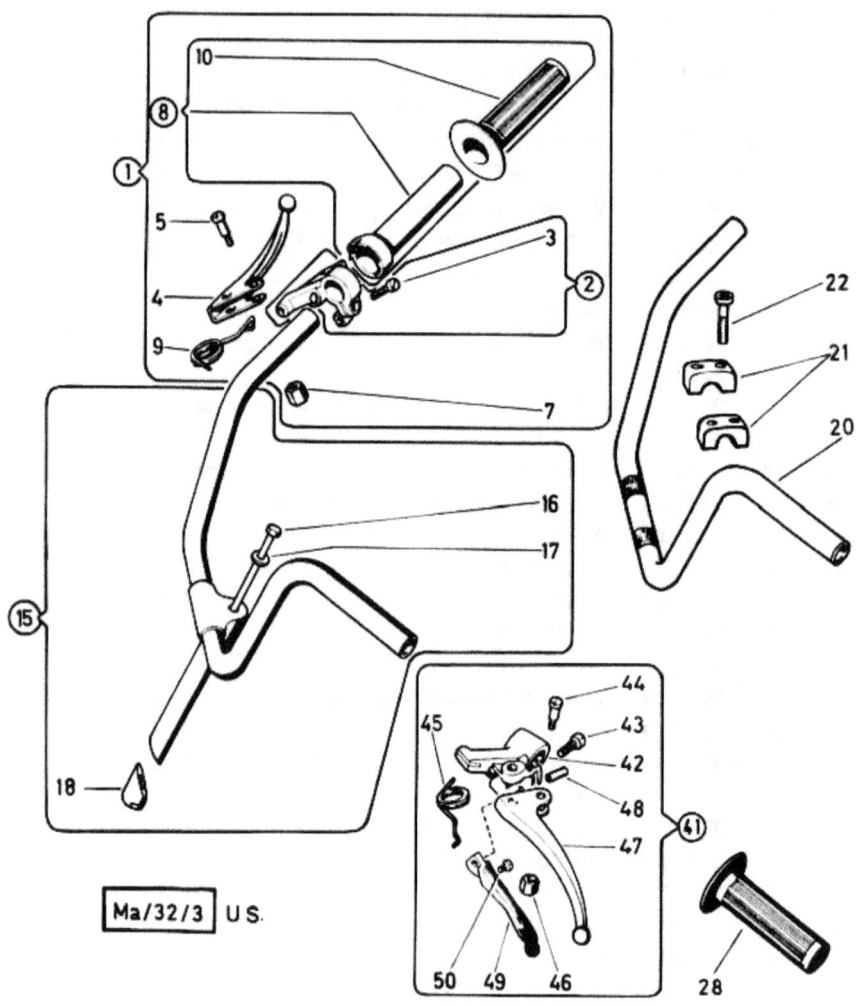

Puch 1-speed Maxi USA

17. HANDLEBAR AND CONTROLS

Bild-Nr.	Ersatzteil-Nr.	Benennung	Requd. No. Model Rigid / Model Maxi, Maxi-S / Model Newport
1	349.1.32.805.0	THROTTLE TWIST GRIP compl. (with parts 2÷10)	1
2	349.1.32.807.0	HOUSING for throttle grip compl. (with part 3)	1
3	050.3222	LENS HEAD SCREW (M6x15)	1
4	349.5.32.006.1	BRAKE LEVER	1
5	050.3227	PIVOT BOLT (M5)	1
7	349.3.32.028.1	PLASTIC NUT (self-locking for threading M5)	1
8	349.1.32.808.0	THROTTLE TWIST GRIP TUBE compl. (with part 10)	1
9	349.1.32.809.1	RETURN SPRING r.h.	1
10	360.2.32.016.1	TWIST GRIP COVER Ø24 (black)	1
15	349.2.32.100.0	HANDLEBAR compl.	1
16	349.2.32.051.1	CLAMPING SPINDLE (M8x1) 194 long - 8.8	1
17	186	WASHER 20/8,4/3,5	1
18	349.1.32.122.1	WEDGE CLAMP	1
20	321.1.32.301.1ˣ	HANDLEBAR TUBE	1 x
21	349.2.30.502.1ˣ	CLAMP	2 x
22	900.1374 ˣ	HEXAGON SOCKET HEAD SCREW (M7x35)	4 x
28	350.3.32.016.1	DUMMY RUBBER GRIP Ø22 (black)	1
41	349.1.32.817.0	BRAKE- AND ACTUATING LEVER compl. (with parts 42÷50)	1
42	349.1.32.818.1	SHACKLE	1
43	050.3222	LENS HEAD SCREW (M6x15)	1
44	050.3227	PIVOT BOLT (M5)	1
45	349.1.32.819.1	RETURN SPRING l.h.	1
46	349.3.32.028.1	PLASTIC NUT (for thread M5)	1
47	349.7.32.017.1	HAND LEVER for brake	1
48	902.4809	SPIRAL PIN 4,7x12 DIN 7343	N 1
49	349.3.32.032.1	HAND LEVER for clutch (power)	1
50	349.1.32.031.1	CABLE CLAMPING SCREW (M4x10)	1

ˣ only for Model Maxi - S

Edition April 1977   SPARE PARTS   PAGE 53

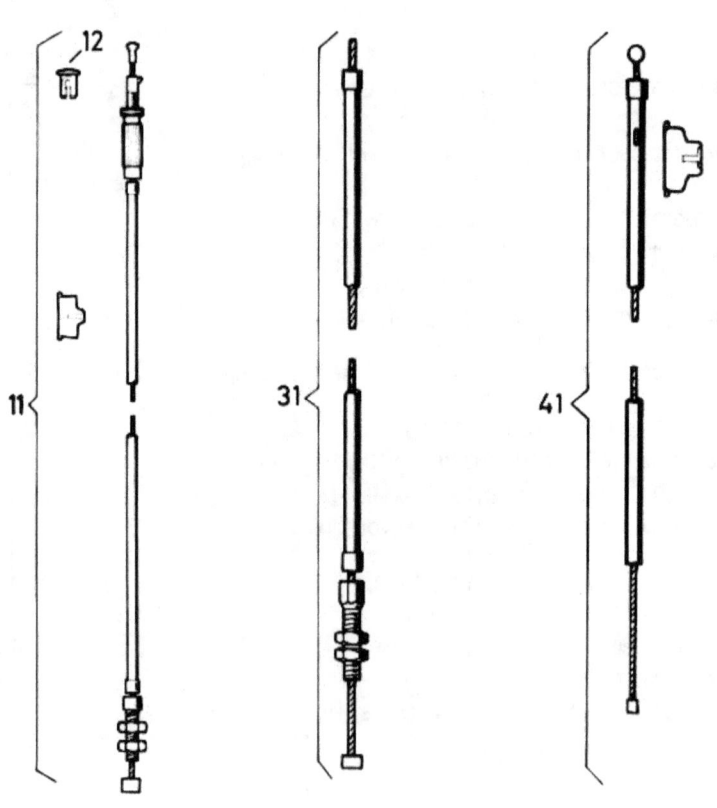

Ma/60/2 US.

Puch 1-speed Maxi USA

18. CABLES

Ref.-No.	Part-No.	Description	Model Rigid	Model Maxi, Maxi-S	Model Newport
11	910.8.18.002.0	FRONT BRAKE CABLE compl. (wire 1010/cover 860)		1	
11	910.8.19.002.0ˣ	FRONT BRAKE CABLE compl. (wire 1010/cover 850)		1 x	
11	910.8.18.001.0	REAR BRAKE CABLE compl. (wire 1648/cover 1500)		1	
11	910.8.19.001.0ˣ	REAR BRAKE CABLE compl. (wire 1650/cover 1490)		1 x	
12	910.0.12.002.1	CABLE RETAINER		2	
31	910.2.11.001.0	CLUTCH (Power) CABLE compl. (wire 1060/cover 810)		1	
41	910.5.10.003.0	THROTTLE (CARBURETOR) CABLE compl. (wire 1026/cover 895)		1	

ˣ only for Model Maxi-S

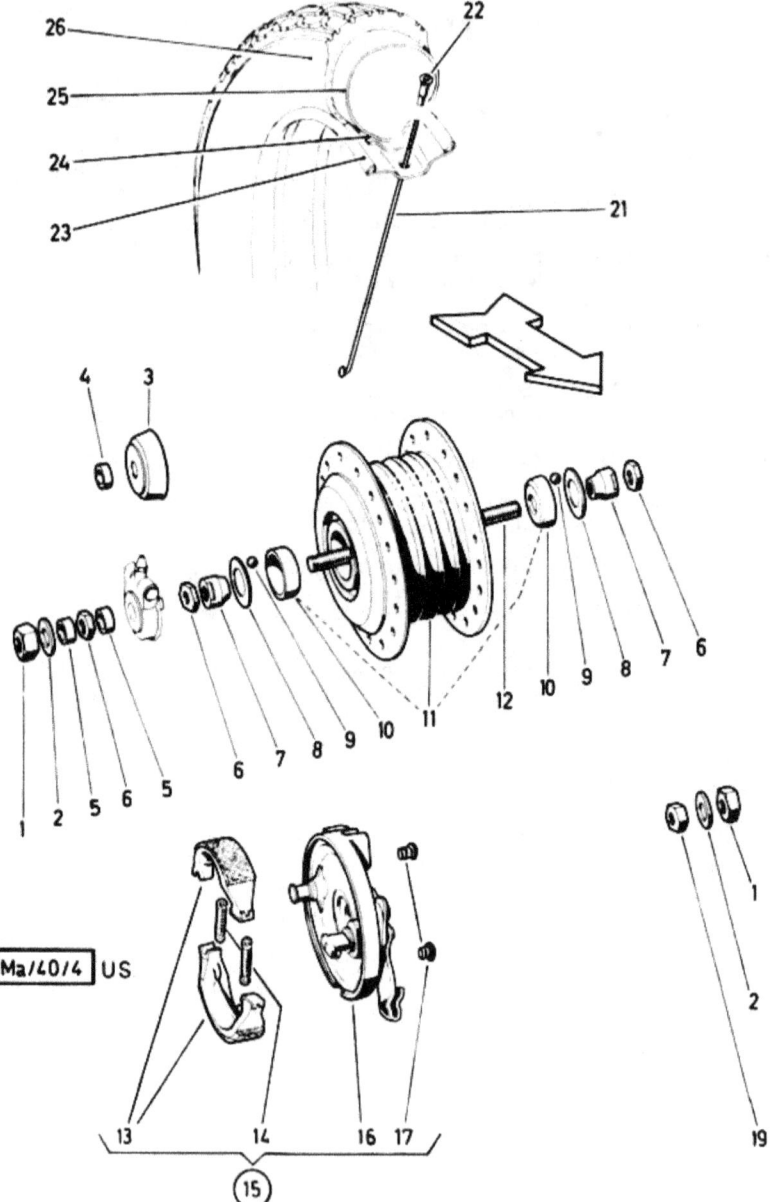

Puch 1-speed Maxi USA

19. FRONT WHEEL

Ref.-No.	Part-No.	Description	Model Rigid Model Maxi	Model Newport
--	349.1.40.800.0	FRONT WHEEL compl. (with steel rim, without tire)	1	1
--	349.1.40.802.0	FRONT WHEEL HUB compl. (Leleu Ø80mm)	1	1
1	349.1.40.016.1	HEXAGON NUT (axle nut) (M11x1, 10mm high, 19SW)	2	2
2	604.4124	WASHER 19/11, 3/0,8	2	2
3	349.1.40.017.1[x]	COVER CAP	1	1
4	349.1.40.005.1[x]	SPACER RING 16/11, 2/4,1	1	1
5	349.1.40.004.1	SPACER RING 16/11, 2/4,7	2	2
6	349.1.40.008.1	HEXAGON NUT (M11x1, 5mm high, SW16)	3	3
7	349.1.40.010.1	CONE Ø18x13	2	2
8	349.1.40.011.1	COVER DISC 29,2/18,5/0,4	2	2
9	22757	BALL 7/32"	22	22
10	349.1.40.006.1	BEARING CUP Ø29x10,5	2	2
11	349.1.40.003.2	FRONT WHEEL BRAKE HUB (with pressed-in bearing cups)	1	1
12	349.1.40.026.1	FRONT WHEEL AXLE, 156 long	1	1
13	349.1.40.015.0	PAIR OF BRAKE SHOES with glued lining	1	1
14	349.1.40.019.1	BRAKE SHOE SPRING	2	2
15	349.1.40.807.0	BRAKE COVER PLATE compl. (with parts 13,14,16 and 17)	1	1
16	349.1.40.807.9	BRAKE COVER PLATE (with part 17)	1	1
17	349.1.40.816.1	PLUG	2	2
19	349.1.40.014.1	HEXAGON NUT (M11x1, 7mm high, SW16)	1	1
21	349.5.40.030.1	SPOKE Ø2,6x188	36	36
22	349.1.40.031.1	NIPPLE M3	36	36
23	349.4.40.033.1	RIM 17" (steel)	1	1
24	901.0894	CHAFING STRIP	1	1
25	901.0863	INNER TUBE 21"x2"	1	1
26	901.0862	TIRE 2-17 (21x2)	1	-
26	902.0834	TIRE 2-17 (21x2) with reflecting side wall	-	1

[x] These parts are omitting when mounting speedometer drive

Edition October 1976   SPARE PARTS   PAGE 57

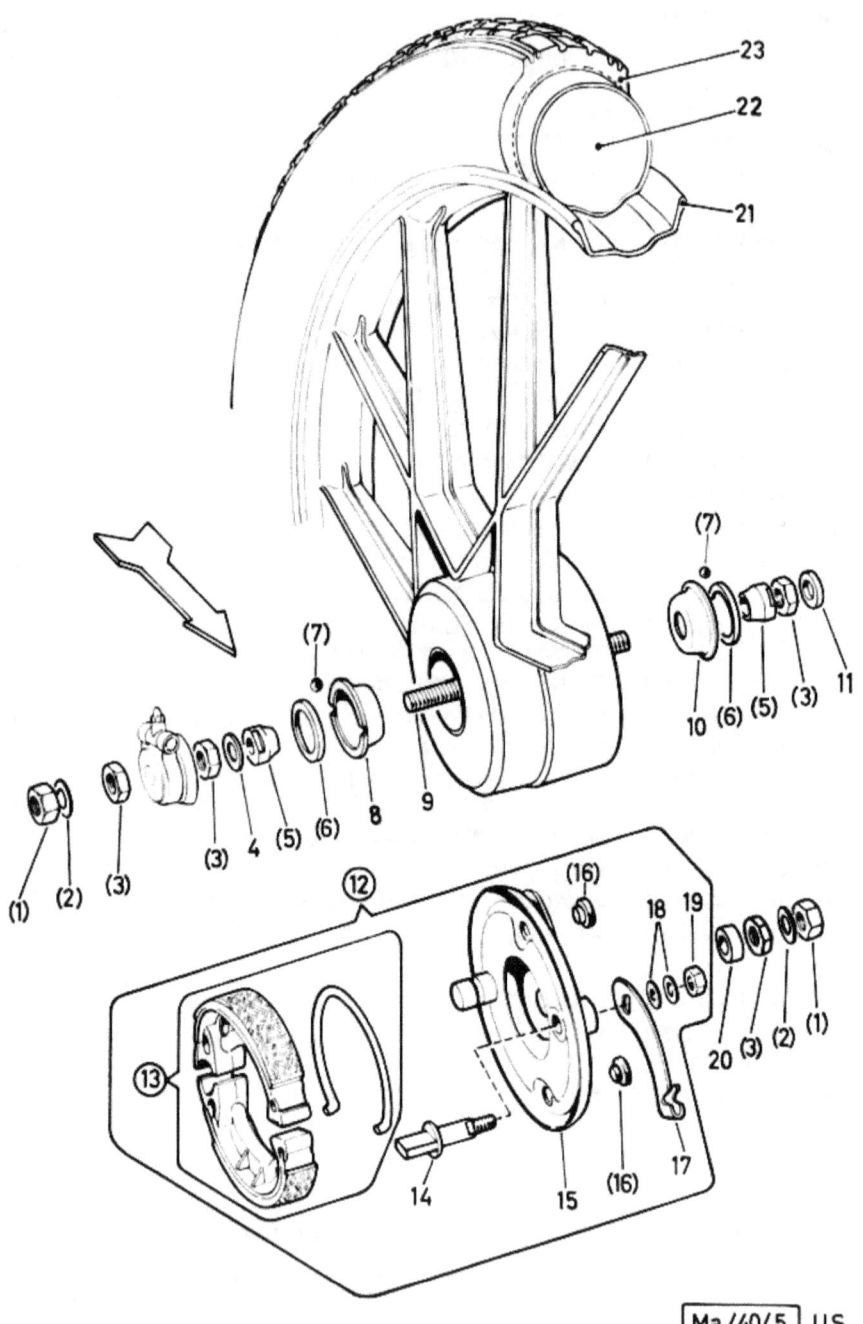

Ma/40/5 US.

Puch 1-speed Maxi USA

19a. FRONT WHEEL
for Maxi-S

Ref.-No.	Part-No.	Description	Reqd.No. Model Maxi-S
--	349.1.40.700.0	FRONT WHEEL compl. (without tire)	1
1	349.1.40.714.1	HEXAGON NUT (axle nut, M11x1 10 high SW 17)	2
2	604.4124	WASHER 19/11,3/0,8	2
3	349.1.40.708.1	HEXAGON NUT M11x1,6 high, SW 17	4
4	900.3938	WASHER 18/12,3/1	1
5	349.1.40.710.1	CONE Ø19x12	2
6	349.1.40.711.1	DUST CAP 28,1/20/3,5	2
7	22751	BALL 1/4"	20
8	349.1.40.705.1	BEARING CUP r.h.	1
9	349.1.40.026.1	FRONT WHEEL AXLE, 156 long	1
10	349.1.40.706.1	BEARING CUP l.h.	1
11	350.1.13.076.1	WASHER 18/12,5/2	1
12	349.1.40.707.0	BRAKE COVER PLATE, compl	1
13	349.1.40.715.9	PAIR OF BRAKE SHOES with brake shoe spring	1
14	349.1.40.709.1	BRAKE CAM, 46 long	1
15	349.1.40.707.2	BRAKE COVER PLATE, loose	1
16	349.1.40.716.1	PLUG	2
17	349.1.40.713.1	BRAKE LEVER	1
18	24795	WASHER 6,4 DIN 125	N 2
19	24773	HEXAGON NUT M6 DIN 934	N 1
20	349.1.40.704.1	DISTANCE RING 16/12/6	1
21	349.1.40.702.2	FRONT WHEEL, loose, (with parts 8 and 10)	1
22	901.0863	INNER TUBE 21x2	1
23	902.0800	TIRE 2 1/4 - 17 (21x2,25)	1

Edition April 1977

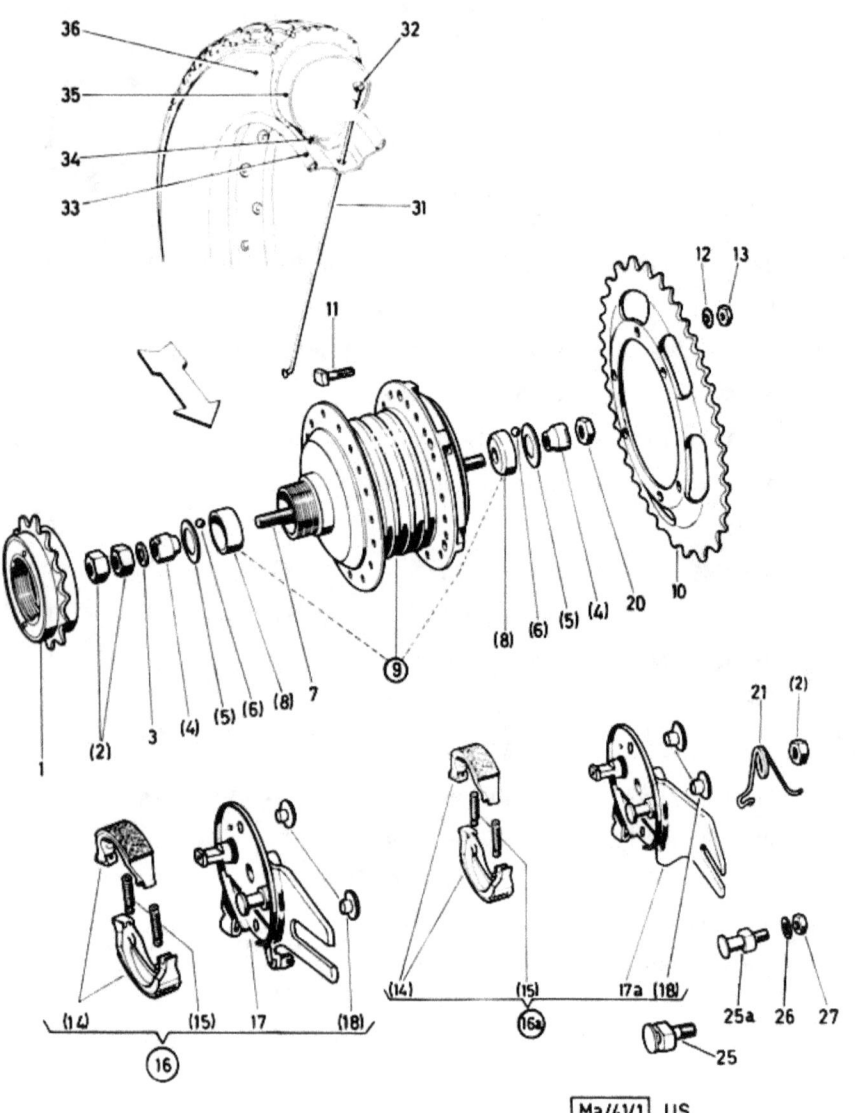

Ma/41/1 US.

Puch 1-speed Maxi USA

20. REAR WHEEL

Ref.-No.	Part-No.	Description	Model Rigid	Model Maxi	Model Newport
--	349.2.41.800.0	REAR WHEEL compl. (45 and 23 teeth) (with steel rim, without tire)	1	-	-
--	349.1.41.800.0	REAR WHEEL compl. (45 and 23 teeth) (with steel rim, without tire)	-	1	1
--	349.2.41.802.0	REAR WHEEL HUB compl. (Leleu Ø80) (with 45 toothed chain sprocket, without idle gear sprocket)	1	-	-
--	349.1.41.802.0	REAR WHEEL HUB compl. (Leleu Ø80) (with 45 toothed chain sprocket, without idle gear sprocket)	-	1	1
1	349.2.41.023.0	IDLE GEAR SPROCKET compl. (23 teeth) (Messrs. Maillard)	1	1	1
2	25015	HEXAGON NUT M12x1 DIN 934	N 3	3	3
3	350.1.13.078.1	WASHER 18/12,5/1,8	1	1	1
4	349.1.41.010.1	CONE Ø20x13,5	2	2	2
5	349.1.41.004.1	COVER DISC 29,2/21/0,4	2	2	2
6	22754	BALL 3/16"	26	26	26
7	349.1.41.026.1	REAR WHEEL AXLE, 180 long	1	1	1
8	349.1.41.006.1	BEARING CUP Ø29	2	2	2
9	349.1.41.003.2	REAR WHEEL BRAKE HUB (with pressed-in bearing cups)	1	1	1
10	349.1.41.045.1	CHAIN SPROCKET (45 teeth)	1	1	1
11	349.1.41.005.1	RETAINING BOLT (M6)	6	6	6
12	900.3267	SERRATED LOCK WASHER A6,4 DIN 6798	N 6	6	6
13	24773	HEXAGON NUT M6 DIN 934	N 6	6	6
14	349.1.40.015.0	PAIR OF BRAKE SHOES with glued lining	1	1	1
15	349.1.40.019.1	BRAKE SHOE SPRING	2	2	2
16	349.2.41.807.0	BRAKE COVER PLATE compl. (with parts 14,15,17 and 18)	1	-	-

Edition October 1976   SPARE PARTS

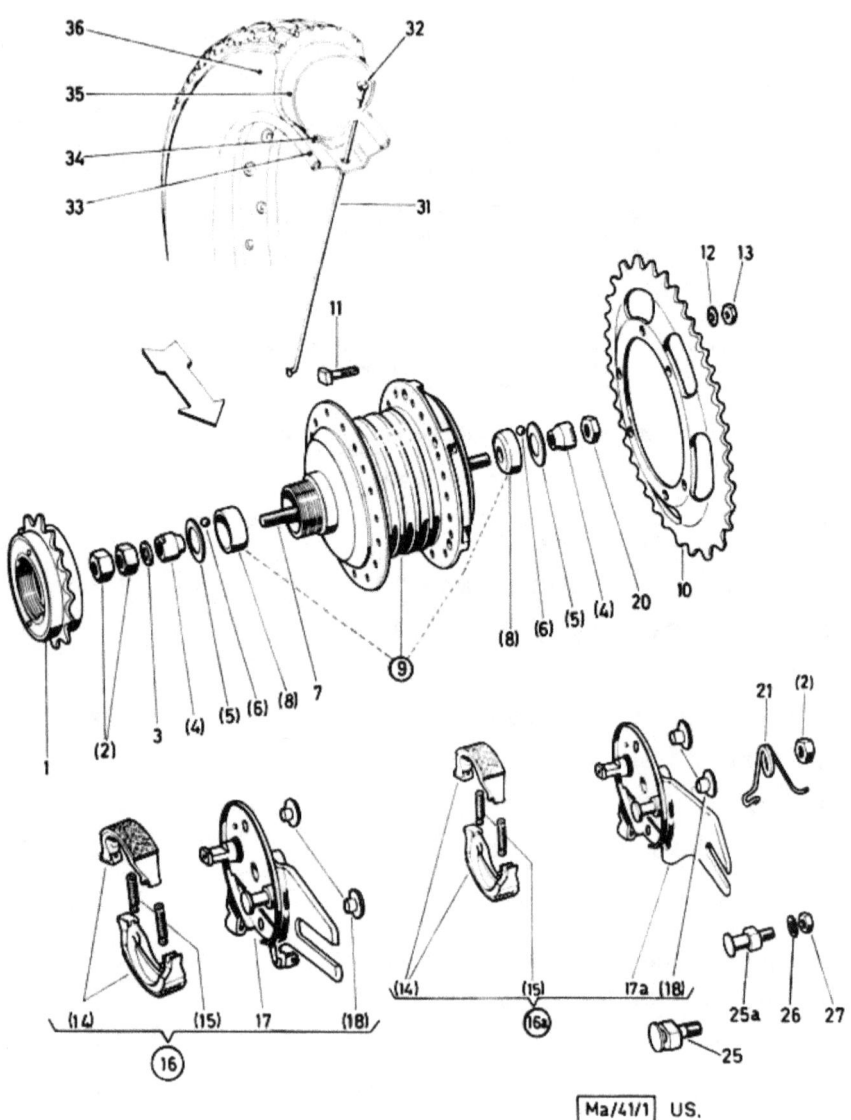

Ma/41/1 US.

Puch 1-speed Maxi USA

20. REAR WHEEL (cont.)

Ref.-No.	Part-No.	Description	Model Rigid	Model Maxi	Model Newport
16a	349.1.41.807.0	BRAKE COVER PLATE compl. (with parts 14,15,17a and 18)	-	1	1
17	349.2.41.807.9	BRAKE COVER PLATE (with part 18)	1	-	-
17a	349.1.41.807.9	BRAKE COVER PLATE (with part 18)	-	1	1
18	349.1.41.816.1	PLUG	2	2	2
20	349.1.41.014.1	HEXAGON NUT (M12x1, 5mm high, 19SW)	1	1	1
21	349.3.41.515.1	RETURN SPRING	1	1	1
25	349.1.41.008.1	BRAKE SUPPORTING BOLT (32mm long)	1	-	-
25a	349.1.41.508.1×	BRAKE SUPPORTING BOLT (38,5 long)	-	1	1
26	22806 ×	TOOTHED LOCK WASHER 10,5	1	1	1
27	24789 ×	HEXAGON NUT M10x1 DIN 934	N 1	1	1
31	349.5.40.030.1	SPOKE Ø2,6x188	36	36	36
32	349.1.40.031.1	NIPPLE M3	36	36	36
33	349.4.40.033.1	RIM 17" (steel)	1	1	1
34	901.0894	RIM BAND	1	1	1
35	901.0863	INNER TUBE 21"x2"	1	1	1
36	901.0862	TIRE 2-17 (21x2)	1	1	-
36	902.0834	TIRE 2-17 (21x2) with reflecting side wall	-	-	1

× for model Maxi and Newport up to ma. 8446632

II Edition October 1976   SPARE PARTS   PAGE 61

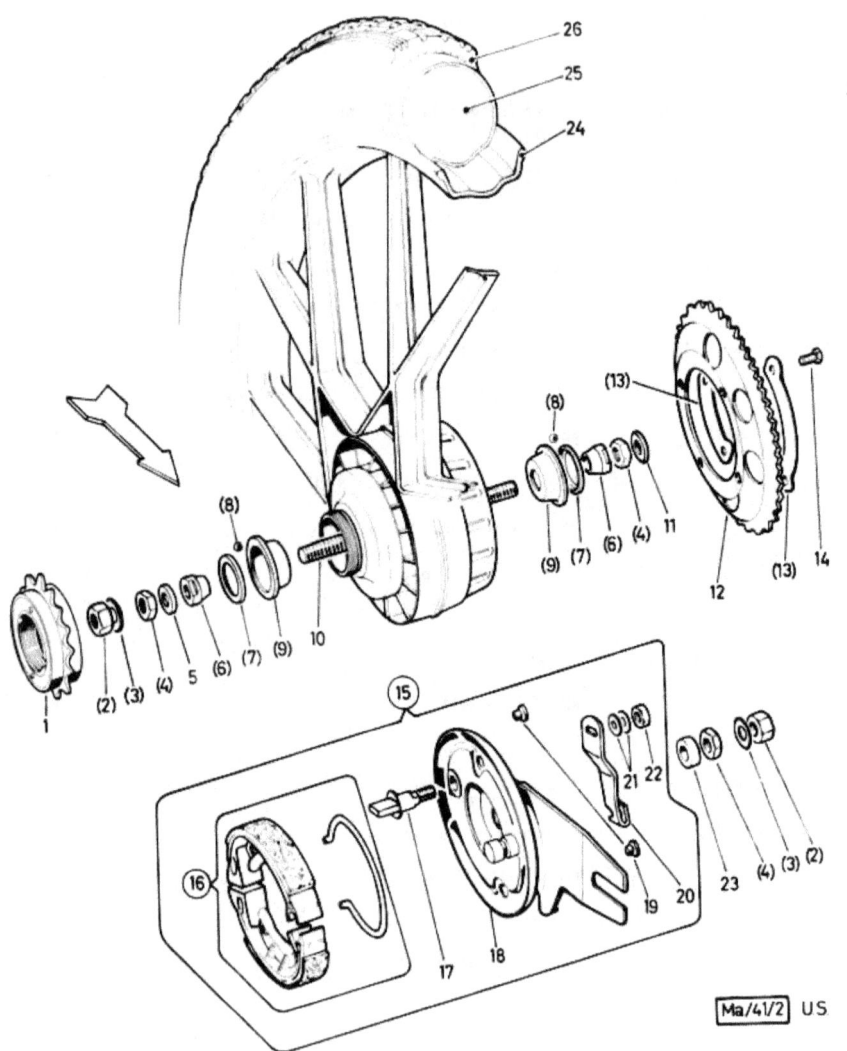

Ma/41/2 US

Puch 1-speed Maxi USA

20a. REAR WHEEL
for Maxi-S

Ref.-No.	Part-No.	Description	Requd. No. Model Maxi-S
--	349.2.41.700.0	REAR WHEEL compl. (45 and 23 teeth) (without tire)	1
1	349.2.41.023.0	IDLE GEAR SPROCKET compl. (23 teeth) (Messrs.Maillard)	
2	349.1.40.714.1	HEXAGON NUT (axle nut M11x1, 10 high SW 17)	2
3	604.4124	WASHER 19/11,3/0,8	2
4	349.1.40.708.1	HEXAGON NUT M11x1, 6 high SW 17	3
5	349.2.41.704.1	DISTANCE RING 16/12/3	1
6	349.1.40.710.1	CONE Ø19x12	2
7	349.2.41.711.1	DUST CAP 25,9/20/3,5	2
8	900.6121	BALL Ø5,5	22
9	349.2.41.706.1	BEARING CUP	2
10	349.2.41.726.1	REAR WHEEL AXLE, 175 long	1
11	350.1.13.076.1	WASHER 18/12,5/2	1
12	349.1.41.745.1	CHAIN SPROCKET, 45 teeth	1
13	349.1.41.718.1	LOCK PLATE for chain sprocket	2
14	900.1132	HEXAGON SCREW M6x16 DIN 933-8.8	N 4
15	349.2.41.707.0	BRAKE COVER PLATE, compl.	1
16	349.1.40.715.9	PAIR OF BRAKE SHOES with brake shoe spring	1
17	349.2.41.709.1	BRAKE CAM, 40 long	1
18	349.2.41.707.2	BRAKE COVER PLATE, loose	1
19	349.1.40.716.1	PLUG	2
20	349.2.41.713.1	BRAKE LEVER	1

Edition April 1977

SPARE PARTS   PAGE 61 d

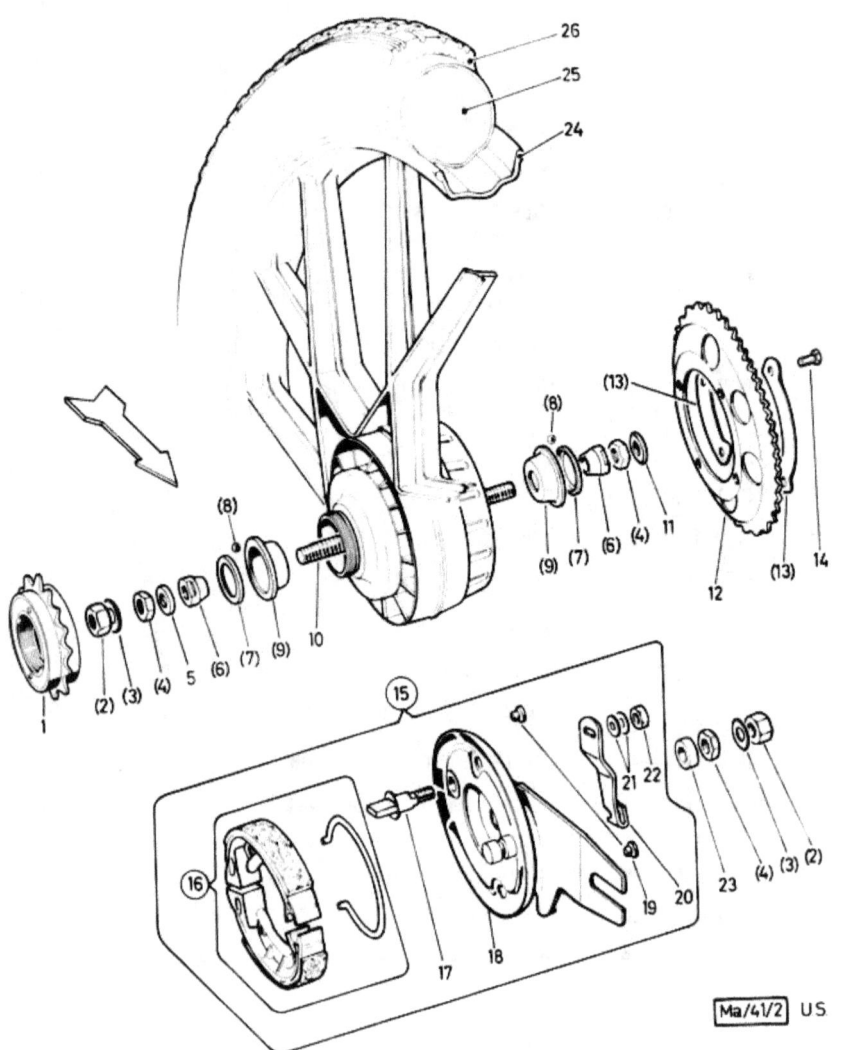

Ma/41/2 US

Puch 1-speed Maxi USA

20a. REAR WHEEL (Forts.)
for Maxi-S

Requd. No.
Model Maxi-S

Ref.-No.	Part-No.	Description	
21	24795	WASHER 6,4 DIN 125	N 2
22	24773	HEXAGON NUT M6 DIN 934	N 1
23	349.2.41.705.1	DISTANCE RING 16/12/7	1
24	349.2.41.702.2	REAR WHEEL, loose (with part 9)	1
25	901.0863	INNER TUBE 21x2	1
26	902.0800	TIRE 2 1/4 - 17 (21x2,25)	1

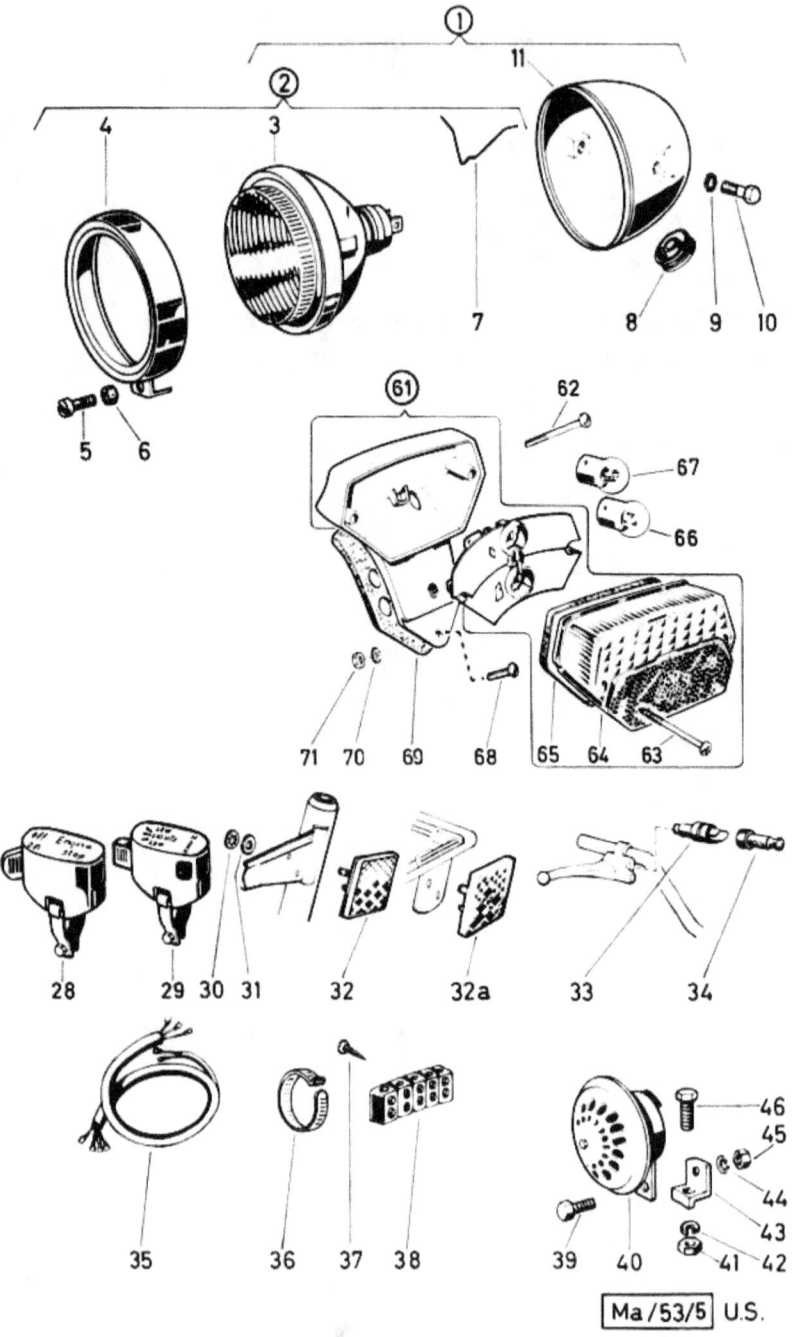

Puch 1-speed Maxi USA

21. HEADLAMP, TAIL-, STOP-LIGHT, RATTLE, HARNESS

Ref.-No.	Part-No.	Description	Requd. No. Model Rigid / Model Maxi, Maxi-S / Model Newport
1	349.1.53.800.0	HEADLAMP compl. (Pagani Nr 2143) (with parts 2÷11)	1
2	349.1.53.802.0	SEALED BEAM UNIT compl. (with parts 3÷7)	1
3	349.1.53.802.2	SEALED BEAM (6 V) loose	1
4	349.1.53.803.0	HEADLAMP RIM compl. (with parts 5 and 6)	1
5	900.1505	RAISED CHEESE HEAD SCREW AM5x16 DIN 85	N 1
6	28547	RUBBER RING 8/4/2	1
7	321.1.53.009.1	SPRING FOR REFLECTOR	9
8	321.3.53.005.1	CABLE SOCKET	1
9	900.3271	TOOTHED WASHER A6,4 DIN 6797	N 2
10	24928	HEXAGON HEAD SCREW M6x16 DIN 933	N 2
11	349.1.53.801.2	HEADLAMP BODY	1
28	349.1.53.830.0	ENGINE-STOP-SWITCH compl.	1
29	349.2.53.817.0	SWITCH compl. (light and horn)	1
30	900.3650	SPEED NUT (SFP 0212) Ø4 up to ma. 1976	8
30	902.4657	SPEED NUT (FC 050) Ø5 from ma. 1977	8
31	901.3956	RUBBER WASHER 15/4, 5/4	8
32	349.1.53.876.1	SIDE REFLECTOR (yellow)	2
32a	349.2.53.876.1	SIDE REFLECTOR (red)	2
33	349.1.55.820.0	STOP SWITCH for brake levers	2
34	413.1.55.122.1	RUBBER CAP	2
35	349.2.57.800.0	HARNESS compl	1
36	364.1.53.227.1	CABLE BINDER	2
37	900.9518	FIXING SCREW B2,9x19 DIN 7971	N 1
38	330.1.57.301.0	SOFT RUBBER TERMINAL (5 rows)	1
39	24927	HEXAGON HEAD SCREW M6x12 DIN 933	N 1

Edition October 1976   SPARE PARTS

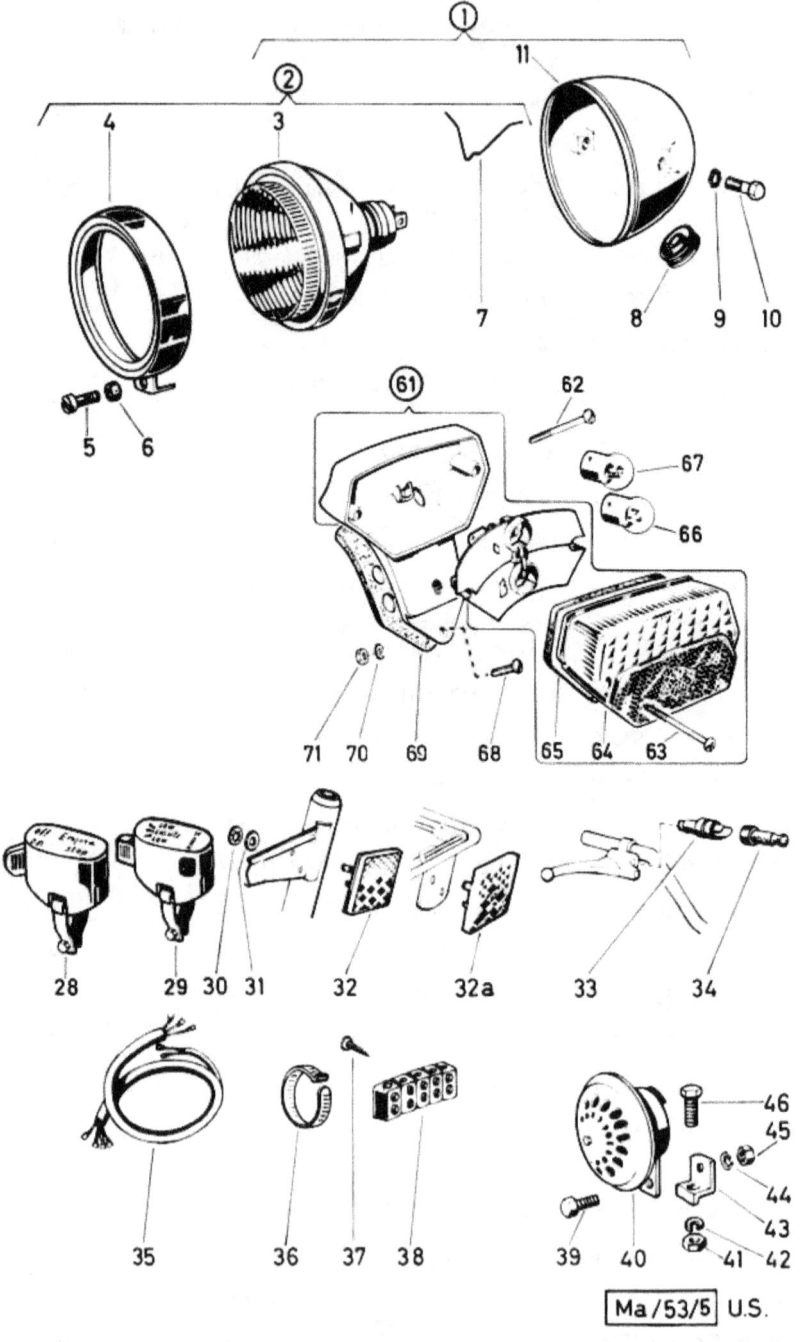

Puch 1-speed Maxi USA

21. HEADLAMP, TAIL-, STOP-LIGHT, RATTLE, HARNESS (cont.)

Ref.-No.	Part-No.	Description	Reqd. No. Model Rigid / Model Maxi, Maxi-S / Model Newport
40	904.0758	RATTLE (Hella with faston plug connector)	1
41	900.2108	HEXAGON NUT M8 DIN 555	N 1
42	26819	SPRING WASHER B8 DIN 127	N 1
43	349.1.56.001.1	RATTLE BRACKET	N 1
44	26834	SPRING WASHER B6 DIN 127	N 1
46	25585	HEXAGON HEAD SCREW M8x16 DIN 933	N 1
61	349.1.55.800.0	TAIL- STOP-LIGHT compl. (ULO)	1
62	900.1546	LENS HEAD SCREW M5x30 DIN 85	N 1
63	337.1.55.107.1	LENS HEAD SCREW (M4,2x55)	2
64	349.1.55.806.2	LAMP HOUSING	1
65	368.1.55.804.1	GASKET	1
66	900.0755	BULB 6V/5W BA 15s for tail-light	1
67	900.0703	BULB 6V/10W BA 15s for stop light	1
68	900.1505	LENS HEAD SCREW M5x16 DIN 85	N 1
69	337.1.55.126.1	BASE PLATE	1
70	900.3255	SERRATED LOCK WASHER A5,3 DIN 6798	N 2
71	24772	HEXAGON NUT M5 DIN 934	N 2

Edition October 1976

SPARE PARTS

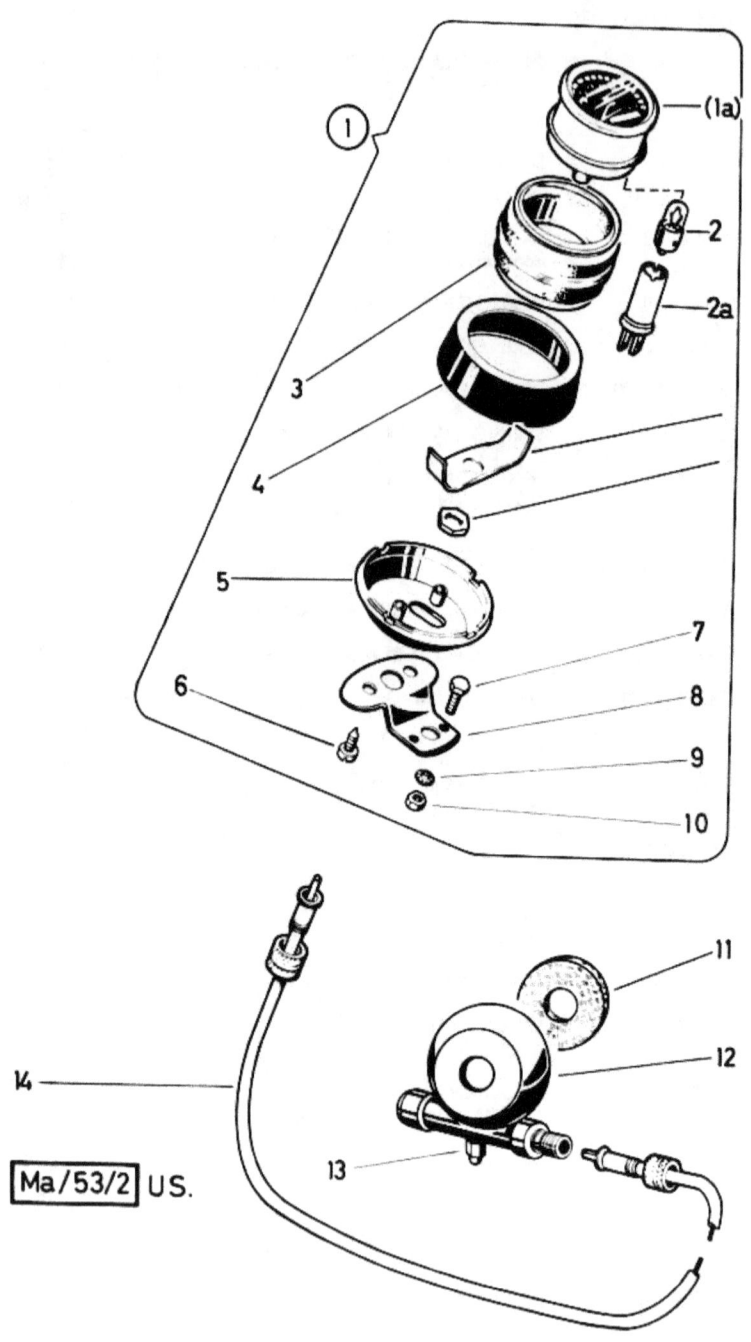

Ma/53/2 US.

Puch 1-speed Maxi USA

21a. SPEEDOMETER WITH SPEEDOMETER DRIVE

Ref.-No.	Part-No.	Description	Requd.No. Model Maxi, Maxi-S / Model Newport
1	349.1.53.820.0	SPEEDOMETER with fastening compl.	1
1a	349.1.53.824.0	SPEEDOMETER compl. (40 mph) Ø60	1
2	900.0762	BULB 6V 0,6W Sockel Ba7s	1
2a	349.1.53.823.2	BULB HOLDER compl.	1
3	328.2.53.530.0	DAMPER HOLDER compl.	1
4	328.2.53.523.1	UPPER PART OF SPEEDOMETER HOUSING	1
5	359.1.53.022.1	LOWER PART OF SPEEDOMETER HOUSING	1
6	900.9502	CHEESE HEAD SCREW Bz3,9x9,5 DIN 7971	N 2
7	25585	HEXAGON SCREW M8x16 DIN 933	N 1
8	321.1.53.027.1	SPEEDOMETER SUPPORTING BRACKET	1
9	900.3265	SERRATED LOCK WASHER A8,5 DIN 6798	N 1
10	24775	HEXAGON NUT M8 DIN 934	N 1
11	050.3.4051	SEALING RING 36/18/5	1
12	349.2.40.050.0	SPEEDOMETER DRIVE compl.	1
13	26821	GREASE NIPPLE	1
14	328.1.53.025.0	DRIVING SHAFT compl. (625 long) (replacement for 360.1.53.525.0)	1

Edition October 1976

SPARE PARTS   PAGE 67

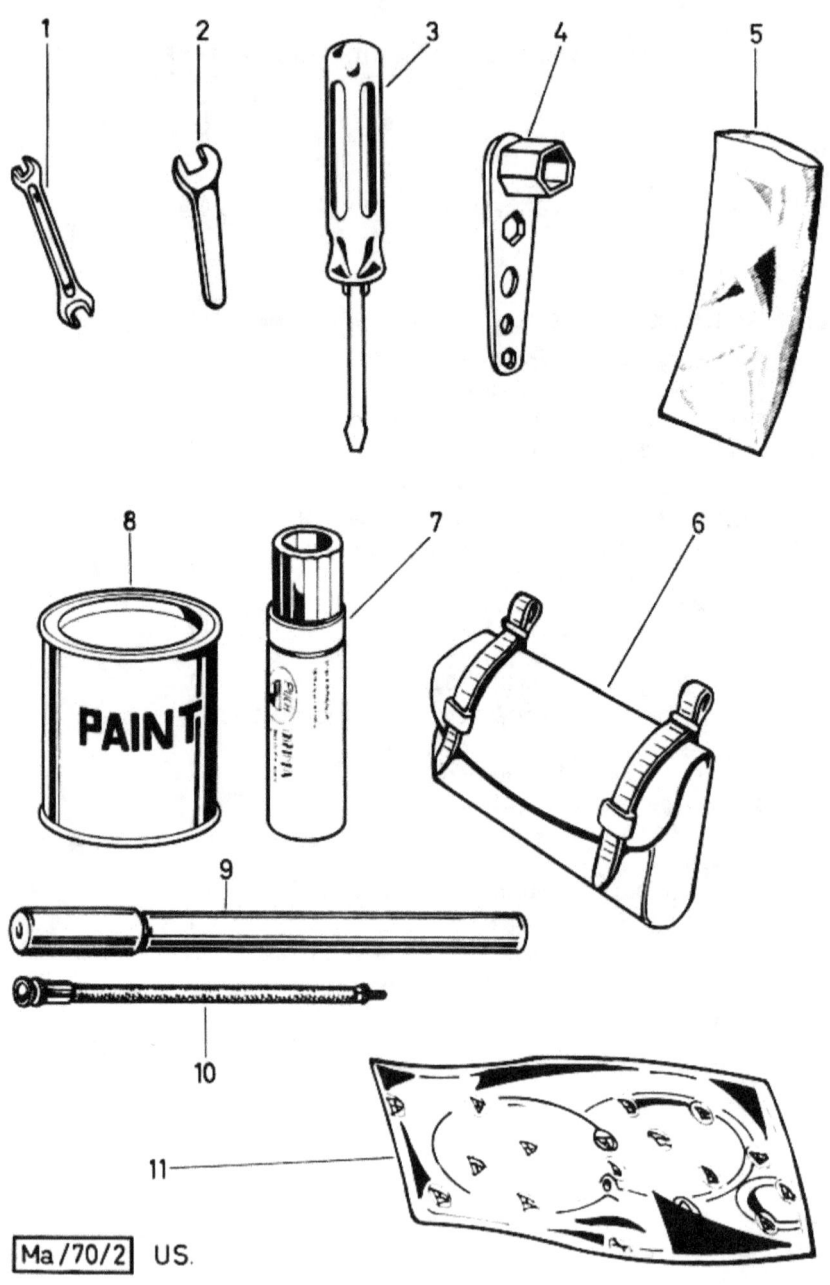

Ma/70/2 US.

Puch 1-speed Maxi USA

22. TOOLS, PUMP

Requd. No.
Model Rigid
Model Maxi, Maxi-S
Model Newport

Ref.-No.	Part-No.	Description			
-	349.1.70.500.0	TOOLS SET			1
1	10181	WRENCH 8/10			1
2	900.7022	ONE END WRENCH 19			1
3	050.2.7021	SCREW DRIVER			1
4	050.7001.2	SOCKET WRENCH (spark plug)			1
5	366.1.70.003.1	TOOL BAG			1
6	600.4.64.004.0	TOOL BAG compl.			1
7	900.0212/09	PAINT STIK, poppy red	(RAL 3002)		as req.
7	900.0250/09	PAINT STIK, white	(RAL 9002)		as req.
7	900.0261/09	PAINT STIK, silver	(RAL 9006)		as req.
7	900.0280/09	PAINT STIK, yellow	(PUCH 1060)		as req.
7	900.0284/09	PAINT STIK, purple	(PUCH 4054M)		as req.
7	900.0291/09	PAINT STIK, green	(PUCH 6064)		as req.
7	900.0208/09	PAINT STIK, black	(RAL 9005)		as req.
7	900.0234/09	PAINT STIK, red	(PUCH 3052T)		as req.
7	900.0267/09	PAINT STIK, blue	(PUCH 5051T)		as req.
7	900.0296/09	PAINT STIK, champagne	(PUCH 1063)		as req.
7	900.0297/09	PAINT STIK, metalic brown	(RAL 8017)		as req.
8	900.0212/10	PAINT, poppy red	(RAL 3002)	(0,276lbs)	as req.
8	900.0250/10	PAINT, white	(RAL 9002)	(0,276lbs)	as req.
8	900.0261/10	PAINT, silver	(RAL 9006)	(0,276lbs)	as req.
8	900.0280/10	PAINT, yellow	(PUCH 1060)	(0,276lbs)	as req.
8	900.0284/10	PAINT, purple	(PUCH 4054M)	(0,276lbs)	as req.
8	900.0291/10	PAINT, green	(PUCH 6064)	(0,276lbs)	as req.
8	900.0208/10	PAINT, black	(RAL 9005)	(0,276lbs)	as req.
8	900.0234/10	PAINT, red	(PUCH 3052T)	(0,276lbs)	as req.
8	900.0267/10	PAINT, blue	(PUCH 5051T)	(0,276lbs)	as req.
8	900.0296/10	PAINT, champagne	(PUCH 1063)	(0,276lbs)	as req.
8	900.0297/10	PAINT, metalic brown	(RAL 8017)	(0,276lbs)	as req.
9	050.7024.0	TIRE PUMP, compl			1
10	050.7023.2	PUMP TUBE			1
11	349.1.10.110.0	GASKET SET			1
--	349.1.72.801.9	NUTS AND BOLTS KIT			as req.

Edition October 1976

Use only <u>genuine</u> Puch spare parts for all repairs

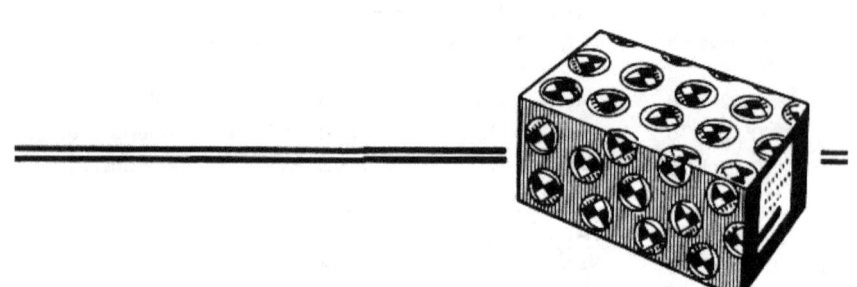